The GENERAL PRACTITIONER *& The Law of* NEGLIGENCE

2ND EDITION

Walter Scott

LLB (Hons)

MBBS, MRCGP, DObstRCOG,

Cavendish
Publishing
Limited

First published 1994 by Business & Medical Publications Ltd.

Published in Great Britain 1995 by Cavendish Publishing Limited, The Glass House, Wharton Street, London WC1X 9PX.

Telephone: 0171-278 8000 Facsimile: 0171-278 8080

© Scott, W   1995

British Library Cataloguing in Publication Data

Scott, W
General Practitioner and the Law of Negligence - (2 Rev Ed)
I Title II Series
344.206332

ISBN 1-85941-023-5

Printed and bound in Great Britain

To my late brother, David Hepburne Scott the schoolmaster, who taught doctors and lawyers long before they learned the mysteries of their professions.

FOREWORD

I am particularly pleased to be able to introduce the second edition of Walter Scott's book, as I regarded the first edition as satisfying an acute need and servicing an important purpose.

The need was for GPs to understand the process of litigation and why patients sue. The service was to try to prevent litigation arising in the first place.

Both points have been enlarged and highlighted in this second edition. Indeed, the author has found it necessary to include a separate chapter on what motivates patients to sue. Understanding this might minimise some of the special distress that arises from medical litigation, the distress having its roots on the unique nature of the doctor-patient relationship. GPs will find the treatment and prevention is obvious from an analysis of the causes.

Scott has rewritten the chapter dealing with clinical matters. Keeping up to date with drugs and procedures is something some GPs may find difficult and they may rely too heavily on specialists' advice. The author illustrates what may reasonably be expected of the ordinary GP today with a variety of recent cases.

Walter Scott is of course a practising GP and an expert who acts on the part of the patient plaintiff. He writes about cases he has been involved in and thus provides an insight which is denied to the defendant doctor and his advisers. Scott takes the reader to the bedside and with a blend of clinical expertise, knowledge of the law and clear analysis of the conflict, he draws conclusions which continue to fulfil admirably the two functions which marked the first edition as a standard text.

GPs will use this book as a dip-in guide as well as a basis for teaching and prevention. It may persuade some GPs to follow in Scott's footsteps and become plaintiffs' experts. That would benefit everyone: patient plaintiffs, by producing a speedier outcome; defendant GPs, by knowing 'the other side' is well-informed; and the rest of us by stopping frivolous ill-based claims.

Dr Nicholas Norwell, MBBS, DA, DCH, MRCGP
Medico-legal Adviser at the Medical Defence Union

PREFACE TO THE SECOND EDITION

Since I completed the first version of this book just a year ago I find myself with nearly 40% more material and a new publisher. It will be apparent from the title that it was originally intended for a medical readership, that is clinicians and medical experts. However, the sales figures for that first edition show that more copies were bought by solicitors and barristers than by doctors. I have therefore tried to change the emphasis a little this time so as to give lawyers more insight into the difficulties facing the doctor and the expectations held by the patient.

Medical experts, when faced with a similar set of facts, often have little difficulty in agreeing what constitutes good practice. The arguments, of course, arise when the experts for the opposing sides have been asked to give their opinions against different factual backgrounds. The lawyers for each side will therefore be particularly concerned to locate all possible sources of evidence of fact and to leave no stone unturned in enhancing its credibility. In this second edition I therefore devoted a chapter to each of these aspects of evidence and have relied heavily on three cases which came to trial last year, namely *McGrath v Cole* (1994), *Fellows v Thomas* (1994), and *Morrison v Forsyth* (1994).

The chapter on the motives for litigation has also been considerably extended in this edition. It has long been recognised that the sensitive and honest handling of a patient is a powerful weapon in the doctor's armoury for preventing litigation. The significance of the doctor's manner and the patient's reaction to it are examined in detail.

Several other textbooks have become available in recent years and are excellent guidelines to the legal advancement or defence of a case. I make no claim to compete with those books. I do, however, firmly believe that my approach helps the reader to appreciate the true nature of events at the patient's bedside or at the doctor's desk. This, after all, is where the alleged negligence occurs and what must be properly understood by all who are involved in the case.

Walter Scott
Slough
May 1995

CONTENTS

PART A

THE SUBSTANTIVE LAW OF NEGLIGENCE

I   THE NATURE OF NEGLIGENCE

Negligence is not a legal concept which is peculiar to medical practice and it is not even confined to the professions in general. It concerns the harm which any person may have sustained at the hands of another who should have taken care not to inflict it.

A successful action in negligence necessitates the demonstration of three elements, and while this part of the book is concerned with a detailed study of those elements it may be helpful to start by providing a very brief outline of them here.

First, there is the existence of a duty of care. This means that the defendant must have realised that the plaintiff might be affected by the activity in question. In a medical negligence case it would be concerned with whether the doctor should have realised that his patient would be affected by the treatment he gave.

Secondly, there is the breach of that duty. This relates to whether the defendant's activity fell below the standard that could reasonably have been expected of him. The question dealt with here would be whether the doctor's management of the case in its widest sense was in accordance with currently accepted practice.

Thirdly, there is the question of causation. This concerns the difficulty of showing that the wrongful act was responsible for the damage. Causation is often the hardest of the three elements to demonstrate in a medical negligence case, and poses what are sometimes insurmountable difficulties for patients. If a woman is knocked down on a pedestrian crossing and her leg is broken, she has no difficulty in showing that the accident was the cause of her injury. This contrasts with the patient who is already ill before he enters the doctor's consulting room. If he fails to survive the illness his widow may argue that he died because of the treatment, but the doctor will argue that he died in spite of it.

Thus any action in negligence needs the fulfilment of these three elements to be successful. The basic concepts are the same for all actions of this type but in medical cases the details of the case will have to be considered against the peculiarities of the profession, the workings of the human body and the natural history of the disease process.

3

II   THE EXISTENCE OF A DUTY OF CARE

SUMMARY

(i)   Introduction

If two people make a contract, they are aware of each other's existence before they even consider making that contract. The terms of the contract are drawn up by negotiation, such that each one knows what is expected of the other. For instance, in a contract for the renovation of a car, the owner knows he will have to pay an agreed sum of money. Similarly, the garage worker will know that he has to carry out agreed repairs and improvements. He will also know that the work has to be of a certain standard and it has to be completed by a certain date. This means that the terms of the contract are agreed, or implied, before either person starts to perform his part of the arrangement. If one of them later thinks that the other has failed to keep to the agreement, there is a ready frame of reference available to assist in deciding whether the allegation can be substantiated. Inadequate payment by the owner can be compared with the agreed price, and late completion of the work can be compared to the original date.

In tort, the relationship is entirely different. The parties may not even know of each other's existence before the act in question takes place, and they are very unlikely to have considered it as a deliberate and planned transaction. No thought is likely to be given to the matter until the accident happens. For instance, a man who is hit in the eye by a carelessly-thrown stone will be unaware of the offender or the missile until he sustains the injury.

These remarks apply to torts generally. They are applicable frequently to defamation, nuisance and occupier's liability. In medical negligence, however, there are two important differences which can set the study of this well apart from that of other torts. One difference is that the doctor always knows of the existence of his patient and the doctor's attention is focused on the patient during the treatment. The other difference is that the doctor's negligence may not cause harm until very much later, or at least the patient may not be aware of it until much later. For instance, in *Pleydell v Aubyn* (1993), a two year old girl with persistent abdominal pains was admitted to hospital by her general practitioner. Delay was alleged in arranging hospital admission and at operation she was found to have suffered a perforated appendix. Twenty five years later she was married and found herself unable to conceive. Investigation by a gynaecologist showed that multiple adhesions had followed the peritoneal sepsis and that these had obstructed her fallopian tubes. She attempted to sue the general practitioner even though it had taken her all those years to realise that his alleged negligence had caused her infertility.

(ii)   The neighbour principle

We have seen how a successful negligence action needs, among other things, the demonstration that a duty of care existed. In other words, it is necessary to show that the defendant should have taken care not to harm the plaintiff in question. At its simplest, a motorist can be expected to take notice of other motorists on the road but he cannot be expected to allow for a pedestrian stepping out from behind a hedge at night. This raises the question of who should be at the forefront of a defendant's mind at any particular moment. The defendant cannot be blamed for damage sustained by someone if he was not in a position to know the other person was there.

The traditional approach appears to have been that a defendant could only be expected to be aware of anyone who could be seen or heard, or who was in close proximity. It seemed out of the question to expect a defendant to make allowances for people if he had never heard of them and they were hundreds of miles away. This changed, however, with *Donoghue v Stevenson* (1932), which laid the foundations of the 'neighbour principle'. In that case, two girls were sitting at a table in a café in Paisley, near Glasgow. One of them had bought some ginger beer and was drinking it from the bottle. When she had nearly finished she allowed her friend a drink. Unfortunately, a snail had been included accidentally in the contents during the manufacturing process. When the second girl found that she had a foreign body in her mouth, she spat it out, realised it was a snail and sued the manufacturers.

There was, of course, a contract between the café owner and the girl who had bought the bottle. There would also have been a contract between the bottler and the café owner. The doctrine of 'privity of contract' prevented the second girl from suing on either of these contracts. She was unable to sue the café owner for selling the contaminated bottle, and she was unable to sue the manufacturer for supplying it in the first place. She was also, incidentally, unable to sue her friend because she had not paid her (given her 'consideration') and therefore no contract existed here either. In any event, the second girl was probably unwilling to do so because she was the first girl's friend and felt she had been allowed to finish the bottle as an act of kindness.

The second girl's only avenue was therefore to sue the manufacturer in tort. In effect, this meant suing in negligence and she first had to show that a duty of care existed between the manufacturer and herself. She met immediate difficulty. The bottler argued that no duty could exist. He had never seen her and did not even know of her existence. Furthermore, his factory was hundreds of miles away from her. On this basis, he could not possibly be expected to know that she, of all people, would drink his ginger beer and be harmed by it.

The principle at the heart of the matter was of such profound importance for the development of English law that, on appeal, it came before the House of Lords. Their Lordships had to decide in general terms what limits should be imposed on the concept of a duty of care. In other words, they had to define the nature of the relationship in such a way that this case, and others which would surely follow in the future, could be given a decision on whether or not the said duty existed. It was Lord Atkin who expressed the difficulty by posing the question, 'Who is my neighbour?'.

The answer he gave was:

> ... persons who are so closely and directly affected by my act that I ought reasonably to have them in contemplation as being so affected while I am directing my mind to the acts or omissions which are called into question.

Put simply, this means that a person's legal neighbour is anyone whom he should realise might be affected by the things he does. It is important to appreciate that Lord Atkin was not concerned with a geographical relationship. Rather, he was concerned with the proximity of the relationship in terms of the activity in question. In the case before him, he was well aware that the girl drank the snail hundreds of miles away from the factory, and that the manufacturers had never heard of her. He made the point, however, that they should have realised that allowing the snail to become included in their bottle might cause someone, somewhere, some distress.

It is clear that a legal neighbour is not the same as a neighbour in the ordinary English sense of the word. A person may be one kind of neighbour, or the other kind, or he may even be both.

(iii) The patient as the doctor's legal neighbour

We have seen how the modern definition of a legal neighbour became established in *Donoghue v Stevenson* (1932). This holds good in any negligence action, and a medical case is no exception. If it can be shown that the doctor should realise that a patient might be affected by the treatment then it establishes automatically the neighbour principle. It goes without saying that this is so. The effect of this is that there is normally no difficulty for a patient who is suing his doctor to demonstrate the first element in his action: that a duty of care did exist.

We normally think of the relationship existing between a general practitioner and a patient who is on his National Health Service list. However, the concept can be extended easily to temporary residents. It is evident that the doctor must realise that this category of patient, as much as the others on his ordinary list, are likely to be affected by how he treats them. It can be extended even further to include the 'good Samaritan'. A general practitioner may be on holiday well away from his own practice area, and attend an accident victim at the roadside. There is no question of the doctor's Family Health Services Authority imposing a statutory obligation on him to treat such a patient, and he may not even be paid for doing so. He does it through the goodness of his heart. If he establishes contact with the patient and takes any part in medical treatment he will have established a duty of care because he will have put himself in a position of realising that what he does might affect the patient. On the other hand, if he decides to 'pass by on the other side', no duty will arise, because no treatment was started.

The question of whether or not a particular person is a patient for the purposes of the general practitioner's obligations to his Family Health Services Authority is covered by paragraph 4 of the 'Terms of Service for Doctors'.[1] The list includes such persons as those already on his list, those whom he has agreed to accept onto his list, temporary residents and those on whose behalf he is

> ... requested to give treatment which is immediately required owing to an accident or other emergency at any place in his practice area.

(iv)   The doctor's legal relationship with his patient

The neighbour principle formulated in *Donoghue v Stevenson* (1932) made it clear that the patient is a legal neighbour of the

---

1   The National Health Service (General Medical Services) Regulations 1992, pp 40-41.

doctor and that a duty of care is therefore owed. This is at its clearest at the bedside on a house call, or when a patient is sitting at the doctor's desk in the surgery. Any treatment, or lack of it, will obviously affect the patient. However, the duty continues to exist even when the proximity, on the face of it, is not as close.

Telephone calls will suffice to show how the relationship holds good even when the apparent proximity is stretched. It is evident that the advice a doctor gives over the telephone is as likely to affect the patient as when it is spoken across the desk.

Suppose a mother speaks to the office receptionist in the first instance about her son's symptoms, and the message is relayed to the doctor in another room. The doctor gives the advice, which the receptionist passes on to the patient. It is apparent that the duty of care still exists, because the doctor should realise that any advice he gives will affect the patient, even though they have not spoken personally.

Similar remarks apply to a failure to follow up the results of investigations. If a patient has a cervical smear taken, a duty of care arises at that stage. It will continue to exist until she is notified of a normal result. If the doctor negligently files an abnormal result, the duty of care will still be in existence, even though the patient had no contact with the doctor at that stage.

The majority of defendants in negligence actions are not trying purposely to make any difference to the plaintiff one way or the other. In a word, they are just careless about their act and give no thought to any potential victim. In *Bolton v Stone* (1951), a batsman hit a ball out of a cricket ground and injured a passer-by, who sought to sue him on the basis that a duty of care existed. The defendant batsman clearly gave no thought to the plaintiff as he struck the ball and had no intention of affecting her in any way. When the case came to trial it was held that no duty of care was owed. The defendant was able to show that the fence at the edge of the ground was sufficiently far away and sufficiently high for him to have quite reasonably thought that there was an almost negligible chance of being able to hit the ball over the top of it. Furthermore, he adduced evidence that his predecessors on that ground had only hit a ball over the fence on six occasions in the preceding 30 years.

Similarly, in *Haley v London Electricity Board* (1964), a partially sighted man fell into a hole in the pavement where street repairs were being undertaken. The electricity board argued that no duty of care existed in respect of partially-sighted people because they represented a minute proportion of persons likely to walk along the pavement. The LEB asserted that their only duty was to fence the hole such as to make it safe for fully-sighted people. Counsel for the plaintiff succeeded in showing that the proportion of pedestrians who were partially sighted was sufficiently high to have given rise to a duty of care towards that group.

The attitude of the doctor to his patient is entirely different. The doctor knows of the patient's existence, has almost certainly made special arrangements to see the patient and is making a positive effort to affect him. He is trying to improve the patient's opportunity for cure by administering the treatment. This means that doctors and patients are a much closer kind of legal neighbour than in most negligence cases. The patient therefore has no difficulty at all in showing that a duty of care exists.

(v)   Delegation of the doctor's duties to a colleague

No general practitioner can be expected to be available to his patients every hour of every day. To ensure proper rest and recreation it is usual for doctors to have a rota system by which they take turns with their partners to be on call. Alternatively, they may avail themselves of a deputising service to assist with out-of-hours cover. The question then arises of who is responsible when something goes wrong with the treatment which was provided by a deputy. This is covered by paragraph 20 of the 'Terms of Service for Doctors'[2] to the effect that the patient's own general practitioner is responsible for treatment given by a deputy unless that deputy is also on the Family Health Services Authority's medical list. This proviso is presumably intended to cover the situation when a partner in the same practice is on duty.

---

2   The National Health Service (General Medical Services) Regulations 1992, p 47.

In this case the patient's own doctor will have passed on the responsibility to his partner.

The wording of the regulations protects the patient who is treated negligently by a locum tenens, where the locum has been appointed by his own doctor on a casual basis and subsequently disappears. In that case the patient is still in a position to pursue his own doctor because the general practitioner retained responsibility for the locum.

Quite apart from the responsibility imposed on the general practitioner by the Family Health Services Authority for out-of-hours cover, the General Medical Council has provided guidelines[3] which carry considerable weight and correlate with the expectations of the Family Health Services Authority. The General Medical Council points out (in paragraph 40) that:

> General practitioners who make use of deputising services have a duty to satisfy themselves that their deputies are registered medical practitioners who have the appropriate experience, knowledge and skill to discharge the duties for which they will be responsible.

In terms of hospital practice, the General Medical Council has similar expectations in that:

> Consultants in hospital practice, and doctors engaged in private practice on either a part-time or a whole time basis, should seek to ensure that proper arrangements are put in hand to cover their duties ...

The General Medical Council has also concerned itself with the relationship between the patient and the doctor who delegates part of the treatment to another professional person such as a nurse or a physiotherapist. Although there is full approval for delegation for these kinds of treatment, the ultimate responsibility remains with the doctor. The General Medical Council expresses its view in terms that:

---

3   The General Medical Council. Professional conduct and discipline: Fitness to practise, April 1992.

... a doctor who delegates treatment or other procedures must be satisfied that the person to whom they are delegated is competent to carry them out. It is also important that the doctor should retain ultimate responsibility for the management of these patients because only the doctor has received the necessary training to undertake this responsibility.

(vi)   The doctor's duty of care to persons other than his patient

It is clear that the doctor owes a duty of care to his patient when he is face to face with him at the surgery premises or on a house call. He also owes that duty when he is giving advice to the patient on the telephone or when he is writing a letter to him with the results of investigations.

We now come to consider whether this duty extends to persons other than the patient with whom the doctor is dealing at any particular time. We have to bear in mind that the patient may have a relationship with persons whom the doctor has never seen, and that the doctor may well be unaware of their very existence.

Suppose a general practitioner sees a child with chicken pox – a common enough occurrence. The question arises of whether it is acceptable for him to confine his advice to the treatment of that child. Should he think of other family members who may develop shingles as a result of contact with the child? In one case, the parents of a child with chicken pox became very angry with the general practitioner who had failed to warn them of this possibility. The child's grandmother came to stay at the house the day after the consultation and it was not long before she developed the lesions of shingles.

A similar difficulty can arise when a young child is vaccinated against poliomyelitis. There is a one-in-two-million chance that a person in contact with a newly-vaccinated individual will develop the disease. Despite this extreme rarity, the British National Formulary gives a clear warning that:

... the need for strict personal hygiene must be stressed; the contacts of a recently vaccinated baby should be advised of the necessity for personal hygiene, particularly of the need to wash their hands after changing the baby's napkin.

In one case, a man had a history of being hepatitis B positive and was erroneously told by his general practitioner, after an up-to-date test, that he was clear. The man relied on this advice and indulged in homosexual relations with another man. The latter relied on the reassurance given to him by the first man, but he later found that he himself had become hepatitis B positive. He advanced a case against the general practitioner of his homosexual partner. It was based on the premise that the doctor should have realised that any negligent advice he gave to his patient might affect other men by inducing reliance on it and influencing their activities with each other.

These examples clearly show that the doctor's duty of care extends to a wider range of people than the patients whom he finds himself treating at first hand.

III THE BREACH OF THE DUTY OF CARE

SUMMARY

(i) Introduction

We saw in the previous chapter that a patient's first task in a negligence action is to show that the doctor owed her a duty of care. We also saw that she was unlikely to have any difficulty in doing so. Even in the so-called 'good Samaritan' situation, the duty becomes established as soon as the doctor becomes involved in any kind of treatment.

That a duty of care was owed will be apparent from the statement of claim. When counsel for the plaintiff drafts this document a paragraph will be included with words to the effect that the defendant 'owed the plaintiff a duty to exercise all reasonable skill and care of the kind to be expected of a general practitioner'. This is included for the avoidance of doubt because that document is part of the pleadings that represent the 'agenda for trial'. The judge may be dealing with other negligence cases which are not of a medical nature and counsel will want to leave no doubt that a duty of care was owed. The statement of claim may also substantiate the existence of the duty by referring to the fact that the patient was on the general practitioner's National Health Service list. The general practitioner has statutory obligations under his 'Terms of Service' with his Family Health Services Authority. Paragraph 12 of the regulations puts the general practitioner under a duty to provide 'all necessary and appropriate personal medical services of the type usually provided by general medical practitioners'.

It is worth quoting the first two sections of paragraph 12 in full as they are central to defining the extent of the duty of care that the Family Health Services Authority expects general practitioners to provide. The relevant part of the contract reads as follows:

NATURE OF SERVICE TO PATIENTS[4]

12(1) Subject to paragraphs 3, 13 and 44, a doctor shall render to his patients all necessary and appropriate personal medical services of the type usually provided by general medical practitioners.

(2) The services which a doctor is required by sub-paragraph (1) to render shall include the following:-

(a) giving advice, where appropriate, to a patient in connection with the patient's general health, and in particular about the significance of diet, exercise, the use of tobacco, the consumption of alcohol and the misuse of drugs and solvents;

---

4   The National Health Service (General Medical Services) Regulations 1992. Statutory Instrument 1992 No 635, Schedule 2.

(b)   offering to patients consultations and, where appropriate, physical examinations for the purpose of identifying, or reducing the risk of, disease or injury;

(c)   offering to patients, where appropriate, vaccination or immunisation against Measles, Mumps, Rubella, Pertussis, Poliomyelitis, Diphtheria and Tetanus;

(d)   arranging for the referral of patients, as appropriate, for the provision of any other services under the National Health Service Act 1977;

(e)   giving advice, as appropriate, to enable patients to avail themselves of services provided by a local social services authority.

It can be seen that in paragraph 12(2) the regulations impose certain obligations on the doctor, but paragraph 3 provides some restriction to these obligations such that they do not become unduly onerous or demanding. The relevant part of paragraph 3 reads as follows:

General

3 Where a decision whether any, and if so what, action is to be taken under these terms of service requires the exercise of professional judgment, a doctor shall not, in reaching that decision, be expected to exercise a higher degree of skill, knowledge and care than –

(b) ... that which general practitioners as a class may reasonably be expected to exercise.

In this chapter we consider the second element in a negligence action, that of whether the duty of care was breached. By this we mean whether the plaintiff received a standard of care which fell below that which she had a right to expect. This is a much more difficult task than showing that a duty of care was owed. This is partly because the standard is so variable and depends on such matters as what kind of doctor the patient was seeing and the period of time during which the events in question occurred. We can now move on to consider the criteria which are used when assessing the level of care that could have been expected. It is only when this has been defined clearly that the plaintiff can attempt to show that it was breached.

(ii)   'The man on the Clapham omnibus'

A contract between two people defines clearly what each has a right to expect of the other. In the example on page 5 we saw how the car owner had a right to expect a renovation to be completed in a certain way and by a certain date. In return, the worker had a right to expect payment of the agreed sum. If either one failed to fulfil these obligations, the other could exercise a legal right, under the terms of the contract, to recover his loss.

Although the general practitioner's relationship with his Family Health Services Authority is one of statutory duty rather than contract, an analogy can be drawn in terms of expectations. The regulations state in paragraph 12 what the authority expects of the doctor. They specify:

> ... all necessary and appropriate personal medical services of the type usually provided by general medical practitioners

although there is some room for argument about exactly what that means in any particular set of circumstances.

In tort, the situation is less clearly defined. There has been no written, or even spoken, agreement about what is expected. Indeed, most plaintiffs in negligence actions expect nothing at all from the defendants before the incident in question. It is only when they do receive something, and that something is unwelcome, that they are even aware of the defendants' existence and think of suing them.

We can illustrate this by reference to the cases discussed on pages 10 and 11. In *Bolton v Stone* (1951), the passer-by was unaware of the batsman, or even of the ball, until he was injured. In *Haley v London Electricity Board* (1964), the partially sighted man was unaware of the poorly-fenced hole until he found himself lying at the bottom of it.

Medical cases are rather different in this respect. The patient and the doctor know that they are going to meet. Furthermore, each has an idea about what to expect, although there has been no previous agreement about the outcome. Indeed, one common cause of complaint is that the patient's expectation of the result of his treatment exceeds that of the doctor's knowledge of what he can provide. Many a practitioner has been able to prevent this kind of situation arising by explaining at the outset the extent of the benefit that can be provided realistically. A patient who is given an explanation of this kind is likely to lower her expectations to a reasonable level and is therefore much less likely to be dissatisfied.

The lack of prior agreement about the rights of a plaintiff against a defendant in an action in tort has led to the concept of the 'reasonable man'. The legal system has to have some sort of test that it can apply to a particular defendant's act to decide whether the plaintiff has good grounds for complaint. It is essential that plaintiffs do not achieve compensation for unreasonable expectations. The test also has to be flexible. Accepted standards may vary from time to time and from place to place.

In one case of negligence, which did not involve any special skill on the part of the defendant, the judge was anxious to find an expression that would illustrate the kind of person whose standard of care would equate with that which could be expected of the defendant. The judge concerned coined the phrase 'the man on the Clapham omnibus'. This has been absorbed into legal phraseology and is used when referring to the kind of person whose standard would be regarded as acceptable. This test would be used in a negligence action which did not involve any special skill or knowledge on the part of the defendant. Needless to say, in medical negligence cases we are very much concerned with special skills and we can now consider how the law ensures that the correct standard is used. It would be unfair to the defending doctor to impose the expectation of too high a standard, and it would be correspondingly unfair to the plaintiff to expect him to accept a lower standard.

(iii) The standard expected of doctors in general

We have seen how the law has a test that is used in ordinary negligence cases to decide if the defendant has breached the duty owed to the plaintiff. That was the 'reasonable man test' and it referred to a quite basic standard in a defendant who was not expected to have any special skill or knowledge.

19

The difficulty, of course, is that patients expect their doctors to deliver a higher standard. Indeed, that is why they go to them for help.

It is evident that a sliding scale must operate when considering the standard expected of different classes of doctors. This is well illustrated in *Philips v William Whiteley* (1938). A woman went to a jeweller to have her ears pierced. Unfortunately, they became septic after the procedure and she endured a fair amount of suffering. She sought to sue the jeweller on the basis that his standard of ear piercing fell short; in other words, that he was negligent. She had no difficulty in showing that a duty of care was owed and there was no doubt that it was the procedure which caused the sepsis. Her case was good on the existence of a duty of care and on causation. It was the second of the three elements, the breach of duty, that posed the difficulty for her. She argued that the technique and the facilities for the procedure were not as good as that which a surgeon would have used. The judge dismissed her claim. He conceded that she had a right to expect a standard higher than that of the ordinary man with no special skill but added that she did not have a right to expect the standard of a surgeon when she attended the jeweller. Doubtless, the lower price paid to the jeweller compared to a higher fee that a surgeon would have charged had some influence on the decision.

Philips v Whiteley shows that the test for judging a particular defendant depends on what can reasonably be expected of him in the circumstances. This particular defendant was not judged against the 'man on the Clapham omnibus', nor was he judged by comparison with a surgeon. In his case, the 'reasonable man' meant the 'reasonable jeweller'.

The concept of ensuring that the standard imposed when judging the defendant is matched to the standards that can reasonably be expected of that particular class of persons received judicial comment in *Bolam v Friern Hospital Management Committee* (1957). The facts of the case are worth summarising because even at the time of writing, nearly four decades later, the judgment provides the yardstick by which the standard of care is judged in every medical negligence case.

Mr Bolam was a patient who suffered from depressive illness. In 1954 his general practitioner referred him to a psychiatrist. The specialist decided to give him electroconvulsive therapy and enlisted the co-operation of an anaesthetist. A decision was taken that muscle relaxants should not be used during the convulsion because there were recognised side-effects. Unfortunately, when Mr Bolam recovered from the anaesthetic he found that both hips had been fractured. He argued that the specialists had been negligent in not administering the relaxants and that, if they had done so, he would probably not have suffered the fractures. McNair J found for the defendant. He considered the standard that Mr Bolam could have expected of the hospital specialists and it is worth quoting the relevant part of the judgment:

> When you get a situation which involves the use of some special skill or competence, then the test as to whether there has been negligence is not the test of the man on the top of the Clapham Omnibus because he has not got this special skill. The test is the standard of the ordinary skilled man exercising and professing to have that special skill.

This 1957 case established the precedent that doctors, and indeed other people with special skills, are to be judged against the standards of their colleagues who do the same kind of work.

(iv) The 'responsible body of medical opinion'

We have considered the traditional approach to the standard of care which was expected of the 'reasonable man'. We also saw how it became refined and narrowed in *Bolam* where the defendant had a special skill upon which the plaintiff relied.[5]

One of the difficulties with medical negligence cases is that there is ample scope for difference of opinion. By this is meant that two doctors, both equally skilled and careful, may have very different views about how to put the patient to an advantage. This has its root in the fact that medical practice is an art as well as a science. All doctors know that there is more to therapeutics

---

5 For a recent discussion about the relevance of the *Bolam* test to different clinical situations, see James Watt in *Clinical Risk*, March 1995, pp 84-85.

than choosing the right drug in the correct dose. Courtesy and kindness go a long way towards making a patient feel better. Every doctor has his own style and personality and he owes it to his patient to bring these factors to bear in whatever way he feels appropriate.

Quite apart from varying technical approaches and different styles, there is a further point which means that doctors must be allowed some room for manoeuvre. The imposition of strict and narrow standards in medical practice would stifle its development. That is not to condone experiments on patients, but there must be some latitude for doctors to exercise their skills in a way that puts the patient to the best advantage. McNair J recognised this point when giving judgment in *Bolam*. He observed that:

> ... a doctor is not guilty of negligence if he has acted in accordance with the practice accepted as proper by a responsible body of medical men skilled in that particular art. ... Putting it the other way round, a doctor is not negligent if he is acting in accordance with such a practice merely because there is a body of opinion that takes a contrary view.

It is from here that we get the expression 'a responsible body of medical opinion'.

No case has yet come before the courts in which a decision has been taken about how many doctors are required before a 'responsible body' can be said to exist.[6] Putting it another way, no precedent has been set to indicate how small a proportion of all doctors the body can be and still qualify as being 'responsible'. Even if a suggested figure was given it would be unusable

---

6   Just as this book was going to press, the Court of Appeal decision in *Defreitas v O'Brien* became available and was reported in *The Times*, 16 February 1995. The Court of Appeal held that a 'small number of medical practitioners' could constitute a responsible body of medical opinion. The plaintiff in this case referred to *Hills v Potter* (1984), in which the judge required that there be a 'substantial' body of opinion and she argued that this word had been used in a quantitative sense. In *Defreitas'* case, it was held that 'the issue could not be determined by counting heads' and that 'it was open to the judge to find as a fact that a small number of specialists constituted a responsible body ...'.

because a survey of the opinions of all the doctors in the country would be out of the question. In *Bolam*, McNair J was making the point that no doctor can have his treatment condoned if it is seriously out of step with what his colleagues would have done. A cynical patient might argue that this gives doctors too much room to exercise their discretion in the management of patients' illnesses, because all a defendant has to do is to find one other doctor to stand up in court and say he would have done the same.

One thing, however, is certain. The defendant's view does not have to represent a majority opinion. McNair J would probably have been quite happy to accept a minority view as long as the group was not so small that it represented an insignificant percentage of the two groups added together.

What happens in practice is that each side will canvass the views of its own experts. The defendant will find colleagues to say that the treatment he gave was reasonable, and the plaintiff will attempt to find experts who will say that it was negligent. If a plaintiff approaches one particular expert and is told that the treatment was perfectly in order, and that his case cannot be supported, he may well seek a second opinion particularly if the first one did not appear to have been properly argued. If the second opinion is of the same view, it becomes increasingly obvious that his case is probably groundless.

Let us suppose, however, that the plaintiff finds two experts who will support his case on negligence. Let us also suppose that the defence has two experts who are of the opposite view, in other words that the treatment was not negligent and that no liability can attach to the doctor for the harm which occurred. In court the plaintiff's advisers will call their own witnesses for examination-in-chief. Counsel for that side will ask questions designed to elicit answers that support the credibility of the witness and the unreasonableness of the treatment that the defendant gave. The proceedings will next involve counsel for the defence subjecting those witnesses to cross-examination. Counsel will attempt to discredit the experience and background of these witnesses and show that their opinions are ill-founded. He may quote from the written opinions of his own experts, disclosed earlier in the 'discovery' procedure, to undermine the reasoning of the witnesses in question. The proceedings will then be repeated, such that Counsel for that side has the opportunity of examining his own witnesses-in-chief, who are then cross-examined by Counsel for the first side.

In this way, the judge has the opportunity to listen to the views expressed by the experts of the opposing sides. Any weaknesses in their reasoning will have been exposed and they will have been tested on the textbooks and literature on which they sought to rely when giving their opinions. This puts the judge in a position to decide upon the standing of the two views expressed. If only the plaintiff's experts appear reasonable, she clearly wins. Conversely, if only the defendant's experts appear reasonable, *he* will win. However, if both appear reasonable, the defendant still wins because he has shown evidence of a 'responsible body' even though there was an equally responsible body who took the opposite view.

It is important to realise that the judge cannot prefer one treatment to the other. In *Maynard v West Midlands Regional Health Authority* (1985), one of the Law Lords in the House of Lords said:

> I have to say that a judge's 'preference' for one body of distinguished professional opinion to another also professionally distinguished is not sufficient to establish negligence in a practitioner whose actions have received the seal of approval of those whose opinions, truthfully expressed, honestly held, were not preferred. If this was the real reason for the judge's finding, he erred in law even though elsewhere in his judgment he stated the law correctly. For in the realm of diagnosis and treatment negligence is not established by preferring one respectable body of professional opinion to another. Failure to exercise the ordinary skill of a doctor (in the appropriate speciality, if he be a specialist) is necessary.

This part of the judgment suggests that however unattractive a minority view appears to the judge to be, he cannot reject it if it is genuinely supported by a significant body of doctors. Despite this apparent acknowledgement by the courts that doctors know more about medical practice than lawyers, the courts have nevertheless succeeded in maintaining their status as the final arbiter with regard to whether or not a particular practice is negligent.

(v)   The opinions of the experts for each side

It is important to remember that expert opinions about the correctness of the treatment in question are given against a factual background which may itself be in dispute. What was, or was not, reasonable is almost certain to depend on the facts of the case.

In *Coker v Dolland* (1993), a girl had been put on contraceptive pills by her general practitioner and shortly afterwards died of a cerebral thrombosis which was attributed to the Pill. Her father alleged that his daughter had made frequent visits to the doctor complaining of severe headaches and tunnel vision. The notes supported this by nothing more than a passing reference to a possible diagnosis of migraine on one occasion. Furthermore, they indicated that there had been good grounds for attributing the headaches to a respiratory infection. Unfortunately, the father died before the case came to trial and much of his evidence had to be excluded because it was hearsay. The defence successfully established that their version of events was more likely to be the correct one. The expert for the plaintiff intended to rely on the warnings in the *Monthly Index of Medical Specialities* (MIMS) and the *British National Formulary* (BNF) that the symptoms alleged by the father, especially being voiced on numerous occasions, were grounds for stopping the Pill and that the failure to do so was negligent. He faced cross-examination by counsel for the defence. When confronted with the evidence of fact that the symptoms may well have had a respiratory basis, he could do no more than agree that the continuation of the Pill was perfectly reasonable and that there was no question of negligence.

Coker v Dolland is a good illustration of how bringing a case to trial is a process by which the areas of dispute are refined and narrowed. The experts for each side had held diametrically opposed views on negligence, and this was caused by their working from different factual backgrounds. As soon as the facts had become established in court, in the defendant's favour, the opinions of the experts immediately fell into line with each other. The expert for the plaintiff had to agree, under cross-examination by counsel for the defence, that there had been no negligence.

(vi)   The standard expected of an individual doctor

At the beginning of this chapter we saw how the law traditionally only imposed tortious liability on a defendant whose act fell below the standard of the 'reasonable man'. We then saw how that standard became refined, in cases of medical negligence, in *Bolam v Friern Hospital Management Committee* (1957). It was made to relate to the medical skills which the defendant offered and upon which the plaintiff relied. But McNair J's judgment was more precise than merely to draw a distinction between lay people and doctors. Let us return to the relevant part of the judgment. He referred to the test as relating to:

> ... the standard of the ordinary skilled man exercising and professing to have that particular special skill.

He was here referring to specialism. The doctors concerned in that case were psychiatrists and anaesthetists, and their treatment would have to be compared with that of other doctors in those particular specialities.

Despite its name, general practice is a speciality. At least it needs special study to master it. It has its own skills and textbooks and its own Royal College. In this sense it is no different from hospital specialities. The important point is that the treatment given by a general practitioner must be compared to the standards regarded as being proper by other general practitioners.

Suppose a patient was suffering from chest pains which were later found to have been caused by ischaemic heart disease. The patient feels that his general practitioner was negligent in not making earlier referral to hospital and he consults a solicitor. If the latter is not particularly experienced he may go to a cardiologist for an expert opinion. A cardiologist will consider the symptoms that were presented to the general practitioner, look at the result of the investigations that were done later in hospital and then may give the view that the general practitioner was negligent in not making earlier referral. The case comes to trial and the plaintiff attempts to sue his general practitioner with expert evidence of opinion given by a cardiologist. If the defending general practitioner can bring the evidence of another general practitioner to the effect that there was no negligence, the plaintiff is unlikely to succeed. The judge will have in mind McNair J's reference to the standard of men 'exercising and professing to have that special skill'.

This is not to say that the opinion of the cardiologist would be of no value to the plaintiff. It will almost certainly be needed for causation. This will involve a study of how much difference, if any, the doctor's alleged negligence made to the outcome of the illness. The cardiologist, if he is advising the solicitor properly as an expert, will point out that a general practitioner's opinion should be sought on liability, while leaving him to deal with causation.

Expert opinions aimed at demonstrating general practitioner liability are not only sought by disgruntled patients, they are also sought by defending hospitals. If a hospital is being sued for the mismanagement of a patient admitted as an emergency by a deputising doctor in the night they may seek to shift some of the blame for the damage on to the general practitioner. They will argue that if the patient's own doctor had acted properly and arranged admission at an earlier stage in the illness, and at a time of day when consultant staff were on the premises, the outcome of the treatment would have been better. If the hospital is successful with this line of reasoning it will be able to reduce the damages payable, because it can call for a contribution from the general practitioner. This means that a general practitioner may find himself defending an action on two fronts. The patient may be suing the general practitioner for not arranging earlier admission, and the hospital may be calling for a contribution to the damages.

Before 1990 it was often the case that the general practitioner and the hospital specialist were represented by the same defence organisation. This made the division of damages academic, because it was all being funded from the same source. However, since the introduction of the 'Crown indemnity' scheme in that year, the difference between various doctors' responsibilities has been brought into sharp focus. The state-funded system will be only too keen to call for a contribution from a defence society. Doubtless, the opposite applies equally strongly.

In one case, an elderly lady fell off a balcony and injured her ankle. She visited her general practitioner, who diagnosed a sprain. Despite the doctor's strapping and prescription for pain-killing tablets the joint continued to be painful and she later attended an accident and emergency department. An X-ray was taken. This showed a fracture, which by this time had been present for several days. The old lady was admitted for operative treatment and the insertion of wires, but the final result was unsatisfactory and she was left with a limp.

She sued the hospital for mismanagement of the operative procedure and for incorrect timing of the removal of the wires. The hospital argued that the principal cause of the poor result was the delay in starting treatment and that this had been incurred by the general practitioner in the first place. The defending hospital was therefore anxious to secure a report on general practitioner liability and approached an expert in that speciality for a view which, they hoped, would support their case and reduce their damages payment by calling for a contribution from the family doctor.

(vii) The solicitor's role in the apportionment of liability

In the previous section we saw how a defending hospital might be anxious to secure an opinion on general practitioner liability with a view to joining the practitioner as a third party who would then, in effect, become an additional defendant. This will have the effect of shifting some of the blame and thereby reducing the damages to be paid by the hospital. If this course of action is successful it will have the effect that the patient will recover a smaller amount from the hospital.

If the patient has not pursued a cause of action against the general practitioner she will clearly recover nothing from him. She may, however, have a case against her solicitor for negligence. If the solicitor failed in his duty of care to involve all the appropriate defendants in the action, the patient may recover from the solicitor the damages which she would have recovered from the general practitioner but for the lawyer's negligence.

For this reason, solicitors are careful to consider involving all potential defendants at an early stage. A decision can easily be taken whether to join them as defendants when proceedings are instituted and the case has become more clearly defined on liability. Consideration may have to be given not only to a hospital and a general practitioner but perhaps also to an optician, for example, if he saw the patient in the first instance, or to a district nurse who may have visited the patient at home.

In one case, a young mother was concerned about her vision in one eye and went to an optician who sent her to the general practitioner who, in turn, referred her to an eye specialist. The surgeon found that she was suffering from a detached retina which responded poorly to treatment because of the alleged delay in referral. The general practitioner had relied on the optician's letter, which had conveyed very little sense of urgency. The patient sought to sue the doctor but the question arose of whether the optician had been negligent in his examination and in the report which he sent to the general practitioner.

In another case, an elderly man complained of a painful foot and an ulcerated toe. The general practitioner visited him, diagnosed peripheral vascular disease and asked the district nurse to attend. She made regular visits over a period of time, to dress the wound. When the doctor visited sometime later he found that the toe had developed gangrene. Although he arranged immediate hospital admission, it was only a matter of time before the leg had to be amputated below the knee. The liability of the doctor for delayed follow-up was not the only question of interest to the plaintiff's solicitor. He also wanted to know if the nurse had been negligent in failing to ask the doctor to review the case earlier in view of the allegedly obvious development of gangrene when she dressed the toe each day.

A solicitor's failure to include a potential defendant is not the only area in which he may find himself being sued for damages that were originally derived from medical negligence. Throughout the life of the case, the solicitor has many deadlines to meet with regard to the service of certain documents. If he fails in one of these, the defendant may apply to the court to have the case struck out for want of prosecution. For instance, a plaintiff approaches his solicitor near the end of the limitation period (three years from the date when the cause of action arose, or the plaintiff acquired the necessary degree of knowledge, whichever is the later) and the solicitor incurs unreasonable delay in issuing and serving the writ. The solicitor may find himself being sued for negligence by his client, with damages assessed at what the client would have recovered in the original medical negligence action had it been successful.

(viii) The selection of the appropriate defendants

It is of the utmost importance that the plaintiff's advisers choose the right defendants.

The selection process may be quite straightforward. Suppose that the patient visits his doctor on one occasion and is given a particular course of treatment which is followed by an adverse result. There can only be one potential defendant here. Conversely, if the patient was seen by a deputising doctor that night and is then followed up by a different partner in the practice the following morning, there will be three potential defendants, although in most cases one of them will probably stand out as being more likely to be liable than the other two. We saw too, in the previous section, how the solicitor will have to be careful to include the hospital if it was implicated, and how each defendant may try to shift some of the blame onto other defendants in the case.

These points will probably be fairly clear at the outset, at least to the solicitor, even if they are not unduly obvious to the patient and her family. As the case progresses, however, other potential defendants may emerge. In the previous section, we saw how a solicitor's failure to include a potential defendant could result in the solicitor himself being sued if that failure was negligent and caused the plaintiff to lose part of her damages claim. Conversely, the inclusion of too many defendants, some of whom can defend the case successfully, will result in the plaintiff having to pay their costs and this could use up a sizeable proportion of her winnings on the successful part of the case.

We can now consider the type of case where the litigation expands against further defendants as it progresses and this will be followed by a mention of the type of case where it contracts.

(a) The expansion of the case against further defendants

A convenient example here is the case of a woman who visited her company doctor for an annual medical examination which was intended to protect her from the adverse effects of her working environment. An unexpected abnormality appeared on X-ray. The company doctor sent the films to a consultant radiologist for comment and he also gave the patient a copy of the same films to take to her general practitioner. The consultant wanted further tests done before he saw the patient for assessment. The general practitioner merely reassured the patient that she need not be unduly concerned about the supposed abnormality because it was probably related to an injury which she had sustained many years previously. Unfortunately, the woman fell ill and died very shortly afterwards. A post-mortem showed that there was almost certainly a causal link between the death and the abnormality which had been shown on the X-ray.

The family initially blamed the general practitioner for providing unjustified reassurance when he was presented with the X-rays. The solicitor therefore obtained the relevant notes and sought expert opinion on the matter. Detailed investigation of the case showed that, far from being just one potential defendant there were three. The general practitioner might have been negligent with his unjustified reassurance. The radiologist might have been negligent by not insisting that he see the patient at first hand for assessment very soon after he received the X-rays. The company doctor might have been negligent in not arranging an appointment for the patient to be seen personally by the radiologist, and he might also have been negligent in not sending a letter, with the X-rays, to the general practitioner, insisting on specialist advice.

(b) The contraction of the case against fewer defendants

In contrast to the case above, where further defendants came to light as the case was investigated, we can consider another case where the opposite happened.

31

A man had been issued with prescriptions for tranquillisers at his general practitioner's surgery over a long period of time. Not all the repeat prescription cards were available with the notes that were disclosed, and there was some uncertainty about whether they had genuinely been lost or destroyed in earlier years, or whether they had been concealed by the defending doctor. In any event, it did prove possible for the plaintiff to show that he had received the tablets during the relevant years, and the defendants had difficulty in showing that they had given proper supervision. The difficulty for the patient's solicitor was that there were several partners in the practice, all of whom might have signed some of the repeat prescriptions and, to make it more complicated, the patient had been attending a different practice just previously and had at one stage even been getting repeat prescriptions from both at the same time.

The patient understandably felt that all the doctors were to blame for his damage to a greater or lesser extent. When this case was considered in detail, it became apparent that there was one particular doctor in one particular practice who had been responsible for the great majority of the prescriptions. The case was therefore narrowed down against him, and the other potential defendants were eliminated. The plaintiff was advised that even if he was successful against that particular defendant, a large part of his damages award would probably be absorbed by having to pay the costs of the others, who would have little difficulty in defending their positions.

(ix) The standard of general practitioners undertaking special procedures

The introduction of Kenneth Clarke's new contract for general practitioners in April 1990 added another dimension to their work. For years, a small minority of general practitioners had had a special interest in minor surgery and they would carry out operations themselves rather than refer the patient to hospital, where patients might be faced with a long waiting list. The new contract provided a fresh impetus for this work. Capitation fees had been reduced, and one of the steps which a doctor could take to maintain his income was to carry out surgical procedures at his practice premises and thereby claim the appropriate fee.

Inevitably, some practitioners are less skilled and less well equipped than their hospital colleagues to whom they would previously have made a referral. This raises the question of whether the patient has a right to expect an equally high standard from the general practitioner as from a consultant general surgeon or a plastic surgeon. In *Philips v William Whiteley* (1938) we saw how a decision had to be reached about the standard of care to be exercised when piercing a woman's ears. It was decided that a lesser standard should be imposed on the jeweller than on a surgeon. If this argument is applied to the area under discussion here, the decision in *Philips v William Whiteley* suggests that a patient cannot demand such a high standard from a general practitioner as from a surgeon.

If this precedent is followed, it raises another issue about general practitioner liability. A doctor owes it to his patient to secure whatever arrangement is, within reason, in the patient's best interests. If the doctor knows that the hospital can serve the patient better, the general practitioner should refer him there.

One of the arguments advanced in *Philips v William Whiteley* was that a lesser standard should be demanded of the jeweller because he charged a lower fee than a surgeon. By the same token, the National Health Service may find that it is cheaper to pay a general practitioner than to pay a hospital surgeon. If this is so, it raises the further question of whether the new contract has lowered the standards which patients have a right to expect.

In one case, a young builder had an enlarged lymph node in the posterior triangle of the right side of the neck. His general practitioner, who had some surgical experience, removed it for histology. In so doing he damaged the accessory nerve in the neck and caused a considerable deficit in the function of the right arm. This was a great handicap to the builder and he sued the doctor for many years of lost wages as well as for pain and suffering. One of the questions which arose in the case was whether the general practitioner should have referred his patient to a specialist. A plastic surgeon or an ear, nose and throat (ENT) surgeon might have been more aware of the risk to the accessory nerve in this vulnerable area of the neck and might have avoided the damage. It was not only the operative technique of the family doctor that was the subject of criticism; it was also the failure to refer the patient to a suitable specialist.

(x) Contemporaneous criticism

Cases are often brought against general practitioners when the events in question took place many years previously. No reference was made in *Bolam* to the question of using the standard of the day when assessing liability. However, it is accepted generally that any criticism must be based on contemporary standards. Putting it another way, there is no case for using hindsight or relying on literature published at a later date.

The importance of contemporary knowledge received judicial comment in *Roe v Minister of Health* (1954). In 1947, two patients were admitted to hospital for operations involving spinal anaesthetic. The ampoules containing the anaesthetic had become contaminated by phenol, which had leaked into them. The anaesthetist was unaware that this had happened and gave the drug in the usual way. Unfortunately, the phenol damaged the spinal cord in both patients and they were paralysed below the waist. The danger of such phenol leakage was first published in 1951, and the case was heard in 1954. The trial judge found for the doctor, but the patients appealed. It was Lord Denning, in the Court of Appeal, who said 'we must not look at the 1947 accident with 1954 spectacles', and he upheld the trial judge's finding.

In *Coker v Dolland* (1993), we saw how there was a criticism of the general practitioner for continuing to prescribe contraceptive pills when the girl allegedly complained of headaches and visual symptoms. The plaintiff's expert in the case was consulted in 1993 and he was able easily to verify that the current editions of *MIMS* and the *BNF* showed that this practice was negligent. The events in question happened in 1986 and although the expert was aware that this danger had been known for many years, he had to obtain copies of the relevant pages of those publications from that earlier year to show the court that his remarks were based on contemporaneous literature.

Coker v Dolland also demonstrated a point on current practice. A criticism arose that no record had been kept of a repeat prescription for contraceptive pills. Counsel for the defendant, in cross-examination of the plaintiff's expert, argued that the keeping of repeat prescription records for the Pill was not current practice in 1986, and that the failure to do so was, therefore, not negligent. The expert disagreed and asserted that reasonable practitioners had been keeping records of this kind for many years, and certainly well before the time in question. In the event, the point was of no significance because the plaintiff had to concede that even if a proper record had been kept, the outcome would have been the same.

When *Pleydell v Aubyn* (1993) came to trial, nearly a quarter of a century had elapsed since the events in question. This was a case where a general practitioner was allegedly negligent in delaying the admission to hospital of a two year old child with abdominal pains. At operation, the symptoms proved to have been caused by appendicitis and the organ was found to have perforated. The plaintiff's expert on causation, a general surgeon, was called to show that earlier admission by the general practitioner would probably have enabled an operation to be carried out before perforation occurred. This involved a study of a series of similar cases admitted to hospital at a similar time to assess the likely outcome of treatment. The expert was able to locate an article in the *British Medical Journal* from 1963 which assisted him in demonstrating his point.

IV INTRODUCTION TO CAUSATION

(i) General background

In earlier chapters we saw how a patient has to establish that the doctor owed him a duty of care and how he has to show that the duty was breached in terms of the treatment the doctor gave. We now come to the third element in a medical negligence action, that of causation. This concerns the study of whether a doctor's negligence is sufficiently likely to have caused the damage to justify compensating the patient. It must be remembered that with the law in its present state, a doctor can only be liable for one type of damages payment, that is, full damages. If the likelihood of the doctor's negligence having caused the harm is not considered great enough to justify this, the doctor pays the patient nothing. Thus the system of compensation can be described as 'all or nothing'. English law does not allow a plaintiff to recover damages in a way that is proportional to the likelihood of the doctor's negligence being responsible for the end result of the treatment and the illness.

(ii)   Comparison with personal injury

Causation in medical negligence is far from straightforward and this contrasts with causation in ordinary personal injury actions. We can cite the example of an employer who is negligent and allows a pool of water to accumulate on the factory floor. An employee slips and fractures his elbow. The plaintiff here has no difficulty at all in proving his case on causation. If it had not been for his employer's negligence, the injury would not have occurred. This contrasts with medical negligence, where the patient is already ill before he sees the doctor and where, even with good treatment, he may suffer some harm in any case. The doctor will certainly be liable if he inflicts any additional harm of his own, but he may also be liable if he fails to mitigate the harm inflicted by nature.

(iii)   'Negative causation'

A plaintiff who is advancing a medical negligence action will have to show that she has sustained some damage and that the defendant's negligence, rather than the illness, was probably the cause of the damage. The battle between plaintiff and defendant on causation will therefore take the form of argument about the relationship between the negligence and the harm suffered. At first sight it would appear that all cases fall into one of two categories. In the first category, which is favourable to the plaintiff, the negligence will have been the cause of the harm. In the second category, which is favourable to the defendant, the negligence made no difference to the outcome of the case.

There is, however, a third and not often recognised category of causation. Cases falling into this group are favourable to the defendant, and the phenomenon can be described conveniently as 'negative causation'. These cases are much rarer than the other two and are only likely to occur in chronic medical conditions for which no beneficial treatment is available at the time of the alleged negligence. In a negative causation case, the plaintiff's position is improved by the negligence. Put another way, her position is enhanced compared to how she would have fared with currently accepted medical management.

Let us consider a rather unusual case which illustrated negative causation. A fives player fell against the buttress on the left side of the court and injured his wrist. His opponent was an orthopaedic surgeon and reassured him that he had only suffered a sprain. Relying on this advice, the player hoped that the supposed sprain would heal quite soon, but he then attended an accident and emergency department six months later, as he still had residual symptoms. An X-ray was taken and the patient was sent home. The film, on inspection by the radiologist the next day, showed a fracture of the scaphoid bone, but the patient was never recalled for further treatment. The X-ray and the report were filed and the patient, hearing nothing, assumed that the accident and emergency doctor had reached the same conclusion as his medical opponent at the original game of fives. Some years later, he sought yet another opinion, the fracture was confirmed and he was offered an operation on the bone. The defending accident and emergency department argued that their admitted negligence in failing to recall him following the X-ray had caused him a benefit. They put it in terms that it was too long after the injury for an operation to have been indicated at that stage. They added that the mere knowledge of the fracture, and the record of it in his general practitioner's notes, would probably have prevented him from being accepted for the highly paid and physically demanding job for which he was engaged shortly after the X-ray was filed negligently.

A plaintiff's usual view of the treatment that she has criticised is that it has caused harm. The defendant, in addition to arguing that he has not been negligent, will assert that no harm was caused. However, there are cases where the plaintiff's life has been enhanced greatly, or even saved, by the treatment that has been criticised. In 'steroid cases', many so-called victims owed their well-being, and even their lives, to the drugs. Some asthmatics, for instance, would have been respiratory cripples, or might even have died, without steroid treatment.

(iv)   The temporal relationship between negligence and causation

Most personal injury actions (for example, motor accidents) are usually concerned with a single act of negligence. The plaintiff's

39

case will therefore be confined to the study of the effect of a careless act which probably lasted for no more than a few seconds. Causation will be straightforward in that the plaintiff must link the damage to that one act.

Some medical negligence actions are similar, in that they are also concerned with a single incident. The general practitioner's carelessly written prescription is a convenient example. We can also cite the receptionist who is negligent in filing a malignant cervical smear report or positive pregnancy test result without notifying the patient. In these cases, too, the patient's advisers will have no difficulty in knowing how to advance the case on causation. It will simply be a matter of showing that the damage was probably caused by that act or omission, even if it did not become apparent until much later.

However, some medical negligence actions follow a different pattern and may make it difficult for the plaintiff to show that negligence and causation coincide. Let us take the example of a young woman who makes several visits to the doctor over a period of time with headaches. The practitioner makes up his mind at the outset that the diagnosis, quite reasonably, is migraine. At subsequent visits, however, the symptoms become worse and other features develop that are suggestive of a cerebral tumour. The doctor persists with his original diagnosis and continues to treat the patient himself without making specialist referral. The plaintiff's expert on negligence may find it impossible to criticise the doctor at the early visits because the expert would have done exactly the same. The expert on causation may have to concede that referral during the later visits would have made no difference to the outcome because the treatment at that stage would have been the same and the prognosis would have been no better.

In this situation, the plaintiff's case is only strong on negligence at the end of the case and is only strong on causation at the beginning. Put another way, there is no area in the case where the two can be made to coincide, and the plaintiff's case is doomed to failure. Sometimes, of course, there is a small area part way through the case where they overlap; this is sometimes described as the 'window of opportunity for cure' (see also pages

51-52). The defendant's advisers, on the other hand, will want to show that the case is only strong on causation at the beginning and only strong on negligence at the end, there being no such 'window' between the two.

(v) Selecting the right defendant for negligence and causation

In the previous section we saw how essential it is, and how difficult it can be, to ensure that negligence and causation coincide in terms of their timing. However, it is equally important to be able to demonstrate that they concern the same defendant. It is insufficient to show that the first defendant is negligent if it made no difference to the outcome, and then to show that the second defendant's non-negligent action caused the damage.

In one rather unusual case, a cricketer was fielding at square leg when he suffered a nasal injury while attempting a difficult catch. He attended an accident and emergency department for treatment, but no investigations were arranged. He later consulted his general practitioner who, although the swelling and pain had settled to some extent, suspected a fracture and made a tardy referral to an ENT surgeon. By the time the sportsman reached that specialist it was too late for optimum treatment and he was left with considerable disability in terms of nasal deformity and obstruction.

He sued the accident and emergency department as first defendant and the general practitioner as second defendant. The A & E department argued that their negligence had made no difference because immediate surgical reduction of the fracture would not have been appropriate. The general practitioner asserted that, although it was the delay incurred by him that had caused the damage, he had not been negligent because the symptoms with which he was being presented were not sufficient to put him on notice that the referral was urgent. The plaintiff was therefore left with the difficulty that his case in negligence and causation could not be fixed on the same defendant.

(vi) Primary and secondary causation

Put in simple terms, causation concerns the study of the effect that the defendant's negligence has on the plaintiff's position. In an ordinary personal injury action it is usually quite straightforward. For instance, the employer's failure to provide goggles for a worker may be the cause of a piece of swarf penetrating the eye when a grinder is being used. Similarly, a pedestrian may suffer a fracture of the spine as a direct result of a motorist's negligence. In medical negligence actions, however, it is important to realise that there are often several steps between a doctor's inappropriate management of the illness and the harm suffered by the patient. The plaintiff's advisers must study these steps very carefully, aided by the medical expert, to ensure that the criticisms being advanced can be linked to the damage that has been sustained.

Let us consider an example to illustrate this point. Suppose a woman visits her doctor with a complaint of pain in the breast. Suppose, too, that the doctor is negligent and fails to carry out an examination. The sequence of questions which the plaintiff's advisers will ask of their expert will take the form of a cascade running something like this:

• If the doctor had examined the patient, would he have detected a lump?

• If he had detected a lump, would he have referred the patient to a surgeon?

• If he had secured an appropriate appointment, would the surgeon have arranged a biopsy or a mammogram?

• If one of these tests had been arranged, would it have shown cancer?

• If it had shown cancer, would surgery, radiotherapy or chemotherapy have been given?

• If any of these treatments had been given, would the woman's prognosis have been better?

A break at any point in this sequence of six steps will tend to weaken the plaintiff's case on causation. However, it is only the last step, the alteration to the outcome of the illness, which is conventionally considered to come under the heading of causation. To emphasise the importance of the first five steps it may be helpful to term those aspects of the case 'primary causation' while reserving 'secondary causation' for the ultimate harm which the patient suffers.

(vii)   The classification of causation

As we shall see in the next three chapters, causative difficulties come in many different forms. We have to remember that the difficulty is something which is facing the plaintiff rather than the defendant. It is the plaintiff who must show that the negligence is sufficiently likely to have been the cause of the damage to justify compensating him.

Although causation can cause considerable difficulties for plaintiffs, it can cause difficulties for those studying the subject as well. It would be helpful if there was some sort of classification to facilitate its study, but unfortunately none seems to be generally available. In an attempt to provide such a classification, it is here suggested that we think in terms of a defendant who, in his attempt to escape liability, will assert:

- that his negligence did no more than to cause the plaintiff to lose the opportunity of cure ('lost opportunity' causation);

- that some unrelated factor could perfectly well have been responsible for the damage ('unrelated factor' causation);

- that his negligence merely made a contribution to the damage ('material contribution' causation).

In the next three chapters we shall consider these approaches in more detail.

V   'LOST OPPORTUNITY' CAUSATION

(i) Introduction

When making a comparison with ordinary personal injury actions (see page 38) we saw that a difficulty which often faces a plaintiff in a medical negligence case is that the outcome of the illness is uncertain even with good treatment. The pedestrian who is crossing the road and whose leg is broken when he is knocked down by a negligent motorist can be quite certain that the injury would not have occurred but for the negligence. It would be absurd to postulate that the development of the abnormality in the leg just happened to coincide with the negligence. Conversely, the patient who attends his doctor is already ill before he enters the consulting room. Indeed, that is the very reason for which he is visiting the doctor. Some illnesses are more amenable to treatment than others, and this produces an element of uncertainty about what the outcome would have been but for the negligence.

    We can here cite the example of a woman who attends her general practitioner because she is convinced she has a lump in the breast. The doctor is negligent and fails to carry out an examination, preferring to rely on his partner's notes, which record a diagnosis of mastitis a year previously. The patient returns to the surgery three months later, has an examination at which a cancerous lump is confirmed and she is referred

45

promptly for specialist treatment. The question will then arise of how much difference the earlier referral would have made. It will certainly have made some difference to the outcome, but the court will have to decide whether that difference is great enough to justify compensating her. If that point is reached, causation will concern any adverse effect on the treatment, such as whether a mastectomy is necessary. It will also concern any worsening of the prognosis and the experts will have to produce statistics comparing the survival rates for treatment given at the earlier compared to the later stage.

To advance her case, the plaintiff will want to show that it was probably the doctor's negligence that caused the damage. Conversely, the defending doctor will want to show that the damage was more likely to have been caused by the illness itself.

This type of case contains, as it where, an element of competition. It is said that the doctor's negligence and the illness which he is treating are competing with each other to be identified as the true cause of the damage. The lack of certainty about the outcome of the illness with good treatment means that we can go no further than to say that the negligence caused the patient to lose the opportunity of being cured. The patient will assert that good treatment would have given him a chance of cure and the doctor's negligence deprived him of that chance.

(ii) The *Barnett* type of case

It is convenient to start our discussion of 'lost opportunities' by considering the type of case where the patient's condition is such that she is doomed in any event. In other words, we are considering a patient who has an illness which is not amenable to treatment and to whom no benefit will accrue even if the doctor provides a good standard of care.

Strictly speaking, this type of case should not be described as belonging to the 'lost opportunity' class, because the patient never had an opportunity of cure. Put another way her illness was such that she had a zero chance of recovery. However, for the purposes of discussion, it is appropriate to classify it like this because the patient believes there was an opportunity. Furthermore, it provides a natural starting point for the more difficult type of case in which the chance of cure with good treatment lies somewhere between nil and 100%.

In *Barnett v Chelsea & Kensington HMC* (1969) a man accidentally drank some arsenic. Some hours later he attended an accident and emergency department and related his history to the nurse in charge. The nurse informed the doctor, who decided not to see or examine the patient, and he was sent home. Shortly afterwards he collapsed and died. A post-mortem confirmed the cause of death as arsenic poisoning, and the widow sued the doctor. In terms of negligence she was successful. Under the principle in *Bolam*, she showed that any reasonable accident and emergency doctor would have attended a patient with this history. She was then faced with having to prove her case on causation. The defence successfully showed that the ingestion of the arsenic had been a sufficiently long time beforehand to have meant that a stomach washout, or any other treatment for that matter, would have been to no avail. The patient would have died in any case. The widow's case therefore failed on causation.

Barnett provides us with a useful example of a plaintiff who understandably thinks that if the doctor had given proper treatment, the patient would have been cured. It illustrates very well how the doctor's negligence often makes no difference at all to the patient. With the legal system as it is, this type of action is bound to fail. Patients often find it very difficult to accept that they have no case against a doctor when negligence is extreme and is easy to demonstrate. The task of explaining this to a dissatisfied patient usually falls to his solicitor. He will have had the expert's favourable report on negligence, but will have to convince his client that, with a negative report from the expert on causation, the case cannot succeed.

Although *Barnett* was a case in hospital medicine, examples of this kind abound in general practice. Every experienced general practitioner has had occasion to visit a man with upper abdominal and lower chest pains, who has perhaps been rather sick and does not feel at all well. Let us also assume that he confesses to overindulgence the previous evening and attributes his symptoms to that. The doctor carries out a detailed examination and finds nothing abnormal apart from obesity, which raises the possibility of an hiatus hernia. He is tempted to agree with the patient's own explanation of the symptoms and diagnoses indigestion. On his return to the surgery he is greeted with the news that the receptionist has received a telephone call from the wife saying that her husband has just collapsed and died. A post-mortem is carried out which confirms a myocardial infarct as the cause of death.

Let us assume that the widow sues on the basis that her husband should have been admitted to a coronary care unit and that, if he had been, treatment would have been put in hand which would have saved his life. She may well be successful on negligence if she can show that the history alone was enough to have warranted immediate admission. When it comes to causation, she may have an impossible task. The post-mortem report may show that all three major coronary arteries were severely affected by atheroma. The doctor may be able to show that the underlying disease process was such that the patient would probably have died in the ambulance on his way to hospital. Alternatively, the patient may have survived the journey but would probably have developed irreversible ventricular fibrillation very soon after reaching the cardiologist. Unless the widow can overcome these difficulties, her case will fail on causation and it will be of little consolation for her to know that it was strong on negligence.

(iii)   The *Hotson* type of case

The so called 'lost opportunity' cases are probably the commonest type of causation difficulty in medical negligence litigation. They occur when the disease process under consideration has an uncertain chance of cure, even with good treatment. In *Barnett* we saw an example of a patient with a condition which had a zero chance of recovery. We now move on to consider the difficulty which arises when the illness is such that good treatment by the doctor provides the patient with an opportunity of cure that is more than minimal but falls short of being certain. In other words, the patient is deprived of a chance which lies somewhere between nil and 100%. The task in resolving this type of case involves deciding how much compensation, if any, the plaintiff should receive when it is impossible to know what the outcome would have been but for the negligence.

The dilemma fell to be considered in *Hotson v East Berkshire Health Authority* (1987), and the House of Lords decision in that case therefore represents the current state of the law on this important topic, but this has not always been so. The legal principles and the case law which preceded it will be reviewed in the next section (see pages 52-53).

In *Hotson*, a boy fell from a tree and injured his leg. He was taken to hospital and examined. No X-ray was considered necessary and he was sent home. Five days later he was still complaining of a painful hip, and his general practitioner sent him back to the accident and emergency department. On this occasion an X-ray was taken and this revealed a fracture of the neck of the femur. Treatment was then put in hand, but a complication developed. Avascular necrosis of the head of the femur was diagnosed and this was followed by considerable long-term disability. The boy sued the hospital staff on the basis that they were negligent in not taking an X-ray at the initial visit and that, if they *had* taken one, the fracture would have been detected and treated such that the avascular necrosis would never have occurred. He succeeded on negligence. He called expert evidence which showed that no reasonable accident and emergency doctor, faced with that clinical situation, would have neglected to have arranged an X-ray.

In terms of causation, he argued that earlier detection would have avoided the later complication. The hospital called expert evidence which showed that even with prompt treatment there was a chance that it could have occurred. Indeed, it went further than this. It produced statistics which showed that in a comparable series of promptly treated cases the complication occurred in 75%. It argued that this meant that the boy, far from being deprived of a certain cure by the negligence, had only lost a 25% chance of cure.

The House of Lords then had to decide how to quantify damages that were appropriate to that degree of lost chance. Full damages (that is, for undoubted causation) had been set at £46,000. At first instance, and in the Court of Appeal, the boy had been awarded £11,500. This was in recognition of the one quarter lost opportunity. The House of Lords, on appeal by the hospital, overruled this decision and awarded him nothing. It held that the 'proportionate' approach was wrong and preferred the 'all or none' solution. They ruled that unless the chances of recovery with good treatment exceeded 50%, the case must fail on causation. The natural consequence of this approach is that even if the chance only marginally exceeded 50%, the plaintiff would be entitled to full damages. It was Lord Ackner who expressed the fear that the proportionate approach would:

> ... give rise to many complications in the search for mathematical and statistical exactitude.[7]

Although *Hotson* was a hospital case, examples of this type of causation abound in general practice. Two will suffice for the purposes of illustration.

A man consulted his general practitioner with a history of abdominal pain and intermittent constipation. Irritable bowel syndrome was diagnosed initially, but some time later the patient was referred for further investigation. He was found to be suffering from bowel cancer and later died. Causation in this case concerned an assessment of the chance of cure with prompt referral. It was accepted that the delay had at least some adverse effect on his prognosis. For the case to be strong on causation, the patient had to show that his chance of cure was 51% or greater at the time that he had shown the general practitioner to have been negligent in not making the referral.

Another case concerned an elderly man who was visited by his general practitioner because one of his toes had developed a black area and become painful. The district nurse was asked to apply dressings at intervals. Some weeks later he was admitted to hospital with gangrene and the leg was amputated below the knee. To advance his case on causation, the man had to be able to show that there was a 51% or greater chance that the leg could have been saved by hospital admission at the appropriate stage.

---

7   For an alternative approach to the assessment of damages, supporting the proportionate approach, see Walter Scott, *The Modern Law Review*, July 1992, pp 521-25. For a view supporting the 'all or none' approach, see Timothy Hill in *The Modern Law Review*, July 1991, pp 511-23.

(iv)   The 'window of opportunity'

Suppose that a woman is attending her doctor over a period of time and wants to sue him on the basis that an opportunity for cure was lost. It will be of the utmost importance that her advisers select the relevant phase in the treatment on which to advance the case. In other words, they will have to identify the 'window of opportunity' in which the case is strong on both negligence and causation.

The treatment received by the plaintiff in *McGrath v Cole* (1994) provides us with a useful example. A young woman has been seen by her general practitioner for symptoms which were initially attributed to a urinary tract infection. Unfortunately, they were later found to have been caused by pelvic inflammatory disease and this ultimately rendered her sterile. She alleges that the doctor had been negligent in failing to refer her for investigation by a gynaecologist and that, if he had done so at an appropriate time, she would have had a greater than 50% chance of avoiding the sterility. There was a succession of visits which had to be considered and they extended over a period of some weeks. She found it difficult to criticise the very early visits, but as the sequence progressed it became easier for her experts to assert that the standard of care, in terms of failed referral, had fallen short of what she had a right to expect. Her difficulty was that, as time progressed, it became gradually less likely that even a prompt referral would have made effective treatment possible.

It is convenient to think of Mrs McGrath's case as being composed of three phases, as follows:

(a)   an early phase, where there had been no negligence;

(b)   an intermediate phase, where there had been negligence and where appropriate management would probably have secured a better outcome; and

(c)   a late phase, in which the negligence continued but the damage was complete, such that even with appropriate management the outcome would have been no different.

It was clear that Mrs McGrath had to advance her case on the basis of the intermediate phase. To succeed, she needed two expert opinions to coincide. Her general practice expert had to be able to say that the failure to make specialist referral at some point in this phase was negligent. Additionally, her gynaecology expert had to be able to say that it was more likely than not that a referral at this stage would have enabled the sterility to be avoided. In a word, the intermediate phase was Mrs McGrath's 'window of opportunity', where negligence and causation coincided.

(v) The historical approach to the 'lost opportunity' cases

We saw how the House of Lords in *Hotson v East Berkshire HA* (1987) held that an 'all or none' approach to causation must be adopted when the doctor's negligence has deprived a patient of an opportunity of cure.

This solution has not always been used. The dilemma was considered originally early in the 20th century in a case of contract law. In *Chaplin v Hicks* (1911), a girl had entered into a contract which meant that she might have won a prize. The defendant was in breach of contract and the girl argued that she should be compensated for loss of the prize. In that case, her chance of winning the prize was assessed and her damages award was expressed in similar terms. This laid the foundations for the 'proportionate' approach to lost opportunity cases.

The question arose again much later, but in a medical negligence case. In *Kenyon v Bell* (1953) a girl suffered an eye injury and lost sight in the eye. Her father showed successfully that the doctor's treatment was negligent. The defence brought evidence to show that, even with good treatment, the chances of saving the sight were less than 50%. The judge decided against using the proportionate approach in *Chaplin v Hicks* and adopted the 'all or none' solution. The girl therefore received nothing.

It was only a matter of time before the rules in medical negligence actions changed again. In *Clark v McLennan* (1983) a woman underwent a pelvic floor repair operation for incontinence very soon after childbirth but the disability continued. She showed successfully that the gynaecologist had been negligent in not deferring the operation until later. The defence were able to show that even if it had been done at the right time, there was a 33% chance of the incontinence continuing. To allow for this, the judge therefore deducted one third from her damages award. Similarly, in *Bagley v North Herts HA* (1986), a mother successfully sued the hospital for negligence following a stillbirth. In that case, the medical evidence showed that there was a 5% chance of her having a stillbirth even with good treatment. In view of this, the judge only awarded her 95% of the full damages figure.

When *Hotson* came to trial, at first instance the judge followed the recent precedents and used the proportionate approach to award the boy 25% of full damages. The hospital appealed, presumably hoping for a reversal to the 'all or none' solution adopted in *Kenyon v Bell*. The Court of Appeal upheld the trial judge's ruling and held that the proportionate approach should apply. It was on further appeal to the House of Lords that the decision was overruled and the current state of the law became established.

VI   'UNRELATED FACTOR' CAUSATION

SUMMARY

   (i)   Introduction..55

  (ii) The *Wilsher* type of case....................................55

(i)   Introduction

In the previous chapter we considered cases where the doctor's negligence caused the patient to lose the opportunity of cure. We saw how the negligence was said to compete with the illness to be identified as the cause of the damage.

We now come to the type of case where the negligence is facing competition, not from the illness in which the treatment allegedly fell short, but from unrelated factors. The important point here is that these other factors just happen to co-exist. They do not form part of the treatment and they have no connection with the illness that the doctor is trying to cure.

(ii)   The *Wilsher* type of case

The dilemma of how to resolve the question of causation in cases where it is possible that the damage was caused by factors unrelated to the doctor's negligence fell to be considered by the House of Lords in *Wilsher v Essex Area HA* (1988).

Wilsher's case involved a baby who had been born prematurely. He was given supplementary oxygen while in the incubator. Unfortunately, the catheter for monitoring the level of oxygen in the blood had been misplaced. It was inserted into a vein rather than an artery and gave erroneous readings. The oxygen delivery apparatus was adjusted based on readings which were too low and the baby received an excess of oxygen. The baby was later found to have become blind. This damage was blamed on the fact that he had been given too much oxygen. There was no difficulty in showing that the hospital had been negligent in allowing the mistake to occur. In other words, the plaintiff succeeded on negligence. Causation was his next hurdle, and he had reason to be optimistic here too, because it was well known that the administration of excessive oxygen to a premature baby could cause blindness, by damaging the retina.

The medical facts of the case were, however, more complicated than this. The baby was also suffering from five other unrelated disorders which were an accompaniment of the prematurity. The defence were able to show that these were also possible explanations for the blindness.

The case came to trial and at first instance the judge held that the plaintiff should succeed on causation on the basis that the excess oxygen was one of several possible causes of the damage. The defendants appealed, but the Court of Appeal upheld the decision. They therefore appealed again, to the House of Lords. This gave their Lordships the opportunity of deciding how to resolve cases where the doctor's negligence is competing with unrelated factors.

It had long been established that the civil standard of proof requires a plaintiff to show that there is a greater than 50% chance that the negligence caused the damage. In *Wilsher*'s case there were six possible causes, only one of which was the doctor's negligence. The defendants showed successfully that one or more of the other five factors were also possible causes. The House of Lords held that the plaintiff should not succeed on causation because he had failed to show it was the excess oxygen which was more than 50% likely to have been responsible for the retinal damage. Their Lordships pointed out that a proper decision on causation could only be taken when a thorough comparison was made between the negligent cause and the other possible causes that were not related to the negligence. Unfortunately, the material that was available at the trial was insufficient for this decision to be made, and a retrial was ordered. This must have caused particular distress to the child's family, as the case had already been running for several years. However, the retrial never materialised because the case was settled out of court.

In *Hotson* we saw how the case was decided in the plaintiff's favour at first instance and on appeal, only to go against him in the House of Lords. *Wilsher* followed the same pattern, except that no decision was ever given in the House of Lords. Nevertheless, the discussion about the principles to be applied had the effect of clarifying the law on that particular type of case, such that a decision on future cases can now be predicted.

Wilsher-type causation is not nearly as common as the *Hotson*-type in general practice, but it could occur in a prescription regime. Suppose that a doctor maintains a patient on several drugs simultaneously and the patient develops a side effect. Now suppose that two of the drugs on the list are known to produce that side effect. Thirdly, suppose that one of the drugs had been prescribed negligently and the other had been prescribed appropriately. In this situation, the patient could only succeed on causation if he could show that there was a more than 50% chance that the negligently prescribed drug was the one that caused the damage.

VII 'MATERIAL CONTRIBUTION' CAUSATION

SUMMARY

(i)   Introduction

In the previous two chapters we considered cases where a doctor's negligence was said to be competing with other possible causes of the damage. We first discussed those where there was uncertainty about whether the doctor's negligence was more likely than not to have caused the patient to lose the opportunity of cure. In *Hotson v East Berks HA* (1987), the patient lost a 25% chance of cure. In *Barnett v Chelsea & Kensington HMC* (1969), the patient had a zero chance of cure such that, in effect, no opportunity was lost. We then considered cases where there was uncertainty about whether the negligence was more likely than some unrelated factor to have caused the damage. We saw how the plaintiff in *Wilsher v Essex HA* (1988) was unable to show that the negligence was more likely than five other unrelated factors to have been responsible for the damage.

We now move on to consider another category of case, and this concerns the uncertainty of whether the negligence made a material contribution to the damage. This will involve the study of cases where the plaintiff has been exposed to a potentially harmful substance but where only part of that exposure was negligent. This difficulty commonly arises in general practice when a patient receives a prolonged course of tablets which results in harm. Some of the tablets may have been properly prescribed and the remainder negligently prescribed. We are then faced with a question of whether the doctor should be liable for the damage which results from the whole course.

(ii)   The *McGhee* type of case

We are here concerned with cases where the defendant is negligent by causing the plaintiff to be exposed to something harmful, and damage results. A difficulty arises for the plaintiff when the defendant is able to show that the harm might have arisen in any event. He will assert that many people develop similar damage without the negligence.

The principle by which cases of this type are resolved is to be found in an industrial injury case. In *McGhee v National Coal Board* (1973), a miner was employed to undertake bricklaying below ground. There was a statutory requirement for the Coal Board to provide showers at the pit-head. This enabled skin irritants such as coal dust and brick dust to be removed at the end of the day's work. In this case, the employers were in breach of their statutory duty in that no showers were available and the employee developed dermatitis. He argued that this had been caused by brick dust irritating his back and shoulders while he cycled home from work in dirty clothes. The defence attempted to counter this by saying that the dermatitis could have developed in any event. It had been known to occur in miners who had showers and clean clothes available at the end of every shift.

The plaintiff was able to call expert evidence on causation to the effect that the lack of showers materially increased the risk of the development of the dermatitis. He won his case on causation, even though there was a lack of certainty about the cause of the harm.

The benzodiazepine litigation provides a convenient example of medical cases where it is uncertain whether a doctor's negligence caused the damage of which a patient complains. Many of the plaintiffs in that litigation complained that the tranquillisers had caused depression and personality changes. Psychiatrists instructed on behalf of the plaintiffs examined them and confirmed that these changes had occurred. In many cases, the plaintiffs had to concede that the changes would have occurred anyway perhaps because they were prone to depression. In line with *McGhee* they would only succeed on causation if they could show that the drugs had materially increased the risk of these adverse effects occurring.

(iii)   The *Bonnington* type of case

At this stage we are still concerned with the defendant whose negligence makes a material contribution to the plaintiff's damage. In *McGhee v National Coal Board* (1973) we saw how it merely increased the risk of the harm occurring. We now move on to those cases where only part of the harm is caused by the negligence, the implication being that the rest of it was caused by something else, for which the defendant cannot be blamed.

Like *McGhee*, the solution to this type of case also has its principle derived from an industrial injury case. In *Bonnington Castings v Wardlaw* (1956), a silicone dresser had been employed for a long period of time in an environment which exposed him to the risk of dust inhalation. He developed pneumoconiosis and sued his employers. He showed successfully that the amount of silicone dust where he had been working was above a safe level and that, as a result, the employers were in breach of their statutory duty of control over working conditions. At first sight his case appeared strong on causation because he had developed a disease which had been caused by the inhalation of dust, for which his employers were liable. However, the workman then found himself confronted with a difficulty. The employers were able to show that he had spent some of his working day in a part of the factory where the silicone dust level was within acceptable limits. There could be no doubt that his illness had been caused by the sum of all the dust he had inhaled. Part of that dust could not be blamed on the employers. A distinction was made between so called 'guilty dust' and 'innocent dust'. Nevertheless, the court held that the plaintiff should succeed on causation on the basis that the 'guilty dust' at least made a material contribution to the damage.

At this point it is convenient to observe the correlation between *McGhee's* material increase in the risk of the damage occurring at all and *Bonnington*'s material contribution to damage, some of which would have happened in any event.

Bonnington-type causation is sometimes encountered in general practice prescribing. In one case, a man was discharged from hospital after an operation to remove a brain tumour. A short course of steroid tablets was prescribed for him to take home with review at the hospital clinic some time later. He was seen in the meantime by his general practitioner, who was negligent and maintained the patient on the full dose of steroids for much longer than the hospital had intended. The patient developed side-effects from chronic overdosage, and sued his general practitioner. This was clearly a case where every single tablet had made a tiny, but equal, contribution to the damage. Even the properly prescribed ones from the hospital had been responsible for their share. In a case such as this, the general practitioner's steroid tablets will be regarded as analogous to *Bonnington*'s 'guilty dust', and the hospital's tablets to his 'innocent dust'. As long as the general practitioner's steroids made a material contribution to the side effects, the court would be likely to find that the patient had proved his case on causation. It would be a case of showing that the number prescribed by the general practitioner amounted to a significant proportion of the total that had been taken.

Prescribing errors of this kind also occurred in the benzodiazepine litigation. In many cases, the decision to initiate the tranquillisers in the first place was very proper. However, it was often followed by numerous repeat prescriptions over a period of many years without the patient being reviewed. If the expert for the plaintiff in such a case was of the opinion that the drugs should have been given for no more than a month, the same type of causation difficulty would arise. The tablets prescribed in that first month will be analogous to *Bonnington*'s 'innocent dust', and those which were subsequently prescribed would be analogous to the 'guilty dust'. Again, the final decision would rest on whether the tablets that had been negligently prescribed made up a significant proportion of the total.

(iv) The *de minimis* principle

It will have been observed that throughout these discussions the word 'material' has occurred from time to time. This was mainly in the context of *McGhee* and *Bonnington*. In the former case, the defendant's negligence was not the definite cause of the harm and in the latter case it was not the only cause. We were concerned with a material increase in the risk and with a material contribution.

The word 'material' was almost certainly used in the judgments of these cases for two reasons:

- to avoid a degree of precision that would set a precedent for future cases. A figure for a proportion which is 'material' in one case may be quite inappropriate in another. Whether a contribution is, or is not, 'material' must be decided on the facts of the case in hand. In practice there is usually little difficulty with the decision. Let us revert to the earlier example of benzodiazepines which were properly prescribed for a month then negligently prescribed for several years. Clearly, the latter group would qualify easily as having made a material contribution; and

- in recognition of the *de minimis* principle. The law does not recognise minutiae. To do so would involve pedantic arguments about microscopic differences. As an example let us alter the facts of the steroid prescription example given in the *Bonnington* discussion, such that the hospital intended the patient to receive 90 tablets and the general practitioner prescribed 100. It would probably be quite easy for the defence to call expert evidence to show that the additional 10 tablets did not make any significant difference. The doctor's negligence would therefore not qualify as having made a material contribution.

VIII CAUSATION AND CONSENT

(i) The effect of consent on causation

In Chapter X we shall see how the standard of care which is required when securing a patient's consent to treatment is governed, at least in England,[8] by the principle in *Sidaway v Board of Governors of Bethlem Royal and Maudsley Hospital* (1985). That case showed that the standard of care expected of a doctor when giving information about possible side effects is assessed by comparing it with the level of information which would be disclosed by a responsible body of medical opinion. In this chapter we are concerned with the effect of a doctor's failure to obtain that consent. In other words, the patient has agreed to the treatment but no mention has been made of a side effect which, in the event, materialised.

All treatments are associated with at least some degree of risk, but in most cases the patient is happy to accept it in view of the almost certain benefit she will receive. If there is a formal discussion, and perhaps even the signing of a consent form, this is likely to take place before the treatment commences. If a risk materialises of which the patient was not warned, the question will then arise of whether the patient would have accepted the

---

[8] The alternative approach, used in America and Australia, is also discussed in Chapter X.

risk had she been so warned. Clearly, if she would have consented to it, the doctor's negligence in not disclosing it made no difference to the outcome.

(ii)   The 'helmet cases'

The so called 'helmet cases' did not occur as part of medical treatment and were not concerned with consent, but they provide a good illustration of how the patient's state of mind at the time the consent is given has a profound influence on causation.

In the 1960s, two industrial injury cases came to trial. *McWilliams v Sir William Arrol* (1962) and *Wigley v British Vinegars* (1964) were both cases in which workers received head injuries when they had not been issued with safety helmets.

It was a statutory requirement for the employers to make helmets available, and the plaintiffs sued their employers on the basis that, if they had been so provided, the injuries would not have occurred. Causation thus appeared quite straightforward, as it was accepted that the helmets were strong enough to have withstood the type of impact in question, and would have prevented the injury. However, the defence argued that many workers, even when helmets had been supplied, did not bother to wear them. They succeeded in showing that these workers, even if they had been given helmets, would probably not have been wearing them at the material time, and so the injury would still have occurred. This meant that the employers' breach of their statutory duty, or their negligence towards their employees, made no difference to the outcome, and so the cases failed on causation.

These industrial industry cases provide the basis for causation in relation to failure to obtain the patient's consent. The patient will argue that she would not have consented to the treatment if she had been warned, but the doctor will counter this by seeking to show that, even if the patient had been told, she would have regarded the risk as worthwhile and would have taken it.

The Australian case of *Rogers v Whitaker* (1992) provides a convenient example of how important it is for a patient to be able to show that a warning would have resulted in his declining the treatment. A woman who had been blind in one eye for many years was offered an operation which, it was hoped, would restore some degree of vision in that eye. She was not warned of the 1 in 14,000 chance of sympathetic ophthalmia developing in the other eye, which could render her blind in both eyes. The fact that she was already blind in one eye, and the fact that she convinced the court successfully that her approach to medical treatment was both cautious and fastidious enabled her to show that, if she had been so warned, she would have refused the operation and would still have retained sight in one eye.

(iii) Consent to sterilisation

The consequences of the doctor's failure to warn his patient about possible adverse results are well illustrated in the context of sterilisation procedures.

In *Thake v Maurice* (1986) a man underwent a vasectomy. Evidence of fact showed that the pre-operative counselling procedure did not include any mention of the risk of recanalisation. This meant that fertility could be regained at a later date without any question of negligence in the original procedure. In the event, the wife conceived, but dismissed her early symptoms of pregnancy, relying on the reassurance that she had been given to the effect that her husband was sterile. When the symptoms persisted and became more pronounced she sought advice and the pregnancy was confirmed. By this stage it was too late to have it terminated and the couple sued the surgeon. In this case, they were not suing him for a poor technique at operation but for failing to warn them of the possibility of later recanalisation. They faced two tasks:

- they had to show that the surgeon fell below a reasonable standard in not so warning them when he obtained the husband's consent; and

- they had to show that, if they had been so warned, the wife would have suspected the pregnancy at a sufficiently early stage to have had a termination and would have requested one.

The first of these points concerned negligence and the couple were successful. The second point involved causation, and the wife was successful here too. She had older children and convinced the court that she would have recognised the symptoms of pregnancy at an early stage and, as she regarded her family as complete, she would have asked for a termination.

Thake v Maurice provides a good example of the effect of litigation on clinical practice. Since that time, couples have been warned routinely about the risks of recanalisation. A cynic would regard this as defensive medicine,[9] arguing that the dominant purpose of giving the warning is to protect the surgeon when he is sued. However, the better view is surely to accept that the case has helped to improve standards of consent when a patient is contemplating sterilisation of himself or his spouse.

In a case which settled out of court, a girl in her twenties consulted her general practitioner about a tattoo on her arm. The doctor offered to remove it and it was alleged that she was told that she would be left with nothing but a very small scar. Unfortunately, the end result of the operation was regarded as being considerably worse than the original tattoo. Quite apart from suing the doctor for negligence in respect of his operative technique, she also sued him for failure to obtain her consent. The case settled out of court as her evidence was very convincing to the effect that, if she had been warned about the possibility of the end result which in the event materialised, she would not have consented to the operation.

(iv) The patient's difficulty

We have seen how the plaintiffs in *Thake v Maurice* had little difficulty in showing that the doctor's failure to warn them caused their damage. If the warning had been given at the proper time the wife would have been in the position of having a choice. Had she been aware of the pregnancy at an early stage she could have elected to continue with it, or she could have asked for a termination. In the event, she convinced the court that she would have opted for the latter.

---

9   For a discussion about defensive medicine, see pp 146-49.

This contrasts with cases where the patient is in a position of having very little choice, usually by virtue of the threat of the possible consequences of the illness if it is left untreated. The plaintiff in *Thake v Maurice* would not have been faced with any undue difficulty or danger if she had had a termination. It was therefore relatively easy for her to claim that she would have acted on the doctor's warning.

The plight of the patient who is in a less enviable position is well illustrated by *Chatterton v Gerson* (1981). A woman was suffering from chronic pain which was very severe. She submitted to an operation which involved an injection near the spinal cord to destroy the nerve fibres which supplied the painful area. Two months later the pain returned and so the injection was repeated, but it provided no relief at all from the pain. Additionally, the patient suffered from numbness in the right leg and this interfered with walking. She sued the doctor on the basis that if she had been warned about the side effects she would not have submitted to the operation and the numbness would never have occurred. Unlike the plaintiff in *Thake v Maurice* she was unsuccessful. The court took the view that her desire for pain relief was so great that she would have regarded the risk as worth taking and would still have wanted the operation.

A case on the avoidance of a future disability rather than the escape from present pain is *Smith v Barking, Havering & Brentwood HA* (1989). A woman was faced with the prospect of a severe disability developing in the future if an operation on her spine was not performed. Unfortunately, this operation was followed by tetraplegia and evidence of fact showed that she had not been warned about this possibility. Again, the court took the view that she would have accepted the slight risk of this happening compared with the much higher risk of the disability which the operation was designed to avoid.

IX LIMITATION AND DATE OF KNOWLEDGE

(i) Introduction

There can be no doubt about the desirability of having a limit to the delay a patient can incur before she brings an action in negligence against her doctor. The lack of any ruling on this subject would mean that patients could start suing a doctor many years after the alleged negligence. This would make it difficult to assess the credibility of the patient's evidence, which is usually based on memory. Furthermore, it would make it difficult for doctors to defend themselves, because notes might have been lost with the passage of time and, indeed, the doctor's memory of the events is even more likely to have faded.

It is therefore important to have a set of rules which provides a limit to the amount of time that a plaintiff can allow to elapse before a case is brought to court. Additionally, a balance needs to be found. On the one hand, the time allowed must be sufficiently long to allow the plaintiff to prepare her case. On the other hand, it must be sufficiently short to prevent the doctor from being put at a disadvantage by being asked to defend a case after an unreasonably long delay.

(ii) Historical background

The need for some sort of ruling of this kind is not peculiar to medical negligence. In personal injury cases, for instance, the need has long been recognised. It was given statutory support by the Limitation Act 1939. This allowed a period of six years. The plaintiff had that length of time from the date on which he alleged the negligence had occurred to the date on which he could start proceedings.

Six years seemed plenty of time, but in due course it was realised that in some circumstances this rule could operate very harshly on plaintiffs.

In most personal injury cases there was no difficulty with this rule. The victim of a road accident knows of his damage the moment the negligence, usually an accident, occurs. Similarly, in the workplace, the employee who has been injured by an inadequately guarded machine will at once be only too painfully aware that he has suffered some harm. The difficulty arises when the case involves negligence that gives rise to damage of a more insidious kind which is not immediately apparent.

Just as the rules for causation in latter-day medical negligence cases were formulated in industrial injury cases in the early post-war years, so too was this point on limitation appreciated. In Chapter VII we saw how *Bonnington* and *McGhee* laid the foundations of causation, in 1957 and 1973 respectively, for cases where the negligence did no more than make a contribution to the damage. In the same way, another industrial injury case, *Cartledge v Jopling* (1963) paved the way for the modern rules on limitation. Just as the manufacturing process in *Bonnington* exposed the plaintiff to harmful dust in the working environment, so did it in *Cartledge*. In that case, the symptoms of the disorder took several years to develop, and the plaintiff was unaware of any damage until long after the six years had expired. The legislation in place at the time meant that his case was therefore statute barred. Faced with this injustice, he took his case to the Court of Appeal. The court acknowledged that this rule was unfair to a plaintiff who had suffered a latent form of harm which did not manifest itself until long after the negligent act. Nevertheless, it was constrained by the current legislation and the plaintiff's claim was dismissed.

Negligence actions for industrial injury have doubtless been fairly common since the Industrial Revolution got under way a couple of centuries ago. At first sight it seems curious that this point about limitation and latent damage was not appreciated earlier. The explanation is, however, probably medical rather than legal. It was not until the middle of the 20th century that industrial health services were set up and this branch of medicine became a speciality in its own right. Once doctors started seeing employees regularly and monitoring their health in relation to their working environment, there was more opportunity for linking earlier exposure to noxious substances with the later development of symptoms. As an example, we can mention bladder cancer caused by aniline dyes used in the chemical industry. Lung disorders include pneumoconiosis in coal miners and bagassosis in cotton workers. Tracing the latter type of disorder to its antecedent cause was probably made even more difficult by the intermittent nature of the symptoms, which took the form of recurrent attacks of wheezing.

(iii)   The present situation

Cartledge v Jopling (1963) focused the legislators' minds on the need to make allowance for plaintiffs who had no means of knowing that they had suffered harm until long after the time of the alleged negligence. This is particularly relevant to medical negligence cases. In some cases, the harm is known immediately, an anaesthetic accident being a simple example. In general practice, the failure to make timely arrangements for specialist

73

referral of a patient with cancer is likely to take a little longer in this respect. Nevertheless, the patient will probably know within a few weeks or months that the delay in referral could have affected the prognosis. Conversely, in some general practice cases it may be a very long time indeed before the harm is apparent. In the benzodiazepine litigation, some patients were not aware of psychiatric damage until they had been on the tranquillisers for very many years. Similarly, long-term steroid administration may result in adrenal suppression years after the allegedly negligent prescriptions have been started.

The Limitation Act 1980 allows for this difficulty and represents the current state of the law with regard to date of knowledge. It differed from the earlier Act in two important respects.

First, the limitation period was set at six years rather than three. Although this halved the time available for a plaintiff to bring her action, the disadvantage was more than compensated by the other difference.

The second point affected the time at which it is said that 'the clock starts to run'. By this is meant 'the time from which the three years is dated'. Under the new Act, time was not considered to run until the patient knew, or could reasonably be expected to have known, about the damage, irrespective of when it was caused. There are two facets to consider here. First, there is knowledge of the existence of the harm and, secondly, there is knowledge that it could have been caused by the act or omission which is alleged to constitute negligence. Let us consider each of these facets in more detail.

(iv)   Knowledge of the existence of the harm

Medical cases are probably the commonest type of negligence action in which the plaintiff may not be aware of any damage until long after it has been inflicted. This is explained by the intricacies of causation and the latent nature of the damage in medical cases. In an ordinary personal injury case there is only one possible cause for the harm. That is the defendant's negligence, and the plaintiff is usually aware of it immediately.

However, medical treatment may extend over a long period of time. The damage may be cumulative and not apparent to the patient until it is well established many years later. A patient is far less likely to notice damage if it has a gradual rather than a sudden onset.

The benzodiazepine litigation produced numerous examples of cases where the damage was insidious. Personality disorders took years to develop and at first appeared to be represent nothing more than a mild variation of the patient's usual self.

A particularly useful illustration of latent damage occurred in *Pleydell v Aubyn* (1993). A two year old girl was seen by her general practitioner several times over the course of a week with abdominal pains in 1966. At the end of the week she was admitted to hospital and found to have appendicitis. Unfortunately, the appendix had perforated and the recovery process was complicated by adhesions in the long term. Over twenty years later she got married having suffered nothing more than occasional attacks of abdominal pain in the meantime. After a year or two of marriage she found herself unable to conceive. On investigation by a gynaecologist it was found that the pelvic adhesions from the appendicitis had caused the infertility. In *Pleydell* the alleged negligence had occurred nearly a quarter of a century before she could have known that she was infertile. Under the old rule on limitation, her action would have been statute barred long before. However, her knowledge of the existence of the harm was not acquired until she found herself unable to conceive. As her case was governed by the 1980 Act the limitation clock in her case did not start to run until she knew of the infertility.

(v) Knowledge of the cause of the harm

It is apparent that, in some medical cases, the plaintiff may not be aware of any damage until long after the time of the alleged negligence. Knowledge of the mere existence of the harm, however, is not enough to fix the patient with 'knowledge' for the purposes of the Limitation Act 1980 and therefore to 'start the clock running'.[10] In addition to the existence of the harm, the patient must know that it was caused, or at least was capable of being caused, by the act or omission which is alleged to constitute negligence. Even if she thought that there were also some other, quite innocent, causes of the damage, such as the illness itself, she would be fixed with knowledge.

In personal injury cases there is usually only one possible cause for the harm, and that is the negligent act itself. Conversely, in medical negligence cases, there is an additional cause to be considered, that of the illness. We must add to this the point that many personal injury cases involve an isolated incident such as a car accident or an industrial accident. By contrast, some medical cases involve negligent treatment over a long period of time. Even the treatment may be aimed at an illness which has an insidious onset and is subject to relapses and remissions. All these points tend to distract the patient's mind from the fact that the negligence may have caused the harm. We must also remember that nearly all patients trust their doctors implicitly. This means that they are far more likely to assume that any harm has been caused by the illness than by the negligence.

Again, *Pleydell v Aubyn* (1993) comes to our assistance by way of an example. We saw on page 75 how more than 20 years elapsed between the negligent house calls and the knowledge of the infertility. Even this realisation, however, was not enough to fix the patient with knowledge because she was unaware of any connection between the two. She understandably assumed that her inability to have children was caused by some naturally-occurring process. It was only when she went to the gynaecologist for investigation that it transpired that the cause was blockage of the fallopian tubes by adhesions. The gynaecologist speculated that these adhesions might have been associated with the earlier appendix operation, the scar of which he saw on his initial examination of the patient. It was not until the girl mentioned this to her mother later still that she was reminded that when she was very young there had been a delay in arranging for hospital admission. Only when the girl had had the opportunity of

---

10 For a detailed survey of the case law on date of knowledge see three articles on 'Limitation' by Charles Lewis in *AVMA Journal* (July 1992, October 1992, Autumn 1993). These articles demonstrate the variable degree of information and understanding which a plaintiff must acquire before a court will hold him to have been 'fixed with knowledge'.

drawing all these threads together in her mind could she be fixed with knowledge that her infertility could have been caused by the doctor's management of her case a quarter of a century earlier.

(vi) Limitation Act 1980

This is the statute to which reference will be made when deciding if it is too late for a plaintiff to bring a claim.

For our purposes the most important parts of the Act are probably ss 11, 14 and 33. In a nutshell, we can say that s 11 deals with the time which is allowed for starting proceedings, and s 14 defines the nature of the requisite knowledge, while s 33 allows a discretionary extension of the time limit in certain circumstances.

Section 11(4) has the effect that the plaintiff must bring an action within three years of either the date of the alleged negligence or, if later, the date that the plaintiff first realised he might have a claim.

Section 14 lays down the rules governing the difficult question of whether a patient has acquired the necessary degree of knowledge for time to start running against him. It states that the plaintiff must know that the injury was significant (s 14 (1)(a)), that it was capable of being attributed to the allegedly negligent act (s 14(1)(b)), and that he knew the identity of the defendant (s 14(1)(c)).

Section 33 allows a court to extend the three-year limit 'provided it is equitable to do so'. Section 33(1) directs the court to consider the injustice that might result for the plaintiff if the discretion is not exercised, but it also has to take notice of any possible prejudice to the defendant that could be caused, for instance, by medical notes having disappeared with the passage of time.

For the convenience of readers, the relevant parts of the Act[11] can be quoted, in an incomplete and abbreviated fashion, as follows:

Actions in respect of wrongs causing personal injuries or death

Special time limit for actions in respect of personal injuries

11.–(1). This section applies to any action for damages for negligence,

(4). the period applicable is three years from—

(*a*) the date on which the cause of action accrued; or

---

[11] Reproduced, in part, by kind permission of Her Majesty's Stationery Office.

(b) the date of knowledge (if later) of the person injured.

Definition of date of knowledge

14.–(1). In sections 11 and 12 of this Act references to a person's date of knowledge are references to the date on which he first had knowledge of the following facts–

(a) that the injury in question was significant; and

(b) that the injury was attributable in whole or in part to the act or omission which is alleged to constitute negligence;

(c) the identity of the defendant; and knowledge that any acts or omissions did or did not, as a matter of law, involve negligence, is irrelevant.

Discretionary exclusion of time limit for actions in respect of personal injuries or death

33.–(1). If it appears to the court that it would be equitable to allow an action to proceed having regard to the degree to which–

(a) the provisions of section 11 or 12 of this Act prejudice the plaintiff or any person whom he represents; and

(b) any decision of the court under this subsection would prejudice the defendant or any person whom he represents;

the court may direct that those provisions shall not apply to the action.

(vii) Recent developments on 'date of knowledge'

We are here concerned with the plaintiff who wants to bring a case more than three years after the allegedly negligent treatment on the basis of s 11(4)(b) of the 1980 Act. For the purpose of the Act, the definition of knowledge appears at s 14, but it is s 14(1)(b) – the 'attributability' sub-section – which has been the subject of different judicial interpretation in recent years. As far as bringing late claims is concerned, the tide in the plaintiff's favour has risen and fallen with the development of the relevant case law.

In *Bentley v Bristol & Weston Health Authority* (1991), a woman underwent a hip replacement operation but the sciatic nerve was damaged in the process and this gave rise to severe symptoms. A second, unsuccessful, operation was carried out two months later and the surgeon explained the whole matter to the patient very soon afterwards. On the face of it she had by this time acquired knowledge of the existence of the harm and the fact that it might have been caused at the time of the operation. Additionally, she knew the identity of the defendant. The operation had been in June 1981 and a writ was not issued for her until September 1988 but the case was allowed to proceed at this apparently late stage. After her initial suspicion of negligence she sought advice but received a negative report from an orthopaedic expert while still within the three-year period. It was only when she received a second and subsequent report which raised the possibility of negligence that she was deemed to have been fixed with knowledge. This enabled her to start proceedings within three years of that second report.

Bentley represented a high watermark for plaintiffs who wanted to bring a claim very late in the day. However, the water level was considered by some to have fallen noticeably with the decision in *Hendy v Milton Keynes Health Authority* (1991), which addressed the question of attributability. In other words, how much factual detail does a plaintiff have to acquire before the criteria of s 14(1)(b) become fulfilled? It was held that the knowledge of attributability only had to be held 'in general terms' and, as if to emphasise this relatively low level of knowledge, the judge added that it was not necessary for the plaintiff to know the 'particular facts of what specifically went wrong or how or where the precise error was made'.

Just two years later, the Court of Appeal considered the questions of attributability and specificity in *Broadley v Guy Clapham & Co* (1993). It observed that *Bentley* had been wrongly decided, but it did not go as far as to approve the relatively modest test of knowledge in *Hendy*'s case.

The tide of limitation was clearly running against plaintiffs who were slow to act until they had very clear knowledge and it continued to fall by virtue of the Court of Appeal's decision in *Dobbie v Medway Health Authority* (1994). In that case, a woman was referred to a surgeon in 1973 because she had a breast lump. At operation the surgeon thought the lump was probably malignant and proceeded to a mastectomy. The biopsy report showed that the lump had been benign and she was informed of this result very soon afterwards. In the years that followed she probably felt that the trauma of losing the breast was to some extent off-set by the relief of not having cancer. As a result, she let the matter rest for a decade and a half until, in 1988, she heard a radio programme about a similar case which had resulted in compensation. This prompted her to see a solicitor and, in 1990, a positive report was obtained from a surgical expert who advised that there had been negligence at the time of the original operation in that a biopsy to confirm or refute malignancy should have been done before the breast was removed. When the case reached trial the defending health authority pleaded that the claim was statute barred because her knowledge had arisen at the time of, or very soon after, the operation and that considerably more than three years had elapsed. Mrs Dobbie argued that her knowledge only dated from her receipt of the positive surgical report in 1990 or, at most, from her suspicions which had been generated by the radio programme in 1988.

It was held, at first instance, that she was out of time. Attention was focused on s 14 of the Limitation Act 1980, and it was held that she knew she had suffered a significant injury (loss of a non-cancerous breast), that she knew it was capable of being attributed to the act (the operation on the breast) and that she knew the identity of the defendant (the surgeon concerned).

Mrs Dobbie appealed, again on the basis that she had not acquired the requisite degree of knowledge until 1988 or 1990. The Court of Appeal dismissed her case. It initially focused attention on the point that 'what she did not appreciate until later was that the Health Authority's Act ... was ... negligent or blameworthy ...', which was doubtless part of her case but it then added that '... her want of that knowledge did not stop time beginning to run'.

It therefore appears that the dismissal of the case at least partly relied on the very last words of s 14(1) of the Act, which states that:

> ... knowledge that any acts ... which involve negligence ... is irrelevant.

The debate about the specificity of the knowledge required to start time running was taken a step further in the very recent case of *Hallam-Eames and Others v Merrett and Others* (1995).[12] That was a case involving financial losses incurred by Lloyds 'names', who alleged negligence by the writers of re-insurance contracts.[13] The Court of Appeal referred to *Broadley* and to *Dobbie*. It observed that those cases:

> ... had been interpreted by the judge to mean that a plaintiff need only have known that his damage had been caused by an act or omission of the defendant.

However, it then went on to be more precise about the area of knowledge required and said that it should include facts which were:

> ... causally relevant for the purposes of an allegation of negligence.

It made the point that it was insufficient for the plaintiff names merely to know that their contracts had been written and that damage had resulted. They also had to know that the contracts had exposed them potentially to huge liabilities before the criteria of s 14 of the Act were fulfilled. Furthermore, they even had to know that those liabilities were incapable of proper assessment or quantification at the time that their contracts were being written.

(viii) The implications of the falling tide of date of knowledge

We have seen how *Dobbie* focused attention on some very important words in s 14(1) of the Act, which have the effect that the plaintiff can be fixed with knowledge without realising that there has been any negligence.

---

12 *The Times*, 25 January 1995.

13 For a helpful discussion about the implications of this case for date of knowledge, see Charles Lewis in *Clinical Risk*, March 1995, pp 82-83.

At first sight it might be thought that this would reduce the number of viable medical negligence claims because it would exclude latecomers. However, fears have been expressed[14] that it could have the opposite effect. The theory is that any patient who thinks that he has had a less than satisfactory outcome to his treatment should seek legal advice and issue proceedings at an early stage so as to protect his position at a later date.

(ix) Separate limitation points within a case

Most cases in medical litigation are concerned with a single act of alleged negligence. The defendant will argue that the incident in question represents the point at which knowledge arises, even though the plaintiff may make efforts to show that it is not until some later date that she became fixed with the requisite degree of knowledge for the purposes of s 14(1)(b) of the Limitation Act 1980. In rare cases, however, there may be two or more negligent acts which are separated by a long period of time. Additionally, they may give rise to different dates of knowledge even though they are both, in their different ways, the cause of the harm that generates the complaint.

In one case, a woman was seen by her general practitioner with chest pains that were attributed to angina and high blood pressure. Four days later the doctor was called again because the symptoms had become much worse and the patient had collapsed. She was duly admitted to hospital and found to have developed a myocardial infarct. She alleged that her doctor had been negligent in that he should have arranged admission at the visit on which he diagnosed angina. There was little room for argument that her date of knowledge coincided with the hospital admission date, and she therefore issued proceedings within three years of that time. Expert general practitioner opinion indicated that the doctor had indeed fallen below proper standards in letting the patient stay at home with the degree of angina and the level of blood pressure from which she was

---

14 For an exposition of this theory, see Simanowitz in *AVMA Journal* (Spring 1994) pp 1–2.

regarded as having suffered, but the plaintiff faced a difficulty with causation. A cardiology expert took the view that, even if prompt admission had been arranged, the infarct would probably still have occurred, though it might not have been quite so severe.

On disclosure of the notes, the plaintiff's solicitor checked all the letters and found one dated six years before the time of the infarct. It was from a doctor who had attended the woman about an unrelated matter whilst she was on holiday. That letter mentioned that the blood pressure was raised and suggested it should be followed up and treated by the patient's own doctor. Unfortunately, the letter had been filed away and no action was taken, even though the woman did visit the surgery in the meantime with various complaints. When preparing her case, she argued that the failure to act on the letter was negligent. She further argued that if she had been investigated and treated properly in the intervening six years the myocardial infarct would probably not have occurred at all. This approach made her case much stronger on causation and she had little difficulty in showing negligence as well. The important point was that her date of knowledge in respect of this negligent act was not at the time the letter was received or filed away, and it was not even at the time of the infarct six years later. She had no idea about the existence of the letter until her solicitor looked through the old papers and told her about it. Her three-year limitation period therefore dated from that point.

(x)   Actual and constructive knowledge

We have seen how a patient cannot be fixed with knowledge for the purpose of the Limitation Act 1980 until she is aware of the harm and at least suspects that it may have been caused by some aspect of the doctor's treatment. It will be in the defendant's interest to show that the knowledge had been acquired at the earliest possible stage. Conversely, a plaintiff who has incurred undue delay in getting her action started, perhaps for personal reasons, may want to assert that she had no knowledge at that early date.

In the cases considered so far we were concerned with actual knowledge. There was little dispute about when it was acquired. For instance, it would have been out of the question for the defendant in *Pleydell v Aubyn* to have argued that the girl could have known that she was infertile in her earlier years.

The difficulty arises when the plaintiff asserts that she was not in a position to find out about the damage or its cause, even though another person in the same situation might have done so. This can arise when the patient claims that he has been labouring under a difficulty which prevented her from finding out. If a case reaches trial on the point of limitation, the judge will decide whether or not the plaintiff was fixed with knowledge at the earlier time asserted by the defendant. The judge will hold that she was fixed with 'constructive knowledge' if it was reasonable to have expected her to have found out that the harm could have been attributed to the defendant's negligence even if, in the event, the plaintiff remained unaware of it.

In *Davis v City & Hackney HA* (1989) a child was born spastic. Even when he approached adulthood it never occurred to him that his disability could have been caused by negligence at the time of his birth. Much later, he became suspicious and investigated the matter. He obtained a medical report from a specialist and this indicated that there had been negligence. In this case the patient was labouring under greater difficulties than most people and the judge held that he could not be fixed with constructive knowledge any earlier than his receipt of the medical report. In other words, 'the clock did not start to run' until that point and this left him with three years to serve proceedings, even though the negligence had occurred many years earlier and some other litigant might have considered it sooner.

X   CONSENT

(i)   Introduction

Consent is an integral part of medical treatment. The doctor must ensure that he has the patient's consent before he starts any activity that is going to affect her. We saw in Chapter II how a duty of care arises as soon as the doctor puts himself in the position of realising that anything he does will affect the patient. The neighbour principle was formulated in *Donoghue v Stevenson* (1932) in the context of a manufacturer and a consumer but we saw how the doctor and the patient are even closer legal neighbours because the doctor is under a duty to do more than merely avoid harming the patient. The doctor owes it to the patient to make a positive effort to put her at an advantage. In other words, far from merely refraining from affecting the patient, he is trying to make a difference to her and it is this difference to which the patient is giving her consent.

In an ordinary personal injury case, consent is clearly irrelevant. It goes without saying that this kind of plaintiff will be content to have no difference made to her. Indeed, it is because a difference, and a harmful one at that, was made that she decided to sue.

Just as an ordinary personal injury plaintiff is certain to be content to go without injury, so a patient is bound to be satisfied with being put at an appropriate advantage. A patient's consent to treatment concerns her agreement to run the risk of the side effects that are an inevitable accompaniment of the benefit that she hopes to obtain.

(ii) Express and implied consent

Consent to treatment can be express or implied. Express consent is given when the patient clearly states that he is willing to go ahead with the treatment. This may take the form of a verbal discussion in which the doctor explains the benefits to be expected and the risks to be incurred. Alternatively, it may be written on paper. This commonly happens when a patient signs a 'consent form' for an operation. Consent forms are usually drafted in very broad terms. For example, they may refer to the treatment that is proposed and then indicate that 'the nature and purpose' of it have been explained by a particular doctor. The form may go on to add words to the effect that the patient:

> also consents to such further or alternative operative measures as may be found to be necessary during the course of the operation and to the administration of a general, local or other anaesthetic for any of these purposes.

The patient will be asked to sign this form, and its lack of precision is clearly a reflection of the fact that the same form is used for numerous different operations.

The existence of a signed form is no more than written evidence that a discussion on consent has taken place. If a case comes to litigation, the defendant's side will be considerably strengthened if he has added some remarks to the form, or perhaps has recorded in the patient's notes that various risks were brought to the patient's attention before the form was signed. As a matter of evidence, the patient may counter the standardised content of the form by attempting to show that no proper explanation or disclosure of risks had ever been given.

In general practice, large numbers of patients are seen in a short time and often for matters which are of no great consequence. As a result consent is not often uppermost in the doctor's mind. Patients are usually unaware of the importance of their consent being secured and so, if the doctor does not raise the issue specifically, it may well receive little or no attention. Written consent is hardly ever obtained or considered necessary in general practice. Even verbal consent is not very often expressed in so many words.

It is here that implied consent is the order of the day. Let us consider the doctor who tells the patient that a blood test is to be taken. The doctor reaches for a syringe and attaches the needle but gives no explanation, probably because the patient has been subjected to the procedure before, and further discussion is considered unnecessary. The patient rolls up his sleeve and lays his arm on the desk such as to offer the front of his elbow to the doctor. No word of consent has been uttered, let alone written on paper, but the patient has implied by his behaviour that he is willing to undergo the test. The difficulty only arises when a large haematoma develops. The patient will argue that by rolling up his sleeve he consented to no more than the passing discomfort of a prick in the arm, and that he had never been warned about the possibility of the haematoma.

Implied consent is given many times every day in general practice. It extends to the realms of examination, investigation and treatment. The patient who lies on his left side with his knees drawn up is consenting to a rectal examination. Similarly, the patient who takes a prescription in his hand and then visits the pharmacist is consenting to take the course of tablets.

Surgical operations under general anaesthetic are probably the field of medicine where consent has the most attention focused on it, as evidenced by the obtaining of consent forms. Conversely, general practice may well be the area where it receives the least attention. Despite this apparent shortcoming, consent is often given by implication. The reason why patients so readily imply their consent is probably because they trust the doctor. They just assume that the doctor will only go ahead with treatment if the benefit he believes he can provide outweighs the risk to which he is exposing them.

(iii) The provision of information when consent is obtained

When the word 'consent' is used on its own it indicates no more than that the patient has agreed to go ahead with the treatment. For the purposes of medical practice, however, we are concerned that the consent should be informed. This means that the patient must be told about the side effects that may accompany the treatment, and agree to be exposed to the risk of these occurring. Inevitably patients have little idea of what damage can occur and, in any case, all their attention is focused on the benefit. That is why they consulted the doctor in the first place. The onus is therefore firmly on the doctor to give the necessary explanations without being asked.

No treatment is completely free of side effects. Even an aspirin tablet can cause gastric bleeding. Some side effects are very unlikely to occur, and some are not at all severe. Furthermore, some patients react differently from others. Quite apart from side effects that are recognised and listed in works of reference, every experienced general practitioner has had a patient who has reacted in an unpredictable and inexplicable way to a treatment.

Despite the undoubted need to tell a patient of relevant disadvantages, it has to be recognised that it would be out of the question to tell him of every side effect that has ever been known to occur. There are two reasons why various points may be omitted from the explanation that the doctor gives.

At a practical level there is the sheer pressure of time. It must be recognised that the giving of information about side effects involves more than merely uttering the words. It involves a discussion about the implications of the side effects, such as how serious they will be, and how likely they are to occur. Indeed, the discussion may not stop there. Other issues may be raised which give the patient cause for concern and about which he will want even more information.

There is, however, another reason why the doctor may decide not to disclose certain risks. The mention of a side effect is likely to have at least some influence in terms of putting the patient off his decision to accept the treatment. He will see the taking of the risk as the price that has to be paid for achieving the benefit. This is particularly likely to happen with very serious side effects. Whether or not the risk is justified depends, at least in part, on how likely it is to occur. It may well be reasonable to take it if the risk is 1 in 10,000 but not if it is 1 in 100. When the risk assessment is presented to the patient in this way, the fact that one side effect is a hundred times more likely to occur than another may make little impression on her. The mere mention of a serious side-effect, such as a stroke, is likely to mean that the patient refuses even to consider the treatment.

It is clear than when a doctor is securing the patient's informed consent he has to strike a balance. On the one hand the doctor must give the patient sufficient information to enable him to come to a proper decision about the treatment. On the other hand, the doctor can withhold information if he thinks the side effects are trivial and rare, and if it is apparent that the mere mention of them will put the patient off the treatment when, in reality, it would be in his best interests to accept it. When reaching this balance the doctor must consider all the possible adverse consequences and decide:

- how serious they are likely to be; and

- how likely they are to occur.

If one of the risks under consideration is likely to occur and would be serious it will deserve a mention. Conversely, if it is unlikely to occur and is trivial there may be a case for omitting it.

The need to disclose risks that are both likely to occur and are serious was well illustrated in the Canadian case of *Reibl v Hughes* (1980). The plaintiff suffered severe narrowing of one of the arteries to the brain and was offered an operation. Although he gave his consent to the operation for the relief of the constriction, he was not told that there was a 10% risk of stroke and a 4% risk of death. In the event, the former risk materialised and he sued the surgeon for failing to obtain his informed consent. The court held that, as the risk was as serious as a stroke, and as the likelihood of it occurring was as high as 10%, the surgeon had been negligent in not warning him. Needless to say, the question of risk disclosure has been covered by English law and we can now move on to a study of that. This will be followed by a discussion about the different approaches that have been adopted in American and Australian case law.

(iv)   The standard of care in consent

The patient has a right to expect a certain standard of care in all aspects of her treatment. The procedure by which the doctor obtains the patient's consent is no exception.

The dilemma of how much the doctor should, or should not, tell his patient reached trial in *Sidaway v Board of Governors of Bethlem Royal Hospital and Maudsley Hospital* (1985). A woman was suffering from a prolapsed intervertebral disc in the neck. Pressure on part of the spinal cord was causing persistent pain in the arm. A surgeon advised that an operation could be carried out, a laminectomy, to relieve the pressure and to cure the pain. Unfortunately, the spinal cord itself was damaged during the course of the operation and the patient was severely disabled. She sued the surgeon.

The damage to the cord was a recognised complication of the operation. The patient was not suing for negligence in the operative technique which was used. Rather, she was suing on the basis that her consent had not been obtained. Put another way, she asserted that she had not been told about the possibility of cord damage. She argued that, if she had been told, she would not have consented to the operation and the damage would not have occurred. This raised the question of whether it was negligent to fail to warn her of the risk.

When the case reached trial the medical witnesses for the defence said that they too would not have disclosed the risk. They justified this on the basis the risk was very slight and to mention it would probably have frightened the patient into refusing the operation. Even though the experts for the plaintiff may well have asserted that they would have told her, the defence experts represented a responsible body of medical opinion that would have withheld the information. In *Sidaway*, the House of Lords held that a doctor is not negligent in obtaining a patient's consent if he only discloses the risks which would have been mentioned by a responsible body of medical opinion. *Sidaway* very conveniently brought the standard of care in relation to consent into line with the *Bolam* principle which provided the standard to be observed in the realms of diagnosis and treatment.

A further point which was raised in *Sidaway* as regards the doctor's discussions with his patient about various treatment options was that:

> ... a doctor [is] under a duty to provide the patient with the information necessary to enable the patient to make a balanced judgment in deciding whether to submit to that treatment.

(v) The advantages of the paternalistic approach in consent

The traditional approach to consent in the UK has been paternalistic. Put another way, it was the doctor who took the dominant role in planning the treatment and he expected the patient to play virtually no part in the proceedings. Indeed, the doctor expected the patient to be quite unconcerned because the patient was not in a position to know about such matters and should content himself with the knowledge that whatever the doctor did it would be to the patient's advantage, for the simple reason that he was the doctor. In recent years, however, there has been a shift of emphasis towards the patient, who now expects to be more fully informed about the proposed treatment and to play a more active part in the decision-making process.

There are at least two reasons for this change, one of which is domestic, and the other has its origin outside the UK. Later in this chapter (see pages 95-97) we shall see how the American case of *Canterbury v Spence* (1972) and the more recent Australian case of *Rogers v Whitaker* (1992) produced a 'patient-orientated' test when a decision was made about how much information the doctor should provide when explaining the treatment. Although those cases would be regarded as no more than persuasive in the UK, it is of interest that they both come from countries which have a shorter legal and social history than the UK's. Hierarchy and tradition are probably more firmly established in the UK and the comparatively recent erosion of such factors is probably at least part of the reason why patients now think that they should be given more information than their parents would have expected.

With regard to the domestic point, we are concerned with such matters as education and the media. Since the mid-1980s there has been an explosion in the amount of medical material in the daily press and on television and the radio. This not only provides factual data about health and disease, but stimulates interest of a more general nature. Indeed, medicine is probably the profession which has more appeal and fascination for the lay public than any other.

These two points taken together, and doubtless other less obvious ones as well, have meant that many patients want a comprehensive package of information. This, of course, is all very well when the doctor has plenty of time and the patient is not under any particular threat from illness. The latter point, however, can be of decisive importance in, for example, a case of terminal cancer. Not all patients with serious illnesses want to be treated as the doctor's partner in planning the treatment. Suppose a woman has been increasingly unwell for several months with a multitude of symptoms and her general practitioner refers her to a specialist for further investigation. Suppose further that tests show that she has cancer and that a range of treatment options is available. Some of the options will be well established and of moderate benefit. Others will be recent developments and of uncertain but potentially greater benefit. The last thing a patient in this situation wants is to be asked: 'Which would you rather have – radiotherapy or chemotherapy? Perhaps both, to be on the safe side?' No, this kind of patient wants the doctor to decide what is in her best interests, taking all of the circumstances into account. She wants the doctor to take over her care in the fullest sense. She wants to be able to trust the doctor and to have confidence in him. Anything less than this will mean that she worries about her treatment as well as about her disease. It will merely serve to undermine her emotional strength at the very time she needs it most.[15]

The author well remembers a patient who, 20 years ago, had secondary cancer deposits in his liver. We can call him Norman. The surgeon, whom we can call Raymond, was much older and more experienced than this general practitioner at the time and did not tell the patient about the true nature of his disease when he was embarking on an abdominal operation to relieve the patient's symptoms. The patient, not surprisingly, said to this general practitioner, 'Walter ... have I got cancer?'

The general practitioner's natural inclination was to be honest with Norman and answer his question truthfully. When the two doctors discussed the matter the next day, Raymond said 'Walter, Norman wants to hear something to his advantage and if you tell him he has cancer he will give up hope.' The general practitioner acquiesced rather uncomfortably with this approach, but after the patient had died some years later he realised that Raymond's paternalistic approach had the undoubted advantage of kindness.

One study undertaken recently[16] failed to find undue support for the modern notion that patient participation in the planning of treatment helps to reduce psychological morbidity in serious disease. Breast cancer was taken as a convenient background against which to study anxiety and depression over a period of time in various groups of women who were offered different

---

15 For a discussion on kindness and cruelty in informed consent, see *BMJ* 1993; 307:119-1201. That article is also a useful study of the difficulties facing doctors who are concerned about consent when they are randomising patients in clinical trials.

16 See Fallowfield *et al* 'psychological effects of being offered choice of surgery for breast cancer', *BMJ* 1994; 309: 448.

levels of involvement with regard to the choice of breast conservation or mastectomy. The study concluded that:

> no significant difference in psychological morbidity existed between the women offered choice and those not offered choice.

The same study also focused on the related point of how much involvement women with newly diagnosed breast cancer really want to have with regard to decisions about their treatment. The figures obtained were very revealing, but perhaps not altogether unexpected. It was found that:

> only 20% wanted an active role in deciding their treatment; 28% preferred to share decision-making, and 52% wished the surgeon to decide.

(vi) The significance of the terms 'consent' and 'informed consent'

In section (iii) we saw how a patient's consent can only be said to have been properly obtained when he has been given enough information to enable her to reach a balanced decision about whether to go ahead with the treatment. The expression 'informed consent' was therefore coined, and this recognised, indeed emphasised, the importance of appropriate disclosure of risks. It was meant to distinguish an improper situation in which a patient had agreed to the treatment, in other words had consented to it, but was unaware of the risks. This could, for the sake of argument, be termed 'uninformed consent' and it is just this situation which gives rise to litigation on the subject.

Unfortunately, the purists have objected to the expression 'informed consent' on the basis that if insufficient information was provided the consent was never given.[17] On the contrary, the

---

[17] For a presentation of this view, see Anthony Barton in *Clinical Risk*, March 1995, pp 86-88.

patient had given her consent. When the suggestion of treatment was made, the patient said 'yes', and said it willingly.

(vii) The American rule in consent

The standard of care in consent in the UK was expressed in *Sidaway*. The rule was based on what a responsible body of doctors would have disclosed under the circumstances. It thus adopted a paternalistic approach. It assumed that the patient only had a right to know what doctors considered that patients should be told. Doubtless this was based on the traditional British approach to medical practice. This has always been on a foundation of trust. It is based on the premise that the patient could regard it as a foregone conclusion that the doctor would know what was best for the patient and that he could leave all the decisions to the doctor. The patient expected to play virtually no part in the management of an illness as the doctor knew much more about it than the patient. It was therefore entirely reasonable for the doctor to be entrusted with the decision about whether to take the risk of exposing the patient to a particular side effect.

This attitude has not, however, always had world-wide acceptance. The USA, with its consumer-led attitude to medical care, inevitably took a different approach. It formulated a 'patient-orientated' rule of informed consent in *Canterbury v Spence* (1972). When considering whether or not the risk of a particular side effect should have been disclosed, the court did not concern itself with what most doctors would have said in similar circumstances. It chose instead to ask what a reasonable patient with that particular illness would have wanted to know. It used a 'patient-orientated' test rather than a 'doctor-orientated' test. It rejected the paternalistic view that had been prevalent in Britain and preferred to base the assessment on the wishes of the patient, thereby shifting the 'balance of power' in the decision-making process away from the doctor and towards the patient.

Much more recently the 'patient-orientated' test in *Canterbury*'s American case was given further support in the Australian case of *Rogers v Whitaker* (1992).[18] A woman had suffered an eye injury as a child and had become blind in that eye. She managed very well with the remaining eye for many years. At a much later date she fell into the hands of an eye surgeon who offered her an operation on the blind eye with a view to restoring at least some of the sight in it. The patient, however, was of an unusually inquiring nature and wanted to be satisfied that, by consenting to the operation, she was not exposing herself to any particular risk. Part of her anxiety in this respect stemmed from the fact that she only had one eye that was of any use and that, if any harm came to it, the consequences would be nothing short of catastrophic. She felt sufficiently reassured to go ahead with the operation. The procedure produced no improvement in the sight of the eye and, far worse, the other eye was affected by sympathetic ophthalmia and the patient was rendered blind. It was an extremely rare complication with an incidence of about 1 in 14,000. She sued the surgeon for negligence both in respect of his operative technique and in respect of his failure to obtain her informed consent.

The action failed as far as the operation itself was concerned. The court found no evidence of negligence. This left the question of how much information was, and should have been, given when the patient's consent was obtained. She argued that she had not been told about the admittedly remote possibility of sympathetic ophthalmia and that, if she had been told, she would not have agreed to the operation, and that she would therefore still have retained the sight in one eye.

Expert evidence for the defence made it clear that a responsible body of medical opinion would not have mentioned that particular complication. On the basis of *Sidaway*, this meant that the patient's consent had been properly obtained. The British 'doctor-orientated' rule had been followed. The judge, however,

---

[18] For a full discussion of *Rogers v Whitaker* and the different duties of disclosure in various jurisdictions, see *Medical Law Review*, 1, Summer 1993 pp 139-59.

applied *Canterbury*'s US rule, which was 'patient-orientated', and found the surgeon negligent on the basis that a reasonable patient in those circumstances would have wanted to know about the risk and that she should have been informed. Doubtless, considerable weight was attached to the fact that this particular patient had made it abundantly clear to the surgeon that she wanted to know about any possible risk regardless of how unlikely it was to occur.

The surgeon appealed on the basis that the wrong test had been applied in assessing negligence in relation to the amount of information that should have been disclosed. The Australian Court of Appeal and High Court dismissed his appeal. It rejected the English *Bolam* test that had been absorbed into the *Sidaway* judgment. It pronounced that the *Bolam* test was only relevant to a doctor's decision regarding the provision of treatment. It was irrelevant where a patient asked for information which he had decided he needed.

(viii) The implications of the American rule on consent for British medicine

Canterbury v Spence, followed by *Rogers v Whitaker*, have paved the way for a 'patient-orientated' rule in informed consent. Those decisions were taken beyond the shores of the UK and it will be interesting to see if, in the fullness of time, they are accepted in Britain such that the *Sidaway* approach becomes outdated.[19] However, as *Sidaway* was a House of Lords decision, it has to be acknowledged that any change is highly unlikely in the foreseeable future. Nevertheless, *Rogers v Whitaker* may have some influence on clinicians' behaviour in obtaining their patients' consent.

Efforts to shift the emphasis from doctor to patient in this field may fall on fertile ground in the UK of the mid-1990s. The government's recent Patients' Charter has emphasised that patients have rights. The media have raised the lay public's level

---

[19] For a fuller discussion of the defendant's appeal in *Rogers v Whitaker*, see *Medical Law Review* 1, Spring 1993, pp 115-19.

of knowledge about treatments to which they may be about to submit themselves. Furthermore, patients expect to play a much more active role in the management of their illnesses, and expect to be given much more information than previously. Taken together, these points mean that English law will be increasingly likely to find that a doctor has been negligent if he has not made a very full response to a patient's inquiry about the risks associated with a particular treatment. Additionally, he is unlikely to be able to hide behind the excuse that the patient did not word the inquiry in a very precise way. The plaintiff in *Rogers v Whitaker* did not specifically inquire about sympathetic ophthalmia, presumably because she had never heard of it. Nevertheless, the Australian judge clearly thought that the general tone of her inquiry was such that the surgeon should have realised that she would have wanted to know about it.

(ix)   Choosing the appropriate level of disclosure

In the earlier parts of this chapter on consent we have seen two very different approaches. On the one hand we have seen how, especially in recent years, some patients want to be given a great deal of information about the options for treatment and the relevant side effects. On the other hand, there is no doubt that some other patients do not want very much involvement at all. It has to be added that in this second group the offer of additional information and participation is not just superfluous, it is actually harmful.

This brings us naturally to the question that is all-important to the practitioner faced with the individual patient. The doctor has to make a decision about what level of consent is appropriate to the patient's personality and his condition. All doctors know that some patients are not particularly forthcoming about their fears and aspirations. Many of them, especially if they are frightened about the threat posed by their illness, hope that the doctor will somehow ask the right question or will appreciate the full implication of some casual remark.

In each case, the doctor must make an assessment of the difficulty. There will be at least two aspects to consider. First, there is the patient herself. We refer here to such matters as her personality and ability to understand the doctor's explanations. In passing, we can observe that one of the strengths of traditional British general practice is that it lends itself extremely well to a good assessment of this point. These doctors, especially those who have been in practice for some years, know their patients very well and are in a favourable position to judge the amount of involvement the patients are likely to want. They are also likely to know the rest of the family and there is no doubt that relatives can be an invaluable source of information for the doctor on this kind of issue.

Quite apart from the idiosyncrasies of the patient herself there is the question of the illness that is to be the subject of the treatment. All doctors will acknowledge that this has at least a tendency to affect the level of consent that will be appropriate.

Let us take *Rogers v Whitaker* (1992) (see page 96) as a starting point for resolving the difficulty. In that case, the patient had suffered surprisingly little disability for many years despite only having the sight on one eye. The proposed operation was intended to improve the appearance of the blind eye and, almost as a bonus, to retrieve some of the sight. In this case, consent was clearly of the utmost importance. The information needed to be very detailed and all possible options, even perhaps refraining from any treatment at all, needed to be considered. This contrasts with the cases of breast cancer we discussed earlier (page 94) where the patients were faced with a life threatening condition about which something had to be done. Some members of that group of women were probably also rather frightened and wanted the doctor to relieve them of having to make a decision. This was in stark contrast to Mrs Rogers' position.

At the risk of making a very broad generalisation, we can perhaps suggest that a relatively full level of disclosure is required for patients who have, for example, conditions that are of cosmetic importance, or are just rather disabling. A further point here is that the treatment is unlikely to be particularly urgent and there is plenty of time for the patient to think about it. A convenient example here is the man who thinks he wants a vasectomy. If the patient seems even slightly hesitant, the surgeon will ask him to return for another discussion some months later. For all the doctor knows, the man may have been under pressure from his wife or his girlfriend and the lapse of time will help to ensure that the patient's unadulterated consent has been obtained.

By contrast, we can suggest that a lower level of disclosure is likely to be appropriate for a patient who has a serious or life-threatening condition. There are two points here. One is that there is likely to be some urgency over the treatment. That is not to say that the doctor will not have time to discuss it, rather it is that the patient has less time to think about it. The second point is that the illness may be having a depressing effect on the patient such that he wants the doctor to relieve him of the burden of making a difficult decision.

(x) Causation and consent

Causation is an integral part of any negligence action. An action for failure to obtain a patient's consent is no exception. By this we mean that it is not enough for the plaintiff to show that his consent was not obtained; he must also show that, if he had been given a proper warning, he would not have consented to the treatment and the damage would therefore never have occurred. We saw in *Rogers v Whitaker* how the patient argued successfully that, if she had been told about the 1 in 14,000 risk of sympathetic ophthalmia, she would not have agreed to go ahead with the operation, and she would therefore still have retained the sight in one eye.

The importance of causation in an action on consent, and the difficulty that could be faced by a patient in this particular area, is the subject of a fuller discussion in Chapter XI.

XI   *RES IPSA LOQUITUR*

(i)   Introduction

In all civil cases the burden of proof is on the plaintiff. By this we mean that the patient has to convince the court that her version of events is more than 50% likely to be correct. In medical negligence cases this can sometimes be very difficult for patients, and this typically happens in hospital cases where technical matters can be quite obscure. Additionally, the patient may be anaesthetised at the time of the alleged negligence and have no means of knowing what happened during a critical part of an operation. There is, however, a method by which a patient can occasionally surmount this difficulty: by resorting to the maxim *res ipsa loquitur*.

Literally translated, *res ipsa loquitur* means 'the thing speaks for itself'. Put another way, the patient attempts to show that the mere fact of damage occurring is highly suggestive of negligence. If the degree of such a suggestion is sufficiently great it may place on the defendant the onus of disproving this presumption of negligence.

(ii) The criteria for the application of *res ipsa loquitur*

The classic case[20] on *res ipsa loquitur* is *Cassidy v Ministry of Health* (1951). A patient was seen by his general practitioner with a Dupuytren's contracture. The constriction of the flexor tendons of two of his fingers was sufficiently severe to warrant referral to a specialist and an operation for its relief. After the inevitable disability in the immediate post-operative phase, he found that not only the operated fingers were stiff but so were the other two. The result was that he had even less use in his hand after the operation than he had before it, and he sued the surgeon for a negligent operative technique. The trial judge found for the defendant on the basis that the plaintiff had failed to discharge the burden of proof. Lord Denning, in the Court of Appeal, held that the maxim *res ipsa loquitur* should apply because the end result of the operation was of itself sufficiently suggestive of negligence. The plaintiff's appeal was therefore allowed. Lord Denning highlighted the defendant's position when labouring under the effect of the maxim in terms that he must 'explain it, if you can'.

In a situation such as this, the defendant will try to escape liability by finding a non-tortious explanation for the damage. Alternatively, the defendant may be able to show that the unfortunate result can perfectly well happen as a side effect of the technique that the patient alleges was used without there being any question of negligence. If the doctor decides on the latter approach, the patient may be able to counter this by asserting that his consent was not obtained because he was not warned about this adverse effect in advance of the operation.

The acceptance of a non-negligent explanation for the damage will clearly help the defendant's case. This kind of attempt to escape liability was made by the defendants in *Lindsay v Mid-Western Health Board* (1991). A child had what was thought to be

---

[20] For quite a detailed examination of the case law on *res ipsa loquitur*, from 1865 to the present day, and with particular emphasis on medical negligence cases, see two articles by Leigh in *J Med Def Union* 1993 No 3 (pp 66-67) and 1993 No 4 (pp 88-89).

an uneventful appendicectomy but shortly afterwards suffered a convulsion which was followed by a permanent brain damage. The plaintiff sued on the basis that there must have been hypoxia at some stage while she was under the care of the anaesthetist. The defendants, however, were able to rebut this explanation with evidence to show that the oxygen supply had been adequate at all material times. Thus it was that neither side could produce a clear and credible explanation for the harm, but there was no getting away from the fact that the girl had gone into hospital with her intellect intact and had come out brain damaged after what was supposed to have been no more than the removal of her appendix. This prompted the plaintiff to argue that she should be allowed to rely on the maxim *res ipsa loquitur* for an award of damages. The defendants attempted to find an alternative explanation and pointed out that mesenteric adenitis had been observed at the operation and that this suggested the presence of a virus. They postulated that a viral encephalopathy must have occurred and that it was this, rather than the negligent deprivation of oxygen, that had caused the convulsion. The judge, however, was not convinced that this explanation was supported by sufficiently strong evidence, allowed *res ipsa loquitur* to apply and found for the plaintiff.

It must not be assumed that *res ipsa loquitur* is readily available to any plaintiff who is having difficulty with his evidence. It is not a rule of law in the sense of a statute, but rather a maxim upon which a judge may agree to allow a plaintiff to rely for the purpose of his evidence if the circumstances of the case justify it.

The importance of the circumstances are well illustrated in a hospital setting. Let us take the example of a swab that is left in a wound. Most patients would think that this was sufficiently suggestive of a negligent technique to allow *res ipsa loquitur* to apply. The court is likely to consider all the circumstances of the case and it may well allow the maxim to apply if the operation was of a routine nature without any undue constraints on the operator. Conversely, it might take a more generous view of the defendant's evidence if the operation had been done as an emergency with numerous attendant difficulties for the surgeon. The court may also be influenced in the plaintiff's favour as far as his evidence is concerned if the circumstances of the case are such that he is having great difficulty in ascertaining the relevant facts about his treatment.

(iii) *Res ipsa loquitur* in general practice

Despite *Cassidy*, the lead case on *res ipsa loquitur*, being a hospital case, the maxim is equally relevant to general practice. As an example we can take what must be the humblest of medical procedures and one that is usually delegated to the nurse, that of ear syringing.

There must be many thousands of cases of ear syringing carried out every day in Britain. Almost without exception the patient experiences relief from the impacted wax with no more than passing discomfort. Indeed, the procedure is of such a routine nature that even the most diligent practice nurse will record no more than the date and the words 'ears syringed'. So, what is the position of a patient whose ear drum is ruptured in the process and who wishes to sue for negligence? As has been mentioned repeatedly throughout this book, he will have the burden of proving that the nurse used a negligent technique and he will have to prove that this was causative of the damage.

The patient immediately faces difficulties. He will have no knowledge of, or means of knowing, the technique that was used. Furthermore, the notes are not likely to be in the least informative. He cannot even assert that the lack of reference to the technique in the notes is of itself negligent. He is, however, well aware that he arrived at the surgery with no more than wax in his ears, and that he has left with a ruptured ear drum. He may feel justified in resorting to *res ipsa loquitur*.

The doctor will then have to produce some other explanation for the rupture that does not involve negligence. The doctor might, for instance, be able to show that the patient had a latent weakness in the drum and that the doctor could not be expected to have known about it. Alternatively, he may be able to show that even with the utmost care there is a recognised incidence of perforation. However, the doctor may be in difficulty here, because the patient will argue that he should have been told about the risk. In other words, his consent was not obtained. The patient will then add the assertion that, had he been so informed, he would not have consented to the risk, and the rupture would therefore not have occurred. If this line of reasoning is successful, the patient will be able to hold the doctor vicariously liable for the damage.

(iv)   Typical *res ipsa loquitur* procedures in general practice

We have seen how the main criterion that a judge is likely to use when deciding whether to allow a plaintiff to assert that *res ipsa loquitur* should apply is whether or not the mere occurrence of the damage is sufficiently suggestive of negligence. But there is another point for which the judge is likely to make some allowance. That is the difficulty the patient has in producing evidence of a negligent technique. This would be relevant in a hospital setting where a patient is anaesthetised at the time of the alleged negligence and cannot know what is happening.

In general practice this is more likely to arise in respect of routine procedures such as venepunctures and removal of lumps in minor surgery. These are the sorts of procedures where it is conventionally regarded as perfectly adequate to record no more than the fact that the operation was performed. This means that the patient, after discovery of the records, will have no means of knowing whether a proper technique was used.

Let us consider the patient who has a sebaceous cyst on the back of the neck and asks his doctor to remove it. The note will probably record very little detail. Suppose the patient finds that he has lost the use of part of his arm after the operation and that this has been caused by damage to the accessory nerve in the neck. The patient will argue that he should be allowed to take advantage of *res ipsa loquitur* because the lack of detailed notes makes it very difficult for him to demonstrate a negligent technique.

In one case, a woman consulted her general practitioner about a lump in the breast. The doctor considered that the lump was probably an innocent cyst and wanted to confirm this by aspirating fluid. The procedure was duly carried out but the patient found it very painful. Shortly after leaving the surgery premises she found herself very short of breath and returned to the doctor who arranged immediate referral to the local accident and emergency department. On investigation there she was found to be suffering from a pneumothorax which had been caused by the general practitioner's needle entering the pleural cavity from the breast. The patient found it difficult to demonstrate a negligent technique because so little was recorded in the notes, and she sought to raise the maxim of *res ipsa loquitur* on the basis that treatment for a breast lump should not, without negligence, involve a leakage of air into the pleural cavity.

In another case a child received an immunisation at her general practitioner's premises. Unfortunately, there was a fierce tissue reaction at the injection site during the next few days. The process had all the hallmarks of sepsis and, despite the efforts of various hospital specialists to control the infection, the girl needed skin grafts to make good the defect on her upper arm. She sued the general practitioner but, with nothing more than a very brief entry in the notes which had been made by the nurse who gave the injection, the question of evidence immediately posed a difficulty. She relied on the maxim *res ipsa loquitur* on the basis that, without negligence, the sepsis would not have occurred. Many years previously, in *Voller v Portsmouth Corporation* (1947), a similar case arose in a hospital setting. A young man with a fractured femur was given a spinal anaesthetic. Unfortunately this was soon followed by the development of meningitis and paralysis of the legs. At trial he was allowed to rely on the maxim because it was evident that the organism could only have gained access to his body through the injection and that this would not have occurred if all proper precautions had been taken.

(v)   The current shift away from *res ipsa loquitur*

Any case in which *res ipsa loquitur* is held to apply automatically creates a difficulty for the defendant. In *Lindsay v Mid Western Health Board* (1991) the defendants attempted, unsuccessfully, to circumvent the difficulty by suggesting an alternative non-negligent explanation for the harm. In recent years, however, a current of opinion seems to have developed whereby it is thought to be unduly harsh on a defendant to insist that he finds an alternative explanation. This school of thought may have its root in the notion that this insistence has the effect, in a sense, of reversing the burden of proof. This goes against the long-established rule that the onus is on the plaintiff to prove his case.

In an attempt to ease this apparent harshness there has been a move in the direction of expecting defendants to do no more than to show that they have taken all reasonable care. This is clearly a much easier task, and amounts to no more than demonstrating the use of currently accepted techniques of treatment supported, for the purposes of evidence, by good notekeeping. It has to be acknowledged that this approach is more realistic because the workings of the human body in health and disease can sometimes be impossible to fathom. It cannot be likened to, for example, a broken-down motor car in which the mechanic can almost always find an explanation.

One cannot help having some sympathy with the defendants in *Lindsay*. It must indeed have been frustrating to know that they would be held negligent unless they produced a plausible explanation for the damage. The general practitioner whose nurse has syringed a patient's ear and which is followed by damage to the drum, is in a similar predicament. He will feel that he should be asked to do no more than to show that the nurse took proper care. He will think it unreasonable to have to prove that, for instance, the patient had some latent weakness which he could not have known about in advance.

XII VICARIOUS LIABILITY

(i)   Introduction

In Latin the word *vicarius* means a substitute. Throughout business and the professions, principal workers delegate tasks to their substitutes. Without such an arrangement it would be impossible for the team to distribute and deliver its skills or goods efficiently. One part of the arrangement is that the employer will decide the nature of the work to be done. The employer will also direct the substitute adequately in his task and will take reasonable steps to ensure that incidental matters, such as the provision of equipment, are not neglected. The other part of the arrangement is that the substitute, the employee, is under a duty to fulfil the employer's directions in return for wages.

If the driver of a bus is negligent and injures a pedestrian the latter may decide to sue for damages for personal injury. As the driver himself may well be impecunious and have not made any insurance arrangements, the pedestrian will be well advised to sue the employer; that is the bus company. If the driver was acting in the course of his employment it will mean that the company is vicariously liable. An employee who is not acting in such course is described as being 'on a frolic of his own' and this will put the employer in the position of being able to deny liability. Put another way, vicarious liability only arises when an employee is negligent while doing the job that he is employed to do. It does not arise when he is doing something outside the scope of his employer's instructions.

We therefore speak of an employer being vicariously liable for the negligence of his substitute, the employee.

(ii)   The justification for vicarious liability

There are two reasons which justify the concept of vicarious liability and both are designed to protect the position of the consumer. One concerns the question of insurance and the other concerns the fostering of a responsible attitude on the part of the employer.

First, let us consider insurance. Many an employee is not in a position to effect insurance which will cover his own negligence. If he is sued successfully, the plaintiff finds himself in a disadvantaged position as regards recovering any losses from an impecunious worker. Conversely, the employer is more likely to be able to arrange insurance to cover the work of his employees. The financial arrangements for the work will fall to the employer and it will be open to him to make an allowance in his firm's charges to cover the cost of the insurance premiums.

The other reason is concerned with the employer's attitude to his substitute's work, and ensuring that such matters as the provision of adequate facilities are not ignored. If an employer knows that he might be sued by the consumer if his employee is negligent he is likely to be particularly careful to ensure that his workers are well placed to complete the task efficiently and safely.

(iii) The difference between employees and independent contractors

The relationship between a negligent worker and his employer is of the utmost importance to a plaintiff who wishes to take advantage of the doctrine of vicarious liability to recover damages for the worker's negligence. We have to distinguish between two different relationships.

(a) Employer and employee

In this situation the employer controls, at least to a large extent, the work which is to be done by the employee, and the employer is responsible for the employee. The employer will thus be vicariously liable for his employee's negligence and will have to compensate a plaintiff who sues successfully.

(b) Independent contractor

This involves a different relationship. The person doing the work is responsible for his own efforts and he is not controlled directly by anyone else. No one is vicariously liable for him because he cannot truly be described as anyone's substitute. In this situation a plaintiff will be unable to take advantage of the vicarious concept and will only be able to sue the worker himself.

The difference between these two types of relationship is illustrated conveniently by comparing a chauffeur and a taxi driver. Both men perform a similar task: they both drive a car to transport a passenger from one place to another. On the one hand, however, the chauffeur is employed by his boss, is provided with the car and probably has a weekly timetable to keep to. On the other hand, the taxi driver owns his own vehicle, and decides how and when he will work. The only part played by the hirer of the taxi is to specify the destination and to pay the fare for the journey.

Suppose these two kinds of driver are negligent in the course of their work and are sued successfully by a plaintiff. In the case of the chauffeur, the employer will be vicariously liable as he has had a large degree of control over the driver's job. Conversely, if the taxi driver is negligent, he will be regarded as an independent contractor to be sued in his own right. The taxi driver's passenger, although he is paying for the journey, can sit back immune from the claim.

(iv) Vicarious liability in general practice

A patient who is dissatisfied with the treatment that she has received from her doctor in general practice will have no difficulty in identifying the potential defendant. It will be the practitioner who administers the treatment. She may, however, receive treatment from other health care personnel such as a nurse, a health visitor or even a doctor *in locum tenens*.

We can now consider the liability of the partners in the practice for the negligence of these other workers.

(a) The nurses

In most cases, the nurse is employed by the partners. She is appointed by them, paid by them and has her weekly timetable arranged by them. Furthermore, she treats their National Health and private patients. In other words, she is an employee in the fullest sense of the word. The partners will therefore be vicariously liable for the nurse's negligence. It is clearly in their interest to ensure that she is properly supplied with equipment and has received appropriate training. Money spent in attending to these matters is a form of insurance that tends to reduce the chances of a claim against her for which the partners will be vicariously liable.

In the years preceding the New Contract of April 1990, it was quite common for the Health Authority to supply a district nurse to a partnership for several sessions each week. She was both appointed and paid by the Health Authority although she treated the patients of the partnership. If she was negligent, the Health Authority would have been vicariously liable and the partners would escape liability.

(b) The health visitors and midwives

Unlike the practice nurse, health visitors and midwives are employed by the Health Authority and so it would be vicariously liable for any negligence by them. The partners in the practice will, again, be free from liability.

(c) The *locum tenens*

General practitioners often employ a *locum* to cover their duties in cases of sickness or holidays. The absent partner may well have appointed the *locum* and be paying him but the analogy with the employed nurse stops at this point. The nurse is working mainly at the direction of the doctor and she will be carrying out the treatment which he has directed. For example, she will administer an injection which he has prescribed or she will remove stitches which he has inserted. Conversely, the *locum* doctor has a much freer hand with regard to the manner in which he treats the patients. It is left to the *locum* to decide how extensive a history to take, how detailed an examination to carry out and what treatment, if any, to administer. This puts him in the position of being an independent contractor rather than an employee, and the appointing partner will therefore not be vicariously liable.

If the *locum* doctor is not insured, and is impecunious, the plaintiff may have difficulty in recovering her losses. There may, however, be an alternative route for the plaintiff to pursue. The *locum* may have been an employee of a commercial deputising service which is vicariously liable for the *locum*'s negligence. The plaintiff is more likely to be successful in suing an organisation, which probably carries insurance and has probably been in existence for some time. This is in contrast to the difficulty the plaintiff will face in pursuing a *locum* doctor of whom no trace might be found some years later.

The partner who appoints a *locum tenens* on a casual basis may, however, find that his Terms of Service make it difficult for him to deny vicarious liability. Paragraph 20 provides that:

> ... in relation to his obligations under these Terms of Service, a doctor is responsible for all acts and omissions of ... any person employed by, or acting on behalf of, him.

This means that the statutory regulations will override the employing partner's efforts to pass liability to the *locum tenens* whom he employed casually.

(d) The office staff

The vicarious liability of a general practitioner is not confined to the negligence of other health care personnel. It extends to all those people who are employed by him, regardless of their qualifications or their role in his organisation. It would, for instance, include office staff such as a practice manager, a secretary, a typist or a receptionist.

Let us take an example to show how a difficulty could arise in this respect. A young woman was taken ill in the early hours of a Saturday morning. The boyfriend with whom she shared a flat took her to his own doctor's surgery thinking, mistakenly, that she was registered at that practice. When the couple approached the receptionist who was on duty that Saturday morning she denied all knowledge of the girl's existence. The receptionist told her she was not registered there and she must see her own doctor. The boyfriend therefore took the patient home again and spent a fair amount of time telephoning various local practices in an effort to find the doctor who was responsible for her. Unfortunately, the girl's condition deteriorated in the meantime and, despite an emergency call for an ambulance, she died before help could be obtained.

The girl's parents launched proceedings on the basis that the receptionist had been negligent. They relied on the boyfriend's account of the exchange which had taken place at the desk when the couple were turned away. They claimed that the history given by the boyfriend, coupled with the manifestly ill appearance of their daughter, should have made any reasonable receptionist arrange for the doctor to see her there and then regardless of whether or not she was registered with that practice. From this point they argued that if the receptionist had acted properly the doctor would have examined their daughter, would have sent her to hospital and that her life would probably have been saved.

Suppose, for a moment, that the parents were to succeed in showing that the receptionist, with the basic training she should have been given by her employing general practitioners, had fallen short of the standard that anyone seeking assistance from a person in her position had a right to expect. This would have the effect that the partners would be vicariously liable for the negligence of one of their office staff. They would be faced with

114

meeting a damages payment on behalf of a patient who was not even registered with their practice.

(v)   Vicarious liability in hospital practice

We have seen how the existence of vicarious liability in general practice is governed by whether the member of staff delivering the treatment is an employee of the partnership, an employee of an outside agency, or an independent contractor. Those principles are not peculiar to general practice and they apply equally well to specialist practice in hospital.

Consultants are employed by the health authority to treat National Health patients in a hospital which is controlled by it. They are employees in the fullest sense, in contrast to their colleagues in general practice, who are independent contractors. This status of the latter group has been guarded vigorously by that branch of the profession ever since the National Health Service began in 1948.

However, if a consultant treats a private patient in a National Health hospital or in a hospital outside the National Health Service, the position is different. Private hospitals do not employ consultants. They neither appoint them nor pay them. They merely allow them to use their facilities in return for payment and the bill is usually sent to the patient. This makes the consultant an independent contractor.

It follows that if a National Health Service patient is treated negligently in a hospital she must sue the health authority, as it will be vicariously liable. Conversely, if the incident occurs in a private hospital she must pursue the consultant personally to recover damages.

XIII. *NOVUS ACTUS INTERVENIENS*

(i)   Introduction

Throughout this book we have seen examples of patients who have shown successfully that their doctors have fallen short of currently accepted standards, and that, sooner or later, some damage has followed which was caused by that shortcoming. This is usually a strong basis on which to start a successful action for negligence.

However, there is one method by which a defendant may be able to escape liability despite being faced with this proposition. It is by showing that some later and unforeseeable event also caused damage and that it was of a kind independent of the original type for which he was responsible. We talk of a 'new act' coming between the original negligent act and the ultimate damage. A *novus actus interveniens* is said to have broken the chain of causation. Put another way, the defendant is still liable in terms of the standard of care but from the plaintiff's point of view the other essential ingredient of a successful action, that of causation, is missing.

(ii)   *Novus actus* in criminal cases

The concept of *novus actus interveniens* is seized upon occasionally by a defendant in a criminal case when he is charged with wounding. The defendant will argue that it was reasonable for him to expect that his victim's injuries would be treated properly by a doctor. If it so happens that the injured person is treated negligently and endures a greater degree of suffering, the accused will assert that he cannot be held responsible for the whole of the damage. He will only admit responsibility for the damage that would have occurred if the injury had been properly treated. In other words, his case will be that the doctor's negligence was unforeseeable and that a *novus actus* eclipsed the harm that he had inflicted.

A simple example will suffice. Suppose an offender knifes his victim in the neck and inflicts a small puncture wound near the carotid artery. The victim then attends an accident and emergency department, where a doctor negligently diagnoses the wound as trivial and sends the patient home with no more than a sticking plaster over a small suture. On returning home, the patient bends down to pick up his child who clutches at the plaster and pulls at the suture. This results in a torrential haemorrhage from the carotid artery which had been weakened by the original injury and the patient bleeds to death. The result is that just hours after the original superficial wound was inflicted the victim is dead and the offender is facing a murder charge. The accused may insist that the A & E doctor's negligence was a *novus actus* which the accused could not have foreseen and which was ultimately responsible for the death.

(iii)   *Novus actus* in medical negligence

Novus actus interveniens is only rarely raised by a defendant in medical negligence and it has virtually never been accepted by a court as a valid argument when considered against the circumstances of the case. Nevertheless, it is worth considering because it is of relevance to a general practice case which reached trial in recent years.

In *Prendergast v Sam & Dee* (1989) a general practitioner intended to prescribe the antibiotic Amoxil for a chest infection. Unfortunately, the handwriting on the prescription was so indistinct that the pharmacist misread it and dispensed the hypoglycaemic agent Daonil instead. The patient duly took the tablets he had been given, but they lowered his blood sugar to a dangerous level and he suffered brain damage. Clearly, there were two people at fault in this case. The general practitioner had been at fault by writing illegibly, and the pharmacist had been at fault by not checking the illegible prescription with the doctor.

The patient sued both the pharmacist and the doctor. At first instance, the trial judge found that both had been negligent in their respective duties of care to the patient, and apportioned damages such that the doctor was liable for 25% and the pharmacist the remaining 75%.

The doctor appealed on the basis that there had been a *novus actus*. He contended that the pharmacist's failure to telephone him about the illegible handwriting had broken the chain of causation. The Court of Appeal held that the concept of *novus actus* was irrelevant in this case because it was foreseeable to the doctor that his bad handwriting could result in the pharmacist prescribing the wrong drug. The doctor's appeal was therefore dismissed.

(iv) The plaintiff's own *novus actus*

So far we have considered cases in which the *novus actus* was performed by someone who was another potential defendant and on to whom the original defendant will attempt to shift part or all of the blame for the damage. In the criminal example given above, the offender will try to escape part of his punishment by shifting the blame to the negligent accident and emergency doctor. In *Prendergast* the general practitioner attempted to reduce his contribution to the damages on the basis that the pharmacist was responsible for the *novus actus*.

However, a defendant will occasionally argue that the plaintiff himself has been responsible for the *novus actus*. In *Emeh v Kensington & Chelsea & Westminster HA* (1985), this very situation arose. A woman underwent a sterilisation operation but later became pregnant. Unfortunately, the child was born with congenital abnormalities and the woman sued the hospital that had been responsible for the original operation. The hospital asserted that the woman had a perfectly good opportunity of seeking a termination as soon as she knew she was pregnant and that this would have greatly reduced the damages payable. They argued that her failure to seek the termination was therefore a *novus actus* for which they could not be held responsible. At first instance they were successful with this argument but the decision was reversed by the Court of Appeal. It was held to be unreasonable to expect a woman to have a termination when she had undergone a sterilisation for the express purpose of never needing to have one done in the future.

(v) The difficulties of a doctor who asserts *novus actus*

We have seen how the Court of Appeal in *Prendergast* and in *Emeh* would not allow the defending doctors to take advantage of the doctrine of *novus actus*. There may well have been something of a policy argument here. Clearly, there is a duty on a doctor, be he general practitioner or gynaecologist, to offer a proper standard of care. It is inherent in the concept of negligence that any shortcoming in this standard will be followed by compensation from the defendant for any damage that results from it.

A point common to both of these decided cases is that the defendants were arguing that another person should have taken special steps to mitigate or prevent the damage that they themselves had caused by their negligence. The general practitioner in *Prendergast* was asserting that the pharmacist should have telephoned him with the aim of averting the damage which he had caused. Similarly, the gynaecologist in *Emeh* was expecting the patient to take what must have been a most unpalatable decision so that the negligent sterilisation resulted in a mere termination rather than the birth of a handicapped child.

XIV CRIMINAL NEGLIGENCE

(i) Introduction

Medical negligence, like negligence in any other sphere, is a matter of civil law. By this we mean that the dispute is between two parties. It is a matter between plaintiff and defendant, on more or less even terms. The rules are that the plaintiff bears the burden of proof. She has to show that the defendant's actions fell below the required standard of care and the defendant has to show that it is more than 50% likely that the negligence caused the alleged damage. The sanction imposed on the defendant is designed to achieve no more than compensation, and this is expressed in terms of money. Negligent damage to an item of property is compensated in terms of the cost of the repair. There is no moral consideration at all and the sanction is in no sense a punishment. The civil law is concerned merely with restoring the *status quo* between the two parties as far as is possible in the circumstances.

These remarks apply to negligence in any sphere and by any person or organisation. The rules are equally applicable to the much narrower area of medical negligence although, as many plaintiffs are only too painfully aware, the mere provision of money often falls a long way short of compensating for a disability resulting from a medical accident.

(ii)   Criminal law

Criminal law is a whole world apart from civil law. It is based on different concepts and applies different rules. It is administered in different courts and imposes different sanctions. Even the practitioners themselves rarely mix the two.

The defendant in a criminal case has, in a way, an easier task than his civil counterpart. His opponent is faced with proving the case 'beyond reasonable doubt' rather than 'on the balance of probabilities'. Put in arithmetical terms, the accused person is innocent unless the case against him is 99% certain rather than only 51% certain.

Conversely, a criminal defendant is not competing on even terms with his opponent. He is not facing an individual person as an aggrieved plaintiff but is defending himself against the full weight of the state and this is apparent from the style of the case name. When a case is cited – for instance, *R v Bateman* – it is only too clear that the Crown, in name Rex or Regina depending on the era, is prosecuting Bateman. This is a reflection of the fact that the nature of the incident in question, the crime, is such that the State should take an interest in it. Crimes such as rape and theft have moral implications and are committed intentionally. Indeed, intent is an essential ingredient of these crimes. On the other hand, torts such as negligence are not usually subject to moral considerations and, far from being intentional, they are the result of carelessness. The State is content to allow the parties to resolve the dispute between themselves and on even terms.

Negligence and crime have been regarded traditionally as different concepts. Part of the reason for the great divide is the state of mind of the defendant. As indicated earlier, no defendant in a criminal trial (other than in 'strict liability' offences) can be convicted unless the necessary intent has been proved. This is known technically as the *mens rea* which is Latin for 'the guilty mind'. Furthermore, it must coincide with the *actus reus*, 'the guilty act'. As an example, we can refer to the Theft Act 1968, which defines theft in terms that:

> A person is guilty of theft if he dishonestly appropriates property belonging to another with the intention of permanently depriving the other of it.

Clearly, intention is essential to the *mens rea* of theft. That the *actus reus* and the *mens rea* must coincide is illustrated by the person who borrows something today and decides to keep it tomorrow. That person is not guilty of theft.

The state of mind of a negligent defendant is a different matter altogether. Indeed, the incident in question may well have arisen for the very reason that the defendant's mind was not focused sufficiently on the plaintiff's well-being. A court will not concern itself with what a defendant was thinking at the time, as the only question to be addressed is whether the standard of care delivered fell short.

Theft and negligence also demonstrate conveniently the difference between the sanctions imposed by criminal and civil law. If a negligent motorist causes £50 worth of damage to another car the matter would be settled by payment of that amount in compensation. If the same person is then found guilty of shoplifting the same value of goods, he is likely to find himself facing a much more severe penalty. The concept of guilt, punishable by the state, is peculiar to criminal law.

(iii)   Gross negligence as a crime

The doctor's wrongful act in respect of his patient almost always comes under the heading of the tort of negligence.[21] It is possible, however, that he could be guilty of a crime if he raped or assaulted the patient. Nevertheless, there are very rare occasions when the concepts of negligence and crime can come together.

First, let us consider for a moment the general practitioner whose receptionist is making an effort to keep the office tidy. She files a cervical smear result which is reported as having shown malignant cells and fails to take steps to ensure that the patient is recalled. If the patient suffered damage as a result, she would have little difficulty in showing that the general practitioner was vicariously liable. An outside observer, however, might well have just a trace of sympathy for the defendant, as it is the sort of mistake that can happen in any office.

---

[21]   For a case in the Netherlands where a gynaecologist was found guilty of murder but received no punishment, see *BMJ* vol 310 (22 April 1995) pp 1028. His lawyer said that 'it was unjust to use doctors as law making guinea pigs'.

Secondly, let us move on to the general practitioner who is consulted by a woman with a breast abnormality and who carries out an examination which confirms a suspicious lump. He tells her that he will write a referral letter to a surgeon with a view to a biopsy. He is careless with the notes on his desk and forgets to attend to it. If this results in delayed treatment for the cancer the patient would again have little difficulty in pursuing a successful claim. Our outside observer would probably be less sympathetic to this doctor, on the basis that he was in some way more blameworthy. In other words, the doctor's attitude to his work could more easily be criticised than that of the general practitioner whose receptionist carelessly filed the smear report.

Thirdly, and lastly, let us consider the general practitioner who is called to a middle-aged man with severe chest pains and who is cold, grey and sweating. The doctor does not bother to examine the man, tells him it is probably 'flu and continues on his rounds. Some hours later the wife calls an ambulance and the patient is taken to hospital. He is found to be dead on arrival and a post-mortem shows that the cause of death is a coronary thrombosis. Our outside observer is likely to have even less sympathy with this doctor because he showed a callous disregard for his patient when he was in obvious distress. By using his basic medical skills he could easily have given his patient a better chance of surviving.

These three examples of the civil concept of negligence show that the defendant's state of mind, although it is irrelevant to the eventual damages award, does tend to carry some weight in an onlooker's assessment. If we can extrapolate the argument sufficiently our observer may think that the defendant's attitude to his patient has reached a point where it is so deplorable that it deserves a punishment in its own right. That would be over and above the compensation that the doctor should award to his patient. This state of affairs would lift the case out of the realms of civil law and it would become subject to the scrutiny of criminal law.

Criminal charges resulting from medical treatment have only been brought in the event of a patient's death, and this gives rise to a charge of manslaughter.

(iv) Evolution of the case law on criminal negligence

We have to go back to the 19th century to find the origin of the case law which concerns doctors who have been charged with the manslaughter of their patients. In each successive case, the court has had to decide how culpable the defendant's state of mind had to be to justify a criminal sanction. In *R v Doherty* (1887), the judge gave the jury an illustration in an attempt to show them how extreme the matter had to be to qualify as a crime. He put it like this:

> Supposing a man performed a surgical operation, whether from losing his head, or from forgetfulness, or from some other reason, omitted to do something he ought to have done, or did something he ought not to have done, in such a case there would be negligence. But if there was only the kind of forgetfulness which is common to everybody, or if there was a slight want of skill, any injury which resulted might furnish a ground for claiming civil damages, but it would be wrong to proceed against a man criminally in respect of such injury. But if a surgeon was engaged in attending a woman during her confinement, and went to the engagement drunk, and through his drunkenness neglected his duty, and the woman's life was in consequence sacrificed, there would be culpable negligence of a grave kind. It is not given to everyone to be a skillful surgeon, but it is given to every one to keep sober when such a duty has to be performed.

The distinction was next considered in *R v Bateman* (1925). A general practitioner undertook the care of a woman for delivery of her child at home. He had considerably difficulty with the procedure and the woman died several days later. A post-mortem showed that there was extensive damage to the anatomy of the pelvis and he was prosecuted for manslaughter. The judge explained to the jury that they must not give a guilty verdict unless they thought that the defendant's actions deserved a criminal sanction. He did so in terms that it depended on whether:

> ... the negligence of the accused went beyond a mere matter of compensation between subjects and showed such disregard

for the life and safety of others as to amount to a crime against the State and conduct deserving punishment.

Twelve years later, *Andrews v DPP* (1937) fell to be considered. A motorist was driving a van when he overtook a car by driving on the wrong side of the road and exceeding the speed limit. During the course of this manoeuvre, he hit a pedestrian who died and he failed to stop after the accident. He was charged with manslaughter and, again, the question arose of ensuring that the defendant's state of mind was sufficiently culpable to impose a criminal sanction. The judge recognised the test enunciated in *Bateman* and reiterated the difficulty in terms that:

> Simple lack of care such as will constitute civil liability is not enough: for the purposes of the criminal law there are degrees of negligence; and a very high degree of negligence is required to be proved before the felony is established.

He went on to select the word 'reckless' as most closely describing the required attitude and he distinguished this from 'mere inadvertence'. Although *Andrews* was not a medical negligence case the same principles have been applied when deciding exactly how culpable the defendant's state of mind has to be to justify bringing the case within the realms of the criminal law.

Forty years later, a similar question arose in *R v Stone and Dobinson* (1977). The defendants were an inadequate couple who undertook the care of the sister of one of them. They were so neglectful of their duty that they starved the woman to death. Again, the *Andrews* test was adopted when deciding whether the state of mind of the defendants was sufficiently deserving of censure to justify imposing a criminal sanction.

Throughout the 1980s there was further case law[22] (*R v Caldwell* (1982), *R v Lawrence* (1982) and *R v Seymour* (1983)) in

---

[22] For a detailed study of the case law on criminal negligence, and its implications for medical practice, see McCall Smith 'Criminal Negligence and the Incompetent Doctor', in *Medical Law Review*, 1, Autumn 1993, pp 336-349. See also 'Medical Manslaughter Redefined', in *Medical Law Monitor*, January 1994, pp 9-10.

which the judiciary strove to find a word or words that would cover all states of mind which called for a criminal sanction when the defendant had not taken sufficient care. Each case produced a definition which slightly extended or restricted the scope of its predecessor but they were, in essence, little different from the expressions used in *Bateman* and in *Andrews*.

(v) Recent medical cases

The latest case to the time of writing involving a medical accident which resulted in the death of a patient and which has been subjected to the scrutiny of the criminal law is *R v Prentice and Sullman* (1993).[23] This was a case in hospital rather than in general practice but it is worth considering because the principles are equally applicable to all branches of medicine.

A 16 year old boy was suffering from leukaemia and was on a cytotoxic regime which involved the intravenous injection of vincristine every month and the intrathecal injection of methrotexate every two months. On the occasion in question the boy was admitted to the ward and the task of administering the treatment was delegated to two junior doctors, Dr Prentice and Dr Sullman. Unfortunately, there was a misunderstanding over the correct procedure for administering the medication and both drugs were injected simultaneously into the spine. The patient died. At first instance both doctors were convicted of manslaughter. The two young doctors appealed and they pursued two avenues:

- that the wrong test had been used when deciding whether they had been sufficiently reckless over the injections to justify a criminal sanction; and

- that insufficient allowance had been made for excuses and mitigating circumstances.

---

[23] For a full report of the judgment, and a discussion of the implications of the case, see [1993] 4 *Med LR* pp 304-317.

In the Court of Appeal, Lord Taylor of Gosforth dealt with these two important points as follows, and held that:

(i) The correct approach when deciding whether or not the state of mind was such as to justify a criminal sanction was that expressed in *Andrews v DPP*. This had, it will be remembered, also been used in the *R v Stone and Dobinson*, 1977 and it appears to have had its root in *R v Bateman*, 1925. Thus, the slightly different tests which were used in *R v Cunningham* (1957) and in *R v Caldwell* (1982) were rejected. Seemingly in an attempt to avoid misuse of the word 'reckless' in the future, his Lordship suggested four categories of, as it were, attitude which would constitute the required state of mind to bring the case within the realms of the criminal law. They were:

(a) indifference to an obvious risk of injury to health;

(b) actual foresight of the risk coupled with the determination nevertheless to run it;

(c) an appreciation of the risk coupled with an intention to avoid it but also coupled with such a high degree of negligence in the attempted avoidance as the jury consider justifies conviction;

(d) inattention or failure to advert to a serious risk which goes beyond 'mere inadvertence' in respect of an obvious and important matter which the defendant's duty demanded he should address.

(ii) On behalf of the defendants it was contended that a number of excuses and mitigating circumstances were relevant. A variety of excuses was offered and they concerned such matters as the inexperience of the operator and a misunderstanding about exactly what the treatment involved. Lord Taylor held that the jury, when the case was tried at first instance, might well have not assessed the negligence as being of a sufficiently severe degree if the trial judge had directed them to take these additional matters into account.

Accordingly, the Court of Appeal quashed the convictions of the two young doctors such that their negligence did not make them guilty of manslaughter.[24]

While the Court of Appeal was dealing with the *R v Prentice and Sullman* it also considered *R v Adomako* (1993). This was a case against an anaesthetist who had been convicted of manslaughter after he was found to have left an anaesthetised patient unattended when part of the tubing became disconnected. Two professors of anaesthesia criticised the defendant's conduct by describing it as 'abysmal' and 'a gross dereliction of care' in allowing several minutes to elapse before he was aware that the disconnection had taken place. This resulted in the patient having a cardiac arrest before the disconnection was even noticed. An appeal was mounted on the basis that the jury when that case was tried at first instance had been wrongly directed. It was held that, although some criticisms in that area were justified in that some points were too complicated for the average layman to understand, 'they were entitled to conclude that his [the anaesthetist's] failure was more than mere inadvertence and constituted gross negligence of the degree necessary for manslaughter'. Thus, *Adomako* provided a convenient contrast to *Prentice and Sullman*. However, the defending anaesthetist then appealed to the House of Lords. Among other points, the House held that:

> The essence of the matter was whether, having regard to the risk of death involved, the conduct of the defendant was so bad in all the circumstances as to amount to a criminal act or omission.'[25]

---

24 For a case in which a doctor was recently found guilty of criminal negligence in America, see *BMJ*, vol 310:760 (25 March 1995). The defendant, a New York internist, was convicted in 1993 of 'reckless endangerment' that resulted in the death of a 78 year old lady in a nursing home. There had been a misunderstanding over the parenteral feeding arrangements for her and this was followed by a delay in hospital admission. The prosecutor described part of the mismanaged treatment as a 'wilful failure' and the doctor was punished by being told to spend 52 weekends at Riker Island prison. The case is said to have 'outraged' the American Medical Association.

25 For a helpful commentary on the House of Lords decision in *Adomako*, see *Med L Rev* [1994] 362-63.

In so doing, the House of Lords approved Lord Taylor's four categories to which reference now has to be made when deciding if a particular state of mind makes the negligence qualify for a criminal sanction.

The distinction that the Court of Appeal drew between these two cases not unnaturally prompted Dr Adomako to appeal yet again. His case came to be considered by the House of Lords and the question was once more faced of whether the jury that had convicted him of manslaughter had been wrongly directed. He based his case on the need to be found guilty of recklessness, rather than gross negligence, before he could be convicted. He argued that this would bring his case in to line with the test used in motoring offences that had resulted in death. The House of Lords rejected his appeal and held that the jury at the trial had been told to use the correct test and it therefore upheld his conviction.

It is interesting that the House of Lords seems to have been as anxious as the Court of Appeal to avoid the use of the adjective 'reckless'. We can only speculate that they may have thought that a single word was at risk of being interpreted in slightly different ways in future cases and that they feared this would introduce an element of uncertainty. Their Lordships may well have thought that it was safer to adopt Lord Taylor's four categories and in *Adomako*'s case they presumably relied on the fourth one (see page 128). It is likely that they had the increasing sophistication of modern medical technology in mind, and that other difficult cases might follow. It will then be open to them to extend Lord Taylor's categories to five or more rather than struggling to tighten the definition of the word 'recklessness' in a way that would lend itself to consistent decisions by juries.

(vi) The current state of the law on criminal negligence

We saw at the beginning of this chapter how a defendant's state of mind is of the utmost importance when deciding if he should be subject to a criminal sanction. We have also seen how 'ordinary' medical negligence cases can involve a variety of attitudes of mind, some of which are more culpable than others. It is apparent that only the most extreme variety of culpable attitude will qualify as a criminal matter rather than a civil matter. In a century and more of case law, the courts have tried to find a word or expression to describe the required state of mind. In pre-war years, *Andrews v DPP* produced a test which has survived many post-war cases and has been accepted in the latest case of *R v Prentice and Sullman*. However, in this last case the Court of Appeal recognised the unusual difficulties that can be posed in cases of medical negligence, especially when these are compounded by circumstantial matters such as inexperience and lack of resources. In an effort to provide all-embracing criteria, Lord Taylor of Gosforth suggested four categories (which have been listed above – see page 128) and which were approved by the House of Lords in *Adomako*, but he did add that he was not 'purporting to give an exhaustive definition'. He was presumably allowing for yet more difficulties which may arise with the continuing expansion of medical technology and patients' expectations.

PART B

THE CONDUCT OF THE LITIGATION

XV INTRODUCTION

(i)   What is medical negligence?

'First, do no harm' was Hippocrates' advice to the medical profession 2,500 years ago. Ever since then doctors have been striving to improve the outcome of their patients' illnesses. Until recently it would never have occurred to the lay public that a visit to a professional person could result in an outcome that was worse than the original illness. It was therefore assumed that any harm which followed the visit was a result of the disease rather than of the treatment.

Hippocrates' treatments were doubtless very limited, and the harm that he risked inflicting was correspondingly small. By contrast, however, the benefits now available to mankind from modern medical technology seem to be almost without limit. Inevitably, this has been accompanied by a considerable increase in the possibilities for harm.

Patients expect certain standards from their doctors. Furthermore, they expect their position to be improved or, if the illness is untreatable, to be left in a position no worse than that allotted to them by nature.

The study of medical negligence involves initially a consideration of whether the patient was provided with a proper standard of care. Secondly, it involves the question of whether any shortcoming in that care was responsible for the harm of which the patient complains.

The conduct of any litigation in which medical negligence is alleged, whether for plaintiff or defendant, needs combined skills. It needs the skills of the doctor to assess the standard of care that has been provided and the outcome of the treatment. It also needs the skills of the lawyer to convert this material into a form which will produce a damages award for the patient or, alternatively, protect the doctor's defence organisation from having to pay that compensation.

(ii) The difference between personal injury and medical negligence

The expression 'personal injury' is normally used to refer to cases in which a person has been injured outside the realms of medical practice. Accidents on the roads and at work are common examples. Medical negligence, in a sense, also involves personal injury because the patient (or plaintiff in legal terms) has suffered an injury that he attributes to an accident during the course of his treatment, and he or his dependants seek to blame the doctor for the damage.

However, there are at least three very important aspects of medical negligence litigation which set it apart from other personal injury work. They make the advancement of a case more difficult and, in this author's view at least, much more interesting. It is as well to recognise the differences before we proceed any further.

In a 'running down' case, the question of whether the plaintiff can succeed in a negligence action concerns the standard of care that was provided at the time of the accident. Once negligence has been proved it is usually a matter of little more than quantifying the damage. Conversely, in a medical negligence case, the past history of the patient may be extremely relevant to a later criticism of the doctor. In one case, a woman developed what was thought by the doctor to be an insect bite on her arm. He treated it as such, but the lesion was reluctant to clear up and later began to fester. Taken at face value it would have been difficult to criticise the doctor for failure to refer his patient to a specialist. However, the knowledge that she had been under hospital care for a malignant condition some years previously, and had lapsed from follow-up, made it easier to criticise him for failure to realise that she was suffering from a secondary deposit in the skin.

The second point that sets medical negligence apart from personal injury is the variable standard of care for which allowance has to be made when assessing liability. In 'running down' cases, there will be little room for manoeuvre as regards the standard of driving to be expected of different defendants. Similarly, in factory accidents, the statutory duties that have been imposed on the employer will make his liability fairly easy to define clearly. With doctors, however, the standard has to be judged according to the class of practitioner involved in the case. By this we mean that a general practitioner must be compared with his colleagues, and a hospital specialist must be compared with colleagues who work in the same branch of medicine or surgery. An appreciation of this point involves a study of the test in *Bolam v Friern Hospital Management Committee* (1957) and this is explained in detail in Chapter III.

A third difficulty with medical negligence cases is that of causation. We are here concerned with the question of whether or not it was the negligence itself which caused the patient's injury. In personal injury work this is usually straightforward. If the accident had not occurred the plaintiff would not have been injured. The patient, on the other hand, is ill before he sees the doctor. Some illnesses are so resistant to treatment that the patient will die even if he is attended by the most skilled and careful doctor. On the other hand, there are many conditions that are self-limiting and the patient will recover even with the worst possible treatment. This makes it difficult to assess causation properly. The plaintiff can only claim for the damage which resulted from the doctor's negligence. At the very least the patient must show that the negligence made a material contribution to the damage (Chapter VII). When we add the complexities of unrelated factors (Chapter VI) and the concept of 'lost opportunities' (Chapter V) it will be appreciated that causation can sometimes present insurmountable difficulties for plaintiffs in this type of case.

(iii) Dual legal relationships

Medical litigation is primarily concerned with tortious liability but the proceedings often extend into the sphere of contractual liability.

As we saw in Chapter I, tortious liability arises where the triad of duty, breach and causation between doctor and patient can be established. Contractual liability will arise when another triad can be established, that of offer, acceptance and consideration. This can occur between a doctor and his private patient. It can also occur between a hospital doctor and his employing health authority. The so-called contract between the general practitioner and his Family Health Services Authority has been the subject of judicial comment in *Roy v Kensington and Chelsea FPC* (1992) where one member of the House of Lords was '... content to assume that there is no contract'.

This was a case involving a dispute between a general practitioner and his Family Health Services Authority. The latter had withheld 20% of the doctor's renumeration on the basis that he was not devoting '... a substantial amount of time' to his National Health Service practice.

The legal relationship between any doctor and his private patient is dual such that contract and tort co-exist. However, the general practitioner is in rather a different position when it comes to a dispute with his National Health Service patient. He may find himself defending an action on two fronts. The patient will be suing the general practitioner in tort, and the Family Health Services Authority will be pursuing him for breach of the relevant statutory regulations. The part of the regulations that deals with the standard of care to be provided to a patient appears in paragraph 12 of The National Health Service (General Medical Services) Regulations 1992. That paragraph defines the duty as being to provide '... all necessary and appropriate personal medical services of the type usually provided by general medical practitioners'.

This is regarded generally as equating very closely with the *Bolam* principle which was discussed in detail in Chapter III. Essentially, it concerns the point that a doctor is unlikely to be held negligent if he has acted in accordance with a responsible body of medical opinion. In other words, the services are of the kind that would be given by a responsible body of medical opinion.

XVI   THE RISING TIDE OF LITIGATION

(i)   Historical aspects

In terms of civil litigation, medical negligence actions have been very much the exception until recently. This goes some way towards explaining why doctors' annual defence society subscriptions remained so low for so long.

There are several reasons why this state of affairs continued undisturbed until recent times. However, changes in these points have made their various contributions to the current surge which, for want of greater accuracy, can be said to have started at the beginning of the 1980s. The layman's traditional view of a doctor was, without question, that of a professional person of the utmost integrity and skill. It was inconceivable that he could fail to achieve the best possible outcome for his patient. It therefore followed that any adverse result that happened to materialise was caused by factors that were outside the doctor's control. Accordingly, any action against him was bound to fail.

If a patient really was convinced that his doctor had been negligent, he is immediately faced the difficulty of finding a medical expert who would say so in court. There was a strong feeling among doctors that they must hold together and avoid speculative criticism of a colleague when it was impossible to be certain of the facts of the case. For some reason, the converse did not apply. The defence societies had no difficulty in finding an expert who would justify the course of action that their member had followed. However, it has now become as respectable, at least in some people's view, for experts to report on behalf of plaintiffs as well as on behalf of defendants. Plaintiffs' solicitors now find it much easier to identify and contact a suitable expert. Organisations such as Action for Victims of Medical Accidents (AVMA),[26] formed in 1982, have been instrumental in ensuring that a plaintiff can find an expert who comes from the right speciality and is sympathetic.

Before the advent of legal aid anyone contemplating litigation had, of necessity, to be able to afford it. Medical negligence actions tend to be considerably more expensive than other types of personal injury case and so it meant that only the richest sector of the community could afford to become involved. Legal aid had the effect that the poorer members of society could join their ranks but the rules of eligibility restricted their numbers to some extent. For this reason it was the middle income group who were most at risk of unbearable expense. It might have been expected that this purely financial reason for the rising tide of litigation would have receded a little in view of contraction in legal aid availability which came into force in 1993, but there still appears to be no slackening in the pace.

The pattern of consulting also had its influence on trends in litigation. Patients are now ready to consult their doctors about a wider range of matters. The concept of illness has been widened from the traditional areas such as a broken leg or pneumonia to include more peripheral matters such as stress at work or cosmetic defects. This broadening of the areas of consultation has increased the possibilities for negligence. Furthermore, it is more difficult for the doctor to justify taking a risk with treatment when the perceived illness is not life-threatening and makes little contribution to the patient's physical distress.

---

[26] For a discussion of the assistance that AVMA can give to a patient, see pp 169-72.

(ii)   The patient's increasing expectations

In the past, patients expected very little from their doctors as a matter of right. Any benefit that accrued from the treatment regime was almost regarded as a bonus in that it was better than having to allow nature to take its course.

In recent years, however, patients have become better informed about medical matters. The media have played a large part in this. Some newspapers, such as *The Times*, carry regular articles on health, which not only serve to generate interest among the readership but also supply a good deal of factual information. An explanation of an illness is provided in layman's terms and is coupled with an outline of the various treatment options. This means that when an individual visits a doctor for a related complaint he has a fair idea of what to expect. When those expectations are not fulfilled, there is a serious risk that the patient will be dissatisfied and will sue. A women's weekly magazine recently appeared with a free booklet called *Family Health* attached to it. Details were listed of the symptoms to be found in various conditions that cause chest pain and how the distinction should be made between 'angina', 'heart attack' and 'indigestion'. All manner of other complaints were also described, together with their probable causes.

Topical issues particularly lend themselves to television coverage. In one case the death from meningitis of a young girl just before Christmas Day was reported in *The Times* and this was followed by details of the death of her schoolfriend who had caught the disease and succumbed just after Boxing Day. Very shortly after New Year there was a government announcement on a breakfast television programme that 1,500 people contract bacterial meningitis every year and that it can be fatal within hours. It even provided a photograph of the typical rash. Media health coverage of this kind is bound to enhance patients' expectations because it focuses their minds on the opportunities for cure if a doctor acts quickly. They probably also feel that with this information available so readily, the doctor should be able to prevent an adverse outcome of that particular illness.

Not all media material is designed to be instructive or educational, however. Some of it can be regarded more as a rather serious form of entertainment. For instance, a television series

143

about cases being treated at a leading teaching hospital in England made viewers well aware of the excellent results that could be achieved by specialist treatment.

Many a general practitioner, especially in middle-class areas, has been embarrassed to find that his patient seems to know more about the illness and its treatment than he does. The doctor may find it difficult to answer all her questions and the patient is then less likely to feel that she has had satisfaction. She may feel that the doctor's ignorance was good reason for specialist referral. When the general practitioner does not accede to the request and an unfavourable outcome follows the patient may be inclined to sue. The recent surge in litigation in Australia is considered in *The first thing we do, let's kill all the lawyers* in *BMJ*: 310 page 1090 (29 April 1995). The medical profession's reaction to the judgment in the case was described as 'uniformly scathing' and was seen as at least part of the explanation for the 'dwindling numbers of doctors in Australia's vast rural areas'.

Consumerism is a feature of post-war society dating from about the 1950s. In those days, well before the recent surge in medical negligence litigation, the masses found that cars, televisions and washing machines had become affordable. Harold Macmillan's famous dictum 'most of our people have never had it so good' in 1957 epitomised the mood of the country at the time. With increasing ownership of material goods which required a certain level of expertise for their manufacture and maintenance, the public became more confident about approaching a firm or an organisation to make a complaint. It was then but a short step from complaining about the hairdresser to complaining about the general practitioner or the neurosurgeon.

Information is now available to patients at even the most basic level. The old style chemist's bottle labelled with nothing more revealing than 'The Mixture' was superseded two or three decades ago by a label specifying the name of the drug, and is now accompanied by a leaflet telling the patient about its indications, contra-indications and side effects. This puts the patient in a much stronger position to question the doctor if he is disappointed in some way about the treatment.

(iii)   The influence of the media

Litigation has on occasion been prompted by the media. The benzodiazepine group action provides us with an example here. Several patients had been treated negligently with the drugs in earlier years but only consulted solicitors after seeing a television programme about the matter. In another case, a woman alleged negligence in relation to course of steroids which had been prescribed for an inflammatory muscle disorder, and freely admitted that it was a radio programme on the subject that prompted her to seek legal advice.

(iv)   Advances in technology

We have seen how media information about technological development has increased patients' expectations about the outcomes of treatment. Those advances are perceived as giving the doctor more opportunity to produce a benefit. However, the more opportunities a doctor has to do good for his patient, the more chance he has of being negligent. The use of steroids in general practice provides a convenient example of the sorts of danger that can arise. There can be no doubt that many asthmatic patients have derived enormous benefit from treatment with steroids. Indeed, many of these patients owe their lives to these particular drugs. However, it is well recognised that steroids can cause side effects and have the potential for causing a patient a great deal of harm. In one case, a patient suffered from very severe asthma which had been resistant to all the usual treatments such as broncho-dilator drugs. The general practitioner therefore prescribed steroids and shortly after this the patient developed diabetes. She sought to blame her doctor for causing diabetes by his negligent prescription of steroids. Fortunately for the doctor in this case he was quite easily able to show that far from complaining about being prescribed the drugs, she owed her life to them. If her case had occurred in earlier years before such drugs were available she would probably have died as a result of the asthma.

The example just given provides an illustration of how modern drugs can be a 'two-edged sword'. However, let us for a moment consider hospital practice; and the field of plastic surgery provides a useful example. Recent advances in microsurgery have made vascular reconstruction a reality on a scale that would have been unthinkable in the mid-1980s. The elderly man with gangrene of his foot or the young farm worker whose hand has been caught in a threshing machine are no longer doomed to amputation automatically. Restoration of the blood supply to the appropriate part of the limb has, in some cases, become a distinct possibility. But any adverse result from this type of treatment opens the surgeon to allegations of negligence on two fronts. On the one hand, if the surgeon decides to amputate he may be questioned as to why no attempt was made to save the limb. On the other hand, if the surgeon does opt for vascular reconstruction and something goes wrong with the minute technicalities of the procedure, he may be asked whether his technique was adequate.

Negligence actions prompted by advances in technology may well become more common as the available improvements are not matched by increased National Health Service funding. Medical technology is, after all, an expensive business. Liver transplant surgery will serve to illustrate the point here. A young boy with a congenital disorder that caused liver failure was advised that a transplant was his only hope. There was just one hospital in London at which the operation could be carried out, but the Minister of Health closed it, as part of a cost-cutting exercise, just before the boy needed the treatment. His father sought judicial review of the Health Secretary's decision on closure. This involved such matters as whether the correct consultative procedures had been followed. There was no question here of a doctor being negligent, but it is easy to see how litigation can become more common if government expenditure fails to match the scientific advances that have been achieved by the medical profession.

(v)   Defensive medicine

Good medical practice dictates that in any particular case a proper history is taken, a proper examination is carried out and proper tests are ordered. Interpretations of the word 'proper' depend on the individual circumstances of the case and would be governed by the *Bolam* principle (see Chapter III). For example, if a patient complains of symptoms of a cold with a tickly cough, and examination of the chest showed it to be clear, the doctor can hardly be criticised for failing to investigate the matter in more detail. Conversely, if the patient gives a history of coughing up blood and losing weight and yet that examination is still clear, it will be relatively easy to criticise the doctor for not ordering a chest X-ray. This is because the symptoms are strongly suggestive of lung cancer.

Many patients' actions against their doctors have been founded on the failure to order a certain investigation, on the basis that it caused the delay in the diagnosis which, in turn, caused the treatment to be less effective. This has led some doctors to practice what has been termed 'defensive medicine' in an effort to protect themselves from litigation. The practice has been most commonly carried out in the realm of laboratory and X-ray investigation, but it could apply equally well to history-taking or examination. The former would involve asking unnecessary questions and the latter would involve examining irrelevant parts of the body. It could even apply to treatment where, for example, an antibiotic is given in a case of obvious viral infection for fear that the diagnosis is bacterial and that the patient will sue if the condition fails to clear up quickly. A cynic might suggest that an additional motive for practising defensive medicine is that it takes less time and effort to tick the laboratory request form than it does to phrase additional questions or explain to the patient what examination is to be carried out. Conversely, these courses of action add nothing to National Health Service expenditure, whereas the additional tests and X-rays certainly do.

Defensive medicine can be defined as the ordering of a test where the dominant purpose is to protect the doctor from litigation rather than to put the patient to an advantage from improved diagnosis.

The difficulty in deciding where one purpose ends and the other begins in any particular case is that opinions may well vary about what tests are clinically indicated. Put another way, there may well be two perfectly responsible bodies of medical opinion, on the *Bolam* principle, about whether it was reasonable to omit the test. The body which thought the omission would have been reasonable may be inclined to hold that the ordering of it was defensive.

Quite apart from negligence, defensive medicine has important implications for causation. All tests involve some degree of risk. At one end of the scale, the general practitioner's venepuncture carries a risk of haematoma formation, and at the other end of the scale the cardiologist's cardiac catheterisation carries the possible risk of a stroke from an embolus. The risk of the harm has to be balanced against the benefit from the result. Provided that the risk was justified, the doctor will be in a strong position to defend himself if it materialises. However, if a test or treatment was not clinically justified, in other words was being done for defensive purposes, the patient would be in a strong position to recover for the damage that was incurred. For example, suppose a female patient with a brief history of abdominal pain and vomiting was seen by a surgeon, and suppose that competent history-taking and examination would have resulted in a diagnosis of a gastric upset to be treated by medication. The surgeon is fearful of being sued, operates for appendicitis and finds the appendix to be normal. In this case, the patient would assert justifiably that this defensive operation had been causative of a scar. She then would extend this in an attempt to recover damages for the time that he had lost from work, the increased chance of intestinal obstruction from adhesions at some later date and even for reduced fertility.

The recent development of defensive medicine in general practice was investigated by Summerton.[27] He found that the commonest defensive practices were increased diagnostic testing, increased referrals, increased follow-up, and more detailed patient explanations and note-taking. He identified some of these factors as 'positive' in that they were beneficial. The others were regarded as 'negative' and were seen as 'a symptom of the fundamental problems inherent within the present judicial and quasi judicial regulatory systems'.

If we adhere to the definition of defensive medicine given earlier in this section we shall have to exclude Summerton's positive factors because these were acknowledged as representing an improvement on previous practice. This removes them from the category of activities in which the principal purpose is to protect the doctor.

When we discussed consent in vasectomy (see page 67-68), in terms of disclosure of the failure rate, we saw how *Thake v*

---

27   *BMJ* 1995; 310 pp 27-29.

Maurice (1986) was followed by an increased tendency for surgeons to give a warning to their prospective patients about possible failure. The recognition of Summerton's positive factors in defensive medicine can be regarded as perhaps the only other favourable development in medical practice that has been prompted by the threat of litigation. Alternatively we could regard the effect of *Thake* as being just another example of a positive factor.

We can conclude this discussion about defensive medicine by saying that, at best, it is a waste of time and money. At worst it increases the patient's chance of physical harm and it increases the doctor's chance of being sued.

XVII THE MOTIVES FOR LITIGATION

(i) Introduction

In the previous chapter we saw that there are many factors implicated in the rising tide of medical negligence litigation, although it is impossible to assess the precise contribution of each of these. We have also seen how a patient is more likely to sue if she has been brought up in a consumer society, is better informed about medical matters, is eligible for legal aid, and can find a lawyer with appropriate skills.

In this chapter we are concerned with the driving forces behind individual cases.[28] Clearly, a negligence action can only provide one reward, that of common law damages which are designed to provide financial compensation for the harm. This contrasts with equitable remedies that are available in other areas of law, such as recission or specific performance in contract law.

---

28 For research into the motives for litigation, see Vincent *et al* in *The Lancet* vol 343 (25 June 1994) pp 1609-13.

It is generally acknowledged that money can never truly compensate for the amputation of a hand or the loss of the sight of an eye, let alone the loss of a life. This perceived failure of compensation may go some way to explaining why there are other motives for medical negligence actions. They do not amount to a remedy prescribed by law but they certainly exert a very strong influence on the mind of the litigant.

(ii)　The doctor's manner

It has long been recognised that the doctor's manner and his attitude to the patient at the time of the complaint can have a far-reaching affect on how vigorously the matter is pursued. The defence societies themselves would be among the first to point out that sympathetic handling of an aggrieved patient, together with helpful explanations of what has happened, can go a long way towards defusing the situation. However, it should be realised that the doctor's manner can have considerable influence at any stage. It can exert its effect, for better or for worse, long before there is any question of a wrong diagnosis or a complaint. The important point here is that the doctor who gives his patient the impression that she is not the centre of his attention throughout the treatment is inviting trouble.

This is well illustrated by a case in which a young child with recurrent abdominal pains was visited several times at home by the general practitioner over the course of a week. It so happened that the doctor was a cricket enthusiast and that a Test Match was in progress at the time. A television set was in the child's bedroom and the sound was turned off at each doctor's visit, but this did not stop the screen from catching his eye during the course of the abdominal examinations. He made several remarks about the progress of the score for each side and who was next in turn to bat. When the girl was admitted to hospital by the duty doctor with a perforated appendix at the end of the week, her parents were left with the distinct impression that the visiting doctor was more interested in the Test Match than he was in his patient's well-being.

Fortunately for the doctor, he had good notes of detailed examination findings with which to defend himself, and the plaintiff's expert found it impossible to make an effective criticism of the clinical assessment at any of the visits. Nonetheless, it was only too obvious from the parents' version of events that they considered his examinations to have been unduly cursory and that this was the driving force behind their complaints.

In *Fellows v Thomas* (1994), the litigation was at least partly prompted by the way the patient's wife felt that she had been treated by a general practitioner. When the case came to trial, counsel for the defence asked her if she had thought of suing at the time of, or soon after, the hospital admission at which her husband was eventually diagnosed as having suffered from a subarachnoid haemorrhage. She answered that she had indeed considered it but felt unable to do so because, being a nurse herself, she was well aware of the anxiety that this could cause to another health care professional. It was only when the doctor made some apparently flippant remark at a later date that she decided that she would sue after all.

In a survey by *Pulse*[29] of the 'characteristics considered most likely to lead to a complaint' it was found that rudeness was identified as a likely cause by 66% of general practitioners. Other causes which family doctors felt might be implicated were burn-out (51%), inexperience (27%) and poor clinical knowledge (26%).

(iii)   The plaintiff's personal objective

There is, of course, only one award which can be provided by the common law and that is a monetary payment, termed damages. As we have seen in other parts of this book, it is strictly related to the loss that has been suffered as a result of the negligence.

In many cases, the litigation is advanced despite the prospect of the ultimate damages award being relatively small. In passing, we can observe that this is only likely to happen in a legally-aided case, because a privately-funded plaintiff has to take a more realistic view of the financial risk to which he is exposing himself.

---

[29]   *Pulse*, 17 July 1993.

However, there can be all sorts of reasons why cases are pressed forward vigorously for what seems like an unduly small award. There is one case which serves to illustrate this point very well. A man had died shortly after alleged negligence by a general practitioner and over the course of a couple of years much work was done on the case by the widow's advisers. At the end of the conference with counsel, at which it was emphasised that any damages payment would be quite small, the lady was asked by the barrister if there was anything more she would like him to achieve. She said to the him, 'Yes, there is one thing which I would like more than anything else in the world and that is to receive a written apology from the doctor who attended my husband in his final illness.'

This case was typical of so many in which sympathetic handling at the time of the original illness, coupled perhaps with open communication immediately after the adverse result, would go a long way towards preventing the litigation from ever starting.

(iv)   The quest for an explanation

Another commonly quoted objective is the desire to find an explanation of what went wrong. When there has been an adverse result of treatment, doctors are often suspected of being less than completely open and honest with their explanations.[30] This tends to generate suspicion in the patient, who needs an explanation to help him come to terms with his disability. The doctor and the patient may find their relative positions polarised such that any information is treated automatically with suspicion. The patient then feels that he must turn to another professional person, the lawyer, whom he can trust to act in his best interest. The patient hopes to find the truth through the discovery procedure and sees the threat of civil proceedings as his only option.

(v)   The desire to prevent negligence in the future

One very common reason given for advancing a case is to prevent the alleged negligence from happening again to somebody else.

---

[30]   For a discussion about the advantages of providing an explanation at an early stage, see Ritchie *et al* in *BMJ* vol 310 (8 April 1995) pp 888-89.

This is a laudable attitude, but a cynic would find it hard to believe that the parents of a brain-damaged child are more concerned about other people's healthy children than they are about their own child. However, it is certainly possible that such a course of action would have the desired result, because an internal hospital inquiry might be prompted by the threat of litigation and this might prevent a similar accident occurring.

(vi)   The plaintiff's reaction to threats and rebuffs

In the field of general dental practice, litigation can be prompted by the threat of debt collection by the practitioner. A bill may remain unpaid for some time because, although the dentist was unaware of anything unusual in the case, the patient was dissatisfied with the treatment. When the patient is later faced with the threat of civil proceedings to recover the debt, he may respond by counter-claiming for breach of contract as well as suing in negligence in relation to the treatment. Dentists have found to their cost that the pursuit of a small debt can occasionally result in having to defend a very large claim in negligence.[31]

Just as the threat of debt collection by dentists can result in litigation for negligence, so can the rebuff of a well-intentioned patient by a hospital administrator. In one case, a young lady was seen by an orthopaedic surgeon for a minor operation on the great toe of one foot. She was duly admitted to hospital but unfortunately the consultant's registrar operated on the wrong foot. When the girl got home and visited the surgery, the general practitioner was very concerned about the error and contacted the consultant who saw the patient very promptly, offered profuse apologies and said he would do a second operation personally at the patient's convenience. The patient had settled down by this stage and was keen to remain under the specialist's care. When she approached the hospital a few days later to arrange an

---

31   For a fuller discussion of the necessity for dentists to take particular care when pressing for payment by patients, see *J Med Def Union* 1994, no 2, pp 38-39.

admission date she met with a rebuff. No further treatment could be considered, she was told, when there was the question of a complaint and litigation might ensue. This action by the hospital authorities prompted the patient to see her solicitor to institute proceedings for negligence.

(vii) The influence of guilt

There are also other, less honourable, motives for litigation against doctors when there has been an adverse outcome of the treatment. The patient or his dependant may bear a grudge against the practitioner, and guilt can motivate a claim as well. Any general practitioner who provides regular attendance at a registered nursing home will be familiar with the situation in which family members hardly ever visit an elderly relative until she is dying. One visit from them during a terminal illness is then followed, after the funeral, by the letter before action. The theory here is that the family are trying to assuage their guilt by blaming the doctor. In one particular case a man was admitted to hospital after a short illness and died a fortnight later. This was a great shock to his wife, who alleged negligence in that she had not been told about the serious nature of her husband's condition. She paid very few visits to the hospital during the fortnight, but she claimed she would have gone much more often if she had been told the reality of the situation. After her husband's death she felt guilty for not spending more time with him in his last illness, and it was probably this sense of guilt that prompted her to sue.

In another case, guilt arose from the way in which a father treated his daughter following the doctor's advice. A small girl was seen by the doctor several times over a period of some weeks with behavioural difficulties and various other symptoms. Despite a detailed examination the practitioner could find no sign of organic disease and recommended the parents to be more strict with the child. When she child was later found to have developed a cerebral tumour which was thought to have been the cause of the symptoms the parents were very angry with the doctor for, as they saw it, making them be unkind to their young daughter.

Again, this sense of guilt prompted legal proceedings for allegedly negligent mis-diagnosis.

Another case which may have been motivated by guilt concerned a young boy with appendicitis. At the first visit by the doctor the physical signs were virtually non-existent, a gastric upset was diagnosed and the parents were reassured strongly. However, the patient's condition deteriorated gradually over the next four days, but the father delayed calling again until the end of that time, although he had been under some pressure from his wife to do so. At the doctor's second visit immediate hospital admission was arranged and the child was found to have a perforated appendix. The father sued the general practitioner. In the event, he had no case in negligence, but it was apparent to his advisers throughout the case that he felt guilty for not having yielded to his wife's pleading to ask the doctor to return earlier. The damages figure would have been quite small, but it was the father's sense of guilt which motivated the claim.

(viii) The effect of legal aid

When a case is at or near trial, the motivation to pursue it can be influenced profoundly by whether the plaintiff is funded privately or legally aided. In the former case, a reasonable offer from a defendant is more likely to be accepted. This kind of litigant is unlikely to want to risk the whole offer and be faced with paying the costs of both sides if her case proceeds and she loses. Conversely, a legally-aided plaintiff will be more inclined to take the risk for the satisfaction of winning. If the plaintiff loses her case it costs her nothing because the Legal Aid Board will have funded her costs and the defendant will be faced with paying his own costs as it is not possible to recover them from the Legal Aid Board. If an aided plaintiff wins, she will gain the damages award and will merely have a deduction for the statutory charge (see page 174) imposed by the Legal Aid Board. Thus, an aided person takes no risk in pressing her case home with the chance of winning.

(ix) The will to sue

There can be no doubt that plaintiff medical negligence litigation is not for the faint-hearted. The road is long, hard and likely to be littered with obstacles. Additionally, the privately-funded client must be prepared to incur very substantial costs over which he has little control. We have seen elsewhere in this chapter how there is far more than mere common law damages, that is financial compensation, to fuel the machinery. The other motives all, in one way or another, relate to the state of mind of the plaintiff. That state of mind is likely to be extreme; indeed, it will have to be to provide the motivation to keep the case moving forward over a period of what may be quite some years. We can conveniently refer to this state of mind as 'the will to sue'. In some cases, this burns so strongly that no amount of discouraging advice from the advisers for that side will dampen it. Put another way, it is blind to reason.

One case illustrated this difficulty very well. A middle-aged woman had a much older husband with a history of high blood pressure and who suffered a severe stroke while in bed with her one night. He was admitted to a geriatric unit by his general practitioner the next day, but he then suffered several more strokes, which were soon followed by a chest infection. Within a fortnight he was dead. There was no post-mortem, but the death certificate recorded 'broncho-pneumonia due to cerebrovascular accident due to hypertension'. The widow was distraught, to say the least. She sued the family doctor and the consultant in charge of the geriatric unit as well as the nursing staff. Her solicitor obtained expert reports to assess the standard of care given by these three potential defendants. All the reports were strongly negative as regards any possible negligence. The widow then reported the general practitioner to the Family Health Services Authority. A hearing was duly held and he was found not to be in breach of his terms of service. The solicitor then put it to the woman that she had no case, but she was not satisfied and insisted on three second opinions. These were all negative as well. She was not eligible for legal aid and had by now spent a great deal of money, but she was insistent that the case must go forward. The solicitor found himself under great pressure to call a conference with counsel as the only way of putting the client's mind at rest that no stone had been left unturned. This expenditure of excessive funds on a hopeless case was caused by the woman's complete inability to come to terms with the loss of her husband. It was an extreme example of the will to sue and in this case it was blind to reason as well.

XVIII THE ADVERSARIAL SYSTEM AND THE ORGANISATIONS THAT SUPPORT EACH SIDE

SUMMARY

(i)   Introduction

We have seen how the English legal system resolves disputes by the use of an adversarial system. This contrasts with the inquisitorial system used throughout most of mainland Europe and is based on Roman law. In England the inquisitorial system is used by a coroner conducting an inquest. The proceedings and evidence at an inquest are designed to establish the identity of the deceased and the time, place and manner of his death. No verdict can be expressed in a way that appears to attach blame to any individual. Thus an inquest is designed purely to establish facts rather than to attach blame.

An adversarial system is one in which one side competes against the other to convince the court that it, and not its opponent, has a just cause of action or, in simple terms, is in the right. In medical negligence we are only concerned with tortious liability, but the adversarial system is also used in other cases such as contractual liability and in disputes involving administrative law. The analogy with criminal law is that in the criminal law field the accused is competing against the State (in name, 'the Crown') when presenting his case.

For the successful conduct of a medical negligence case it is of the utmost importance that all matters receive skilled attention that is properly co-ordinated. This applies as much to procedural matters as to the presentation of evidence.

No litigant, whether doctor or patient, can hope to conduct his case personally, and it is the job of his solicitor to supervise the case and to ensure that all other people who are enlisted to help are working in a harmonious fashion. It may therefore be helpful to consider the function of the lawyers, medical experts and other agencies who act for each side.

(ii)   The solicitor for the plaintiff

When a disgruntled patient wants to sue a doctor, the first move is a visit to a solicitor. The patient may be tempted to use the solicitor who has helped here with other legal matters in the past, such as house conveyance or drawing up a will. However, she would be wise to consult a solicitor who is well versed in medical negligence as it is such a specialised business. Additionally, the patient will probably be competing against a defendant who is represented by an organisation such as the Medical Defence Union or the Medical Protection Society. These bodies have a century of experience behind them and concentrate a large part of their time and resources on the business of defending doctors from claims of alleged negligence.

When the patient attends her solicitor, the latter will take details of her allegations and this is often recorded in what is known as the solicitor's 'attendance note'. He may also interview other witnesses, such as the patient's wife or husband who may have been present at the time of the incident in question.

Having assessed the patient's allegations in detail the solicitor will obtain the medical notes partly to bolster his client's allegations but also to assess what kind of defence is likely to be raised.

There are numerous aspects to the work of the solicitor for the plaintiff and we shall now consider some of them.

(a) Discovery of documents

Until the advent of the Access to Health Records Act 1990, patients often met with considerable difficulty in obtaining their notes. Doctors and their advisers were sometimes reluctant to co-operate with a polite request and this left the patient with no option but to resort to the 'discovery procedure'. There is a provision in the Rules of the Supreme Court Act 1985 for a potential plaintiff to obtain discovery of all documents relating to her treatment, provided she can give sufficient reason for the request. That request would cover the general practitioner's clinical notes, prescription forms, X-ray request forms, pathology results and even the nurse's notes. If the doctor refuses to accede to this request, the plaintiff's solicitor can apply for a court order to obtain discovery. If the doctor still refuses, he is 'in contempt of court', which means he may be open to criminal proceedings.

At first sight it might appear that the discovery process would mark just the beginning of what will inevitably develop into the long-drawn-out process of litigation. The reality, however, is very different. The defence societies find that, of all the cases in which their members are asked to disclose the notes to plaintiff solicitors, it is only a small minority that develop any further. The inference to be drawn here is that many criticisms are prompted by matters other than possible negligence. It may need nothing more than a lack of courtesy or an inadequate explanation to provide the first spark of a complaint. One case (discussed in detail on pages 152-53) appeared to have been triggered by a doctor appearing unduly interested in a Test Match on television next to the child's bed when he was visiting a case of undiagnosed appendicitis. In this kind of case the technical aspects of the care may be beyond reproach, and when the solicitor receives a strongly negative report from the plaintiff's expert the case will die immediately.

Despite the frequency with which cases fall away at such an early stage, there is no doubt that doctors can be quite fearful of how matters will develop. In one case, a solicitor advised his client to ask the general practitioner for copies of the notes when he next visited the surgery. The complaint was based on alleged tardiness in securing the result of a blood test, which the doctor had ordered sometime previously. The doctor was keen to blame the laboratory for losing the sample temporarily and before he would agree to release his own notes he insisted that the patient sign a disclaimer note. The doctor wanted the patient to promise that he would not sue him but would confine the proceedings to a case against the hospital. Needless to say, the note was unenforceable, but it did little for the doctor's credibility.

(b) Legal privilege

The only documents a doctor is entitled to refuse to disclose are those that are subject to 'privilege'. Legal professional privilege is a system whereby one side can refuse to disclose any letters or reports that were written in contemplation of litigation. As an example, the contemporaneous doctor's note would not be privileged, but a letter he wrote to his defence organisation after the complaint arose certainly would qualify.

The reasoning behind the principle of legal professional privilege was discussed in *Waugh v British Railways Board* (1980). That was not a medical negligence case, but the judge made the point that there were two objectives to be achieved in deciding what papers should, or should not, be made available to an opponent and used as evidence in court.

The first objective was to ensure that both sides have access to all documentation relevant to the dispute, so as to ensure a fair result. It also makes a dispute more likely to settle at an early stage, out of court, because the defendant may realise that he has no hope of winning and will make an offer. Similarly, the plaintiff may realise that his allegations are unfounded and withdraw his case.

The second objective is to ensure that any litigant can visit his solicitor and discuss everything openly and frankly without the fear that the other side will eventually have access to some point that is adverse to him. If there is any likelihood that there is any risk of this kind to the litigant, the solicitor will find it difficult to make the best of the case for him.

As a case progresses and the prospect of trial looms, the two sides will be getting their respective experts to prepare reports in a form which is fit for disclosure. Although all expert reports are supposed to be independent and objective there is, inevitably, a certain amount of room for manoeuvre (see pages 277-78 on the preparation of the report). The plaintiff's advisers will want a report that puts the best possible gloss on the case without its author being made to feel uncomfortable in any way. The defendant's advisers will be similarly minded, and it may well be that a report that ultimately is disclosed for use at trial is a second or subsequent draft. This has the effect that the earlier draft(s) will be subject to privilege and cannot be used as evidence in court.

This very situation arose in *McGrath v Cole* (1994) when counsel for the defending general practitioner was conducting his cross-examination of the plaintiff's gynaecology expert. It became apparent from the line of questioning that the gynaecologist had prepared several earlier drafts of his final report and that he had probably changed his mind about various matters after discussion with solicitors. Counsel for Mrs McGrath tried to persuade the judge to interrupt the approach on the basis that those earlier documents were subject to privilege. His opponent was, however, allowed to proceed, and the judge held that the doctrine of legal professional privilege does not prevent opposing counsel from probing the expert's state of mind at the time he was rewriting a report.

(c) The letter before action

This is a formal letter which the solicitor for the plaintiff writes to the doctor concerned. It puts the doctor on notice that a case will probably be advanced against him in the near future. It will also contain a demand for sight of all relevant notes, coupled with the threat of a court order for discovery if they are not forthcoming.

The receipt of this letter may well be the first indication of a complaint about an incident that occurred many years previously. Any doctor reading such a letter in his morning post is almost bound to feel a shudder down his spine, especially as it may well be couched in terms that make the case sound far worse than the doctor believes, or indeed knows, it to be. The difficulty here is that the solicitor writing the letter has only his disgruntled client's version on which to rely, because he will not yet have seen any medical records.

The doctor is wise to respond promptly to the letter before action, but he usually asks his defence organisation to deal with it on his behalf. Indeed, defence societies are reluctant to let their members respond of their own free will, for fear that they will do so in a way that later prejudices their position. It is usual for copies of all relevant notes to be forwarded to the plaintiff's solicitor under cover of a letter which gives no hint of what form a defence might take. The provision of any sort of explanation merely gives the other side more material from which to work, and may even be taken as some form of admission of liability.

(d) Obtaining notes from persons who are not parties to the action

If a patient is complaining about the treatment he has received from his general practitioner, one of his prime concerns will be to obtain the general practitioner's notes. However, there may be other medical records that the patient needs for his case, which were made by people whom he has no intention of suing.

As an example, we can cite the child who is admitted to hospital by the general practitioner, allegedly very late, with appendicitis. At operation, it is found that the organ has perforated and this means that a more extensive operation has to be carried out and the child takes longer to recover. The mother may well be extremely grateful to the hospital for all their care in saving her child's life and mitigating the effects of the delayed admission. Nevertheless she will want to obtain the surgeon's notes. The operation notes will be necessary to define the extent of the damage. Additionally, the clinical findings in the admission notes may help to show that a proper examination by the general practitioner a short time earlier should have prompted admission.

In this case, the surgeon, not being a defendant, will be relatively unconcerned about disclosing his notes. To ensure that they are received without undue difficulty, the patient's solicitor will often make it clear in his letter that no case is being advanced in the surgeon's direction. This leaves the surgeon with the uncomfortable feeling that he has cooperated in advancing a case against his friend and colleague, the general practitioner. Any ill feeling between them can usually be dissipated on the basis that the defence organisation is handling the matter, and takes all the decisions about what material to send to the other side. In this sense, the defence organisations tend to act as a kind of buffer between a litigating patient and his doctor, but in general practice this is probably not particularly effective because of their close relationship if the patient continues to attend the same practice.

(iii)   The barrister for the plaintiff

We have spent some time seeing how a solicitor will discuss the case with his client and how he will take various steps, such as obtaining notes and interviewing other witnesses, to make a preliminary assessment of the case. If the solicitor is well versed in medical negligence litigation, he will by now probably have formed at least a provisional view of the strength of the case. However, he will have to point out to his client, who may well be in a distressed state and full of acrimony, that the litigation can provide no redress for ill-feeling. This means that the patient's case can only succeed if it is based on sound legal principles. Many cases have been generated by such matters as the doctor who never lifts his head from the prescription pad when the patient walks into the room, or who fails to give any kind of explanation about the treatment. Conversely, many potentially strong negligence cases have probably never been advanced because the doctor, at an early stage, spoke carefully to his patient and gave an impression of kindness and courtesy.

Having made an initial assessment in this way, the solicitor will next instruct a barrister. This is often described as 'sending the papers to counsel'. We saw earlier how the solicitor should be well versed in medical negligence cases, and the same remark applies to the barrister. The latter will now be in possession of the

167

patient's statement of events, the medical notes and the solicitor's letter of instruction giving his initial views. The barrister's function at this stage can be summarised briefly in the following points:

(a) Initial assessment

The barrister must make his initial assessment of the merits of the case, when considered against the harsh reality of conducting it in court against a determined and skilled opponent. This is in contrast to the amiable and supportive discussion the solicitor may have had with his client across the desk, with no adversary present to make the patient feel threatened.

(b) Additional material

The barrister must decide what other material or evidence is needed. For instance, if a case is being advanced against a hospital, it may not have occurred to the patient or her solicitor that part of the fault lay with the general practitioner or ambulance service for incurring a delay in the admission arrangements. If this were to happen, it would be essential to obtain the records of those other health care personnel.

(c) Additional opinions

The barrister must ensure that all relevant medical opinions have been obtained to support the client's case. In the example just quoted, the solicitor may have already obtained a report from a suitable hospital specialist on the standard of care given when the patient was admitted, but counsel will point out that a general practitioner's report or an ambulance crew's report is needed. A failure to cover all aspects in this type of case lays the client open to the risk that she will fail to recover full damages from the hospital because the latter may be able to shift some of the blame on to the general practitioner whom the patient failed to include as a defendant.

(d) The conference with counsel

The barrister must advise whether to call a 'conference with counsel'. This is a meeting of the plaintiff and all his advisers, both legal and medical, for the purposes of resolving areas of doubt and assessing the case with more certainty. It is nearly always held in counsel's chambers and is often the first opportunity that the patient has to meet the barrister who is going to argue his case in court. Holding a conference is a relatively expensive exercise, especially if it involves a Queen's Counsel or 'silk', his junior, the solicitor and his trainee, and perhaps three medical experts who have had to travel from other parts of the country. Opinions and advice expressed in letters and reports are certainly much cheaper but it is this author's experience that many cases that appear fairly weak on paper have a strong basis when discussed across the table. This is probably caused mainly by the limitations of the written word. Indeed, every doctor knows that a careful history taken at the bedside can put a whole new gloss on the description given in a letter written by a colleague.

(iv)   Action for Victims of Medical Accidents

Almost every general practitioner belongs to a defence organisation. It is usual for partnership agreements to insist upon current membership. The member is reminded of the support he is entitled to receive when his annual demand for a substantial subscription arrives. At other times, he may well receive reminders of a less personal nature in the form of a quarterly journal, or he may hear of a close colleague who has become involved in litigation. Furthermore, he knows that in the 1990s his chances of facing a complaint are increasingly likely.

Conversely, many members of the public rarely see a doctor, and those who do are hardly ever aware of anything amiss with the treatment. Many patients go through the whole of their lives without any contact with the legal system, unlike most doctors, who buy houses, make wills and enter into partnership agreements. This means that many lay people have little idea of where to start when they want to make a complaint or to bring legal proceedings. They fear that seeing a solicitor might be beyond their means, and that dealing directly with the medical authorities is likely to meet with a rebuff.

Until the early 1980s, these considerations made it extremely difficult for many a dissatisfied patient to start an action against his doctor. Added to this was the perception, often realised, that the doctor's colleagues would 'close ranks' and think to themselves 'there but for the grace of God go I'.

In an attempt to redress the balance, Action for Victims of Medical Accidents (AVMA) was founded in 1982. It is a charitable organisation and was founded on the enthusiasm of a group of people whose concerns were epitomised in a television documentary about a woman who underwent some gynaecological surgery during which part of her bowel was punctured. Her unexpectedly slow recovery was dismissed by the surgeon as being caused by 'minor complications' (from which the documentary took its name), the true nature of which was never disclosed to her. This focused AVMA's mind on several important issues which hitherto had received little attention. They concerned such matters as ensuring that cases of medical negligence were referred to solicitors who were sufficiently interested and skilled to conduct them. It was commonplace for clients in the early years to seek AVMA's help after two, three or more firms of solicitors had mismanaged their case when, at least on the available medical evidence, it was quite strong.

As a health charity, AVMA recognises that accidents will continue. Its philosophy is based on the firm belief that a legal approach to a patient's injury may well not be in anyone's best interest. Other solutions, such as the provision of an explanation of what went wrong, and an apology where appropriate, come very high on its list of priorities.

From its early days, AVMA has developed a highly organised system to help plaintiffs and their advisers. Any patient who approaches AVMA will be given some basic advice without charge, although he will be asked to make a donation to the charity if possible.

If it is felt that the patient's case may have a sound legal basis, he will be put in touch with a solicitor who has been approved by AVMA as having the necessary skills and commitment to take it. When the case is ready to be referred to counsel, AVMA may make a recommendation there as well. Throughout the life of the case, the lawyer who has received the referral will have at least some degree of supervision. To support the system, AVMA run a 'lawyers' service' to which solicitors can subscribe. This enables them to obtain advice about any aspect of this kind of litigation, whether it be how to find a neurosurgical expert who is sympathetic to plaintiffs, or whether a general practitioner normally has access to a district nurse's notes. This service extends to include courses of medical lectures for lawyers, and an annual conference which is attended by members of both professions. There is also a quarterly journal to which many eminent doctors contribute, with particular reference to highlighting areas of special risk in medical practice. The journal also has brief accounts of cases that have been settled out of court, and articles for lawyers on the conduct of litigation generally.

In addition to medical lectures for lawyers and the annual conference, AVMA also organise specialist conferences. These are usually centred on some medical speciality such as cerebral palsy or orthopaedics, and there is an emphasis on the pitfalls of medical practice in those areas. Importance is attached to good communication skills and the giving of proper explanations to patients about the treatment they are about to receive and the risks to which they will be subjected.

AVMA's case workers handle letters of complaint from aggrieved patients in the first instance and make a preliminary assessment of whether there is likely to be a case worth advancing. Some complaints will have been generated by nothing more than insensitive management by a doctor, and the case worker will explain to the client that this is no basis for an action in law. Alternatively, the case worker may think that there is a case to be investigated, and will then recommend a solicitor on AVMA's panel who has perhaps handled cases in the same medical speciality before. If the solicitor is in any difficulty interpreting medical notes or understanding a medical expert's report, the case worker will also be able to assist with these matters.

When AVMA was first formed one of its main difficulties was finding medical experts who were prepared to act for a plaintiff. There was a strong feeling that a doctor reporting on a patient's behalf was tantamount to criticising a colleague. However attitudes have changed since then, with the result that, at least in some people's opinion, it has become as respectable for a doctor to report for a plaintiff as for a defendant. AVMA has been able to compile a list of medical experts in various specialities who can be approached by the plaintiff's solicitor with confidence. The list is updated regularly to ensure that the quality of reporting is sufficiently good to enable a case to be analysed properly.

(v)   Community Health Councils

A Community Health Council is a statutory body to which a disgruntled patient may resort for advice. These organisations were first established in 1974 as part of the National Health Service, and their role is defined in the relevant Statutory Instrument as:

> ... to keep under review the operation of the Health Service in its district and make recommendations for the improvement of that service or otherwise advise any relevant District Authority or Family Health Services Authority upon such matters relating to the operation of the Health Service within its district as the Council sees fit.

There is usually one Community Health Council for each health authority. Each one has at least two full-time members of staff and about twenty voluntary members, who can claim expenses.

The staff of a Community Health Council cannot provide legal representation and they cannot give a legal opinion on a complaint. Despite this restriction they can certainly offer advice and support of a general nature, and they can represent the complainant at a service committee hearing in relation to a general practice case. Additionally, they can help the complainant decide what are his best options when faced with the myriad of National Health Service complaints procedures. If a patient is dissatisfied with the treatment received from his general practitioner, one of the staff members may help by writing a letter to the doctor or the Family Health Services Authority on the patient's behalf but this cannot amount to the formal investigation of a complaint. Some patients feel overawed by the medical establishment and fear that even the Family Health Services Authority may not be entirely sympathetic to their case. If such patients are not minded to see a solicitor they may feel they have an ally in the Community Health Council who can go a long way towards helping them to resolve their difficulties.

(vi) Legal aid

Since Victorian times there has been a strong tradition that impecunious patients and litigants should receive help from their professional advisers without charge or at a reduced fee. However, it was not until after the Second World War that the payments to doctors and lawyers began to be funded by the State. In 1948 the introduction of the National Health Service Act made provision for free treatment of a patient who was ill but was unable to afford to consult the doctor. The next year, the Legal Aid and Advice Act 1949 made a similar provision for litigants who were unable to fund their cases. There was, however, a fundamental difference in that many aided litigants had to pay contributions according to their means. This was done on a sliding scale such that only the very poor were exempted from making any contribution at all. Over the years the income limits for qualifying for legal aid have risen to allow for inflation, but have not always kept pace with it.

When a plaintiff visits his solicitor, the question of legal aid in respect of the proposed medical claim will be addressed. Details will be taken of the individual's income, savings and other financial circumstances. A calculation will then be made about whether he qualifies and what his contribution will be.

Inevitably, this has the effect that the very rich and the very poor are the ones who can afford to litigate, with those of moderate means being most affected by financial constraints. In recent years a member of this last group of litigants has been dubbed a 'minela' (Middle Income, Not Eligible for Legal Aid). This effect is probably seen in its most acute form in medical negligence cases, because the proceedings tend to be expensive and the actions often last a long time. A privately-funded person may well have to do much more than cover his own expenses. If he loses the case he will have his opponent's expenses to meet and he will have had no control over the work his opponent has commissioned, or how much it cost. The plaintiff's only hope in having this limited is that the Taxing Master of the High Court may disallow some of the expenses. It is common, after taxation, for an opponent's bill to be reduced to about 75% of its original amount. By the same token, if the privately-funded party wins, he may find his own expenses being taxed such that he only recovers the lower amount in his winnings. A legally-aided plaintiff is immune from these financial pressures. He can advance his case in the knowledge that he is protected from additional expense over which he has no control.

We have seen how a privately-funded plaintiff who wins his case may not recover the whole of his costs from the defendant. There may have been a 'shortfall' caused by the taxation process. The plaintiff has, however, already spent this money and if he had taken out a bank loan to fund his case, he would have to repay that amount out of the damages award. If the plaintiff is legally-aided the Board applies the same principle. It will recover the 'shortfall' by applying its 'statutory charge'. This means that an aided plaintiff who wins his case may not receive the full damages award because the Board will recover the full amount that it advanced to fund the case. If the costs against the defendant are reduced by taxation it is the aided plaintiff who bears the loss rather than the legal aid fund. A simple example will illustrate the process. Suppose a patient has £40,000 advance to fund his case and that he wins a damages award of £100,000 with costs against the defending doctor. Suppose also that the Taxing Master disallowed £10,000 of the patient's costs such that he was held to have only been justified in spending £30,000. The Legal Aid Board would take £30,000 from the defendant's costs and £10,000 from the patient's award, so as to recover the £40,000 it had originally advanced. This leaves the patient with £90,000 rather than with the full figure of £100,000.

Having a financial status that is within the required limit is not the only criterion a plaintiff has to satisfy to secure legal aid to fight a case. The Legal Aid Board makes an assessment from a medical and legal point of view, of how likely the claim is to succeed. The barrister dealing with the case gives his advice on this point and he is under a duty to the Board to advise against the funding of a case if in his view the claim is unlikely to succeed. There could be a medical or a legal reason for an unfavourable assessment. Medical reasons would include those where, for instance, the case was clearly impossible to advance on causation in that the alleged negligence had made no material difference to the outcome of the treatment. Similarly, limitation might prove an insurmountable obstacle from a legal point of view if the patient had known of his damage for more than three years. In addition to the likelihood of a case succeeding, the Board also has to assess the economic viability of the claim and ensure that any possible damages award justifies the expense of pursuing it.

This is a convenient point to mention so called 'nuisance claims'. Suppose a plaintiff advances a case which has at least some merit and, perhaps because he has access to legal aid, shows every intention of pursuing it. The defendant may be confident that, if the case reaches trial, he will almost certainly win. The defendant may, however, be facing a claim which is very expensive to defend and is out of all proportion to any potential damages payment. A defendant in this predicament may be inclined to offer a settlement on a commercial basis. He will certainly regard the claim as a nuisance but will prefer to make a small loss to clear the matter rather than spend a much larger amount fighting it all the way to court. He will also have in mind the question of whether his opponent is privately funded or is in receipt of legal aid because in the latter case the defendant will be unable to recover his costs when he eventually wins the case.

The original 1949 Act was replaced by the Legal Aid Acts of 1974 and 1979, and in April 1993 there was a marked contraction in the availability of legal aid. An applicant's circumstances were calculated such that his contributions were considerably higher, and many of those who qualified previously for full funding had to make contributions. Additionally, aided persons were told that they would have to continue their contributions throughout the life of the case, which could run to several years. At the time of writing it is too early to tell what the long-term effect will be, but it is likely to have some far-reaching effects on how the litigation is conducted. It may well hasten the advent of conditional or contingency fees. In the latter situation the lawyer makes no charge for his involvement with the case, but takes a percentage of his client's award if he wins. With the conditional fee arrangement, the lawyer also receives no payment if he loses, but receives an uplift in his charges if his client wins. Thus, the lawyer's financial gain with contingency fees is related to the size of the ultimate award, whereas in the conditional arrangement it is related to the work he does. As the lawyer knows that either of these arrangements will produce no reward at all for him if his client loses he may well become less enthusiastic about investigating a case that appears to have little chance of a successful outcome or where the work involved seems to be out of proportion to any possible damages award. In the UK, the conditional fee system seems likely to materialise in the not too distant future. The contingency arrangement has been commonplace in the USA for some years.

(vii) Group actions

Some medical negligence actions, particularly those being conducted against pharmaceutical manufacturers, have a great deal in common with each other and will involve identical points of law. It should therefore make for conveinience and economy if they are grouped together.

Several examples of this type of claim have arisen in recent years. We can mention those which have been pursued against the manufacturers of Opren, Myodil, the corticosteroids, vaccines and, perhaps the best known of all, the benzodiazepine tranquillisers. In all these cases there were large numbers of plaintiffs, but just one or two defendant manufacturers. All the claims were based on similar grounds in the sense that every patient alleged that he had suffered from side-effects of the drug and that this had been caused by the negligence of the manufacturers. In some of the groups the number of plaintiffs ran to tens of thousands and it would have been out of the question for every case to have been heard in court. A plan was therefore made to select a few 'lead cases' which were thought to be representative of the rest of the group. All aspects of those cases were investigated in detail and the principles drawn from them were applied to the others. This involved legal points such as limitation (see page 71 *et seq*) and causation (see page 37 *et seq*). It also concerned manufacturing and clinical matters such as whether products had been adequately tested and whether proper guidelines had been issued for prescribers. We should perhaps observe, in passing, that no case against a pharmaceutical company has yet reached trial on the question of negligence. The tranquilliser group also provides an example of this type of case. It met its demise when it ceased to derive any support from the Legal Aid Board and therefore never reached trial.

Loveday v Renton (1988) was chosen as the lead case for damage allegedly resulting from diphtheria-tetanus-pertussis (whooping cough) vaccine. In that case the plaintiff, Susan Loveday, found that her case never reached court on the question of negligence because causation was tried as a preliminary issue. Unfortunately for her, she failed on this point because it was held that the DTP vaccine was probably not the cause of her brain damage. Conversely an Irish case, *Best v Wellcome & Others* (1991),[32] showed that some cases could succeed on causation, although the plaintiff in that particular case lost his claim because he failed to demonstrate the necessary temporal relationship between the giving of the vaccine and the onset of the symptoms.

Although some group actions are directed primarily against manufacturers, it is inevitable that clinicians, in effect the prescribing doctors, will find themselves implicated in the litigation. The benzodiazepine action provides a useful example here. Ativan, made by Wyeth, and Valium, made by Roche, accounted for most of the cases, although there were other examples amounting to a dozen or so of other less commonly used members of that group of drugs. The manufacturers were required by law to produce 'data sheets' for the guidance of clinicians and these had to contain material information about such matters as dose, contra-indications and side effects. Part of the case against the manufacturers was that, particularly in the early years, the sheets had failed to mention the addictive properties of the drugs when they were being taken on a long-term basis, even though there was evidence that such a risk

---

[32] For a helpful discussion about the implications of this case, see Keegan, *AVMA Med & Leg I*, April 1991, p 15.

existed. In the years following the updating of the data sheets in this particular respect, doctors continued to use the drugs and this led some of the manufacturers to feel that at least part of the blame should be shifted on to the prescribers because they had ignored the guidelines. Large numbers of general practitioners found themselves facing actions which had been brought by their patients. Although many of the tranquillisers had been prescribed initially as far back as the early 1960s, the doctors themselves did not become vulnerable to criticism until perhaps 20 years after this point.

In an effort to co-ordinate the case against the prescribers of benzdiazepines, a panel of experts was formed. It considered possible criticisms of the prescribers, such as the failure to monitor prescription regimes over a period of time, and the question of whether the drugs were withdrawn from a particular individual too rapidly or in an otherwise inappropriate manner.

With any group action it is very important to achieve a uniform approach. If the number of cases in any particular class is not too great it is usual for them all to be handled by one firm of solicitors. Alternatively, if the numbers are very high there will be one firm who acts as a steering committee to ensure co-ordination between the firms who are taking individual cases.

Legal aid is an important consideration in a group action. It is essential to be able to demonstrate legal merit and reasonableness. Put another way, the Board will want to ensure that the cost:benefit ratio of the claim will justify the funding. In this type of action, the Legal Aid Board will only consider funding if the claim has a reasonable prospect of success and the damages are likely to be sufficiently high for the Board to recover its outlay by way of the statutory charge. Actions against drug manufacturers tend to be protracted, complicated and expensive. For this reason any action of this kind is likely to need a large number of successful claimants for it to be worthwhile financially. The fact that the claims have a great deal in common means that the generic work tends to have fixed costs regardless of the number of claimants. It would be prohibitive for the Legal Aid Board to fund this work against the possible winnings of just one individual. The more claimants involved, the easier it will become to justify funding the generic research. The Board will find it very unattractive to fund an individual litigant but may consider funding if numbers are sufficiently large. It follows that, to borrow an expression from the world of physics, there has to be a 'critical mass' of eligible claimants before any aided claim of this kind becomes a viable proposition.

(viii) The defence organisations

The earliest mutual defence fund in the UK was formed in 1885 and in those days litigation was of minute proportions. It has to be remembered that this was late Victorian England and it was generally considered inconceivable that a professional man, let alone a doctor, could do a sub-standard job of work. The role of the defence organisations therefore amounted to little more than putting the occasional crank in his place if he became a nuisance or dared to challenge the authority of the medical establishment.

This level of activity continued largely unchanged for many decades, despite the social upheaval brought about by two world wars, until shortly after the inception of the National Health Service in 1948. It was from about this point that the general public no longer regarded their doctors as being infallible. It is difficult to know why this change took place, but it was probably a combination of increasing consumerism and increased awareness of medical matters. The latter was particularly fuelled by the media who found that their readers, listeners and viewers were fascinated by the workings of the human body and what could be done to rectify its defects. Until 1977, no personal injury award had exceeded £100,000 but a decade later it had exceeded the £1 million barrier.

In the early 1980s there was no slackening in the pace of complaints against doctors, with the result that the defence bodies had a burgeoning task on their hands. Inevitably, annual subscriptions rose exponentially. There was a 33-fold increase, from £40 in 1978 to £1,350 in 1989. This was caused by a combination of increasingly large damages awards and the expense of having to defend an increasing number of cases. Although there has been a slight fall in subscriptions since the late 1980s it has not been brought about by a reduction in claims but by the introduction of the 'Crown indemnity' scheme (1990), in which the State absorbs the cost of defence for hospital doctors.

For the general practitioner, and indeed for hospital doctors, the defence organisation is the first port of call when he needs help to deal with a complaint. Unlike the patient who has little idea of where to turn, or which solicitors to choose, the way is clear for the doctor. He will be in touch with his defence organisation at an early stage, whether as a result of an acrimonious telephone call from a patient, or whether he is in receipt of the letter before action from the patient's solicitor. The defence societies, in broad terms, take over the conduct of the case. For instance, they will give advice on disclosure of notes. Until recently medical records were not available on demand, and a patient had to provide a proper reason for wanting access to them. However, in November 1991 the Access to Health Records Act 1990 came into force, and this meant that patients had a right to have copies of the practitioner's notes, provided that the treatment in question was after that date when the Act was implemented. As well as being a very important source of personal support for the defending doctor, the societies also deal with many procedural matters, such as deciding when to instruct solicitors and they will sometimes even accept service of the statement of claim.

The organisations with which we are concerned in England are the Medical Defence Union[33] and the Medical Protection Society, the former having the slightly larger membership. North of the border, the Medical and Dental Defence Union of Scotland is the principal body. All these organisations have broadly similar functions and for years they kept their subscriptions roughly in line with each other. When they were at a relatively modest level there was little difficulty with this, but larger discrepancies have arisen lately which have at least partly been caused by different methods of levying subscriptions. With the pressures of increasing litigation, the societies have made slight alterations to their philosophies of approach based on different beliefs as to how best to tackle the difficulty, and this has also affected

---

[33] For an interesting account of the history of the Medical Defence Union from 1885 to 1973, see two articles by McNamara in *J Med Def Union* 1993, no 4 (pp 84-86) and 1994, no 1 (pp 21-22). The articles make it clear that the function of that organisation has changed enormously since the end of the 19th century. It has been a question of keeping pace with the ever changing nature of the legal threat to doctors in practice.

subscription rates. A junior hospital doctor with earnings below a specified limit, would be charged a relatively modest amount. On the other hand, an established practitioner who had no limit to his income, and was working in a high-risk speciality, would find himself paying a very much higher figure.

Defence organisations are staffed by doctors with administrative support. Most of these doctors are not legally qualified, although they do have at least some grounding in the law of negligence, in health service law and in complaints procedures such as general practitioner service committee hearings. They have usually spent some years in clinical practice so they are familiar with the difficulties that can face doctors and well placed to advise and support their members. The staff are also able to help their members with matters that are not related strictly to litigation. Practitioners frequently seek assistance and support in relation to attendance at inquests and at medical service committee hearings. General practitioners are only too well aware of the increase in these hearings in recent years: they have seen a rise from 1,088 in 1981 to 2,205 in 1991.

(ix)   The solicitor for the defendant

A patient suing his doctor can enlist the help of any solicitors' firm of his choosing, although he will be well advised to consult one that is well versed in medical negligence matters. Conversely, the defending general practitioner's case falls automatically into the hands of his defence organisation, and the latter normally has one particular firm to which it refers all its cases. The Medical Defence Union uses the firm of Hempsons and the Medical Protection Society uses Le Brasseur J Tickle. Thus there are literally hundreds of plaintiff firms in England but only two defendant firms for general practitioners.

The advent of 'Crown indemnity' (1990) has resulted in health authorities employing firms of solicitors of their own choosing (often local firms). They rely on these solicitors when their employed hospital doctors are facing a negligence claim. Although these firms are primarily concerned with defending their clients from allegations of negligence they also, like the defence organisations themselves, give advice on other legal matters, such as partnership agreements and disputes with employing hospital authorities.

(x)   The barrister for the defendant

Unlike solicitors, barristers are in independent practice even though they work in a set of chambers with other barristers. When the defending doctor's solicitors want to instruct counsel any one of a large number of barristers may be chosen.

Counsel for the defendant will have the task of responding to the statement of claim that has been served by the plaintiff. Counsel will formulate the defence and the request for further and better particulars. If the case is reckoned indefensible, he may well have to calculate the amount of damages it might be reasonable to offer in settlement. If the case is to be defended, the offer may take the form of a 'payment into court'. This is a tactical move, which limits the amount of costs the plaintiff can recover on winning if the ultimate award at trial fails to exceed the 'payment in'. If no payment into court has been made, the plaintiff will be awarded the total damages figure decided by the judge and he will also receive reimbursement of the costs, subject to taxation by the court, incurred in bringing the proceedings. The defendant will therefore be faced with paying the damages sum together with the costs of both sides. However, if there is a 'payment in' and at trial the final damages award is less than the 'payment in', the plaintiff will be liable for the costs of both sides during the interval between the 'payment in', and the trial itself. Inevitably, most of the costs of an action are incurred in the period of time that immediately precedes the trial. This rule is designed to encourage a plaintiff to accept a 'payment in', for fear that he will be exposing himself to the risk of a large costs bill if he continues with unreasonable expectations.

XIX   CLINICAL MATTERS

SUMMARY

(i) Introduction

It is not the function of a book such as this to state with any authority at all what are, or are not, proper standards of medical practice in various circumstances. The standards of the day are set out in medical and surgical textbooks. Whether or not there has been a shortcoming in a particular case can only be achieved by a full examination of all the available evidence of fact and opinion.

The *Bolam* principle will be applied in an attempt to establish liability in each case as it arises. The principle enunciated in *Bolam v Friern Hospital Management Committee* (1957) was discussed in some detail in Chapter III. In essence, it concerns the point that a doctor is unlikely to be held negligent if he has acted in accordance with a responsible body of medical opinion. In this chapter we can focus on some of the difficulties doctors face in a clinical setting and examine the approach that lawyers take in solving them.

(ii) Keeping up to date

Every patient visiting a doctor has an expectation, indeed a right, that the treatment he receives will be reasonably up to date. A treatment that would have been perfectly acceptable in 1970 would not necessarily be so in 1990. This became very apparent in the benzodiazepine litigation, when the plaintiffs were unable to show that prescribing general practitioners had fallen short of proper standards in the years before the manufacturers' data sheets gave the appropriate warnings. The data sheets which were circulated before the mid-1980s provided very little in the way of specific warnings about the dangers of addiction in patients who were maintained on the drugs in an excessive dosage or for an unduly long time. Many a practitioner, although not particularly diligent in the supervision of a patient's tranquilliser intake, was able to rely on these early data sheets to show that allegations of negligent prescribing were unfounded. Relevant information may be contained in textbooks, journals, drug company leaflets, notices circulated by the Department of Health, regular editions of the British National Formulary, and even in lectures given at postgraduate medical centres.

The difficulty may be more acute for older practitioners, who are faced with patients needing a treatment that had never been envisaged when they were at medical school. Hormone replacement therapy (HRT), demanded now by many women of middle-age and beyond, is an example of an approach to the management of a patient that could not possibly have featured on the medical student's curriculum in the early post-war years. Doubtless the same remark applied a generation earlier to doctors who qualified in the pre-antibiotic era, and to whom the development of a quinsy (a peri-tonsillar abscess) was a common occurrence. Development of such a condition nowadays would immediately raise the question of whether the doctor had been negligent in not prescribing an antibiotic when the patient presented with a sore throat.

The question of whether or not a particular antibiotic was appropriate at the time of the alleged negligence reached trial recently. In *McGrath v Cole* (1994), a woman was given Amoxil in an attempt to treat pelvic inflammatory disease. Unfortunately, the organisms proved resistant to the drug and the woman later found herself to be sterile. The treatment had been given in 1982 and the defendant argued that such an antibiotic was a perfectly acceptable treatment for the disease in that earlier year. Conversely, the plaintiff asserted that by this date it was known that there could be resistant organisms and that additional antibiotic therapy should have been prescribed if referral to a specialist was not to be made.

In another case, which never reached court, a young man had for some years been seeking help for very badly stained teeth. After visiting a succession of dentists he found one who pointed out that a possible cause for the condition was the administration of the antibiotic tetracycline in childhood. This particular danger had first become known in the early or mid-1960s. The plaintiff was therefore dependent on being able to show that the knowledge of the doctor, who at the time of the prescriptions had been in practice for many years, should have been sufficiently up-to-date to know that this particular antibiotic should be avoided in childhood.

The sheer bulk of material available to doctors raises the question of how much they can be expected to have read when a decision has to be taken about treatment. There is no hard and fast rule about this, but in general terms a general practitioner may be expected to take notice of journals that are ordinarily read by his colleagues, and letters that are circulated to him by the Department of Health or the Family Health Services Authority.

(iii)   The rarity of the diagnosis as a defence

'Common conditions commonly occur' is a time-honoured adage of medical student education. This aphorism is designed to reduce the likelihood that the doctor will overlook the condition from which the patient is, at least from a statistical point of view, most likely to be suffering.

The remark applies particularly strongly in a general practice setting. Doctors here see innumerable cases of common conditions, but hidden among the multitude is the very occasional rare one. When this is added to the fact that the symptoms of the latter may closely mimic those of the former, it is not surprising that a doctor may feel he has a strong defence when he fails to administer treatment that is appropriate to the rare condition.

In one case, a teenage girl was seen several times by her general practitioner with earache and deafness. Some years later she developed paralysis of the face and was referred to a hospital specialist, but her symptoms persisted. After various other specialists had reviewed the girl and carried out numerous tests it was found that all her symptoms were being caused by a very rare tumour of the brain. The general practitioner could not possibly have been expected to have diagnosed such a condition correctly but this would not, of itself, amount to a defence. The test for negligence by the general practitioner concerns whether he should have made an earlier referral on the basis of the symptoms and the examination findings alone.

In another case, an elderly man visited his general practitioner over a period of time with recurrent headaches, but repeated examination showed no abnormality. The patient was reassured and given symptomatic treatment. At a later visit he complained of a lump on his head and the doctor was able to confirm a mass in the scalp. It was not thought to be serious. Various diagnoses were suggested such as a cyst or an innocent fatty lump. Unfortunately, it later started to ulcerate and on hospital referral was found to have been caused by a very rare bone tumour of the skull. The man sued the doctor on the basis that he should have been referred to a specialist as soon as the lump appeared. The doctor pleaded his defence on the ground that in a whole professional lifetime he was very unlikely ever to see such a case. The plaintiff countered this by arguing that no responsible doctor should reassure a patient about a lump anywhere on the body without taking reasonable steps to establish the diagnosis. No such steps had been taken in this case and, indeed, specialist referral would have been the doctor's only option.

The rarity of the diagnosis is sometimes used by defence counsel to discredit the evidence of the plaintiff's expert. The latter may find it difficult to give a convincing opinion on the management of a condition of which he has to admit he has had very little experience. He can go no further than to say what he would have done when faced with the same circumstances as the defendant without knowing the diagnosis. This will concern such matters as the length of the history, the patient's general condition and the presence of specific physical signs. To support the case, he will have to argue that these factors alone were such that no responsible body of medical opinion would have failed to take the course of action that he asserts was proper.

In this type of case, the course of action is likely to be specialist referral. The plaintiff will almost certainly be unable to say that the doctor should have made the correct diagnosis but she may be able to argue that the doctor should have realised that she was sufficiently ill to have needed hospital investigation.

It can be seen that the rarity of the diagnosis is no defence. The test for negligence is whether the symptoms and signs being presented to the doctor at the time should have prompted specialist referral.

(iv) Differential diagnosis in clinical practice

Accuracy of diagnosis is one of the most important parts of a doctor's work. Unfortunately, it can also be one of the most difficult and demanding. With the best will in the world, no doctor can get it right first time, every time. The bizarre presentation of some illnesses can tax the clinician's mind severely. To this must be added rather more mundane constraints, such as lack of time and resources.

We therefore have to be realistic and accept that in many cases the desired degree of precision is impossible. Furthermore, some conditions are self-limiting and relatively trivial, which means that exactitude can be rather academic as it will not affect the treatment or the outcome.

Any doctor, when faced with a patient in whom the diagnosis is uncertain, will consider a range of possibilities. The condition from which he thinks the patient is most likely to be suffering will be at the top of his list. Below this will be other possibilities, in decreasing order of likelihood. We refer to this range of possibilities as the 'differential diagnosis'. It is reached not on the symptoms alone, but by taking other factors into account such as the patient's age, sex, past history, family history or even his occupation. We can consider rectal bleeding as an example. This could perfectly well be caused by piles in a woman of 20 or in a man of 70. However, in the latter case, cancer of the lower bowel would feature much more prominently in the differential diagnosis. This is because the malignant cause is much commoner in the older than in the younger age group. Again, the patient who complains of chest and upper abdominal pains may quite reasonably be considered to be suffering from a hiatus hernia. In some cases of this nature, however, the differential diagnosis would include ischaemic heart disease. The potential danger from the latter condition could mean that appropriate steps should be taken to eliminate it.

Having taken an initial view on the differential diagnosis, the general practitioner may feel that the degree of uncertainty is such that he must undertake various investigations. If he is seeing a heavy smoker with a recent history of a bad cough and bloodstained sputum he may have good reason, from other points in the case, for thinking that lung cancer is unlikely to be the cause and that bronchitis is the probable explanation. Despite this, he may still want to narrow down his differential diagnosis by arranging a chest X-ray to eliminate the malignant condition.

The important point is that cancer is a possible, although unlikely, contender for the diagnosis, but to miss it would be disastrous for the patient.

The results of a general practitioner's examination and investigation may lead to a view that a patient might be harbouring some serious condition that merits specialist referral. The specialist himself will go through the same thought processes to formulate his differential diagnosis. He will take the history again and will carry out his own examination. He will then decide whether his own investigations, which are likely to be more sophisticated than those of the referring general practitioner, are necessary. For instance, a gynaecologist seeing a woman with a history of recurrent abdominal pains may feel that his specialist expertise in the out-patient clinic is sufficient to merit reassurance and return of the patient to the care of her general practitioner. Alternatively, he may see fit to undertake a laparoscopy to eliminate the possibility of endometriosis.

The reason for drawing up a differential diagnosis is to ensure that the treatment given is the most appropriate in the circumstances, when a precise diagnosis is uncertain. To revert to our earlier example, it would be out of the question to investigate all patients complaining of a cough on the basis that they might have lung cancer. On the other hand, if one particular patient has a cough which gets worse over a period of some weeks and is then accompanied by bloodstained sputum and weight loss, it would be neglectful not to consider a malignant diagnosis as being quite likely, and to investigate accordingly.

It can be seen that the formulation of a differential diagnosis is, in essence, a balancing exercise. On the one hand, it is wasteful of time and resources to investigate every patient in detail when there is good reason to believe that they can be started on treatment without further ado. On the other hand, it is dangerous to ignore the possibility of potentially serious conditions simply because an innocent one is, at least from a statistical point of view, more likely to be the real explanation for the symptoms.

The balancing of the risks when drawing up a differential diagnosis was considered when *McGrath v Cole* (1994) reached trial. In that case, a young woman consulted her general practitioner with abdominal pain and urinary symptoms. She had recently been discharged from hospital having had a dilatation and curettage for an incomplete miscarriage. The doctor recorded in his notes that the cervix was tender on internal examination. It was argued by counsel for the defending general practitioner that it was entirely reasonable to dismiss this physical sign as being nothing more than an after-effect of the cervical dilatation which had been necessary to evacuate the retained products of conception. From this it was asserted that it was equally reasonable to treat the symptoms as being caused by a urinary infection. Unknown to the doctor at the time of the consultation, the girl was in the early stages of pelvic inflammatory disease which, inadequately treated by the urinary antibiotic which he had prescribed, later rendered her sterile. At trial, the plaintiff's case was that the combination of abdominal pain, urinary symptoms and cervical tenderness should have made the doctor consider pelvic inflammatory disease as part of a differential diagnosis, even though a urinary infection is a much commoner condition. This thought process should then have made him realise that to ignore the possibility of the serious condition was to expose the patient to the risk of sterility which, in this case, materialised.

(v)   The lack of physical signs as a defence

A physical sign is an abnormal finding that the doctor detects as part of his clinical examination of a patient. The expression is not normally used to include points to which the patient would refer in the account that she gives of her symptoms. It certainly does not include the results of investigations involving the use of special apparatus or the taking of body samples.

For instance, suppose that a woman complains to her general practitioner that she has a lump in the breast. The presence of the lump and whether it was tender would probably be expressed by the patient but the physical signs would include such matters as confirmation of the existence of the lump, the dimensions, the exact position in the breast, whether it was attached to the superficial or deep tissues and whether any glands could be felt in the armpit. Investigations would include points such as the results of a biopsy of the lump or the report of a chest X-ray.

Many conditions are associated with no physical signs at all. Coronary artery disease is a good example. A man of 60 with a history of intermittent chest pains since the previous day may be suffering from indigestion, angina pectoris or myocardial infarction. Examination of pulse, blood pressure, heart and abdomen will probably reveal no abnormality and his general condition may be perfectly satisfactory. The general practitioner faced with such a case may feel he has taken all reasonable steps to exclude an infarct, especially if the patient reassures him that the symptoms have improved somewhat at the time of the consultation. When the wife wakes that night to find her husband dead beside her and the post-mortem reveals a massive clot to have been the cause, she is likely to feel that she has a strong case. The defending general practitioner will argue that there were no physical signs, the patient felt slightly better at the time and, in any case, it would be out of the question to refer every case of chest pain to a cardiologist.

The experts in a case such as this will have to give evidence of opinion as to whether, with the history available to the general practitioner at the time, they would have made specialist referral or perhaps taken some other course of action such as asking the practice nurse to take a cardiograph at the surgery. If they decide that the latter course should have been adopted they will then have to deal with the difficulty of deciding how likely it is that significant changes would have shown on the tracing in the short time that the pain had been present and, if not, whether they would still have made the referral.

It can be seen that the lack of physical signs does not of itself amount to a defence. The test for negligence is whether the whole clinical picture is such that a different course of action should have been taken. This could amount to nothing more than the eliciting of a history that is suggestive of a particular disorder which needs further investigation.

Bova v Spring (1990) provides a useful illustration of a case where the only physical signs the doctor could detect were attributed to a relatively benign diagnosis that had been suggested by the patient himself. He found no signs to suggest a more serious diagnosis, allowed himself to be lulled into a false sense of security, and reassured the patient accordingly. Mr Bova called his general practitioner early one morning with a history of chest pains since lifting a concrete block a week previously. He also mentioned that his chest hurt when he moved and that he had been breathless. Additionally, he had spent the previous day in bed thinking he had a cold and had been shivery in the evening. The doctor found 'exquisite tenderness' of the chest wall but the lungs were clear to examination. He acquiesced with the patient's diagnosis of a muscle strain and dismissed the other symptoms as being caused by a virus infection. He felt it unnecessary to make definite follow-up arrangements. Two days later the patient collapsed and died. A post-mortem showed that he had died of suppurative lobar pneumonia.

In *Bova*'s case the doctor had coupled in his mind the presence of the chest wall tenderness and the lack of lung signs. He had used this thought process to eliminate a serious cause, that of pneumonia. Expert evidence for the plaintiff showed that chest wall tenderness was not necessarily untypical of pleurisy and that signs of pulmonary consolidation may well follow several hours later. In view of this the judge held that the doctor should have visited the patient the next day for review. He found that if this follow-up had been arranged, physical signs in the chest would by then have developed and that prompt treatment would probably have saved the patient's life.

Many serious illnesses, such as ischaemic heart disease, can exist with hardly anything by way of physical signs. *Bova v Spring* shows how the doctor must not allow his mind to be put at rest by signs suggestive of a trivial condition when the history suggests the possibility of a more serious illness.

(vi)   The failure to appreciate the severity of the illness

During the course of a working day, and a night when he is on call, the general practitioner sees a whole range of illnesses. At one end of the scale he will be asked to see children with minor respiratory infections and, at the other end of the scale, will be dealing with cases of cancer and heart disease. Additionally, what is trivial at first may later become serious. Furthermore, serious disease often appears trivial in its early stages.

Many conditions, even serious ones, are accompanied by a paucity of symptoms and signs. We have considered the lack of physical signs as a defence on page 190, but we are here concerned with the situation where the patient presents with symptoms that are not characteristic of a condition which the general practitioner recognises as being amenable to treatment by him. The question then arises of whether the patient should be suspected of harbouring something more serious, and whether specialist referral should be made.

In the Canadian case of *Dale v Munthali* (1977), a general practitioner was asked to visit a man with a fever, aches and pains all over the body, vomiting, diarrhoea and difficulty in hearing. The doctor seemed to take little notice of the hearing difficulties, or at least he had no record of it in his notes when the case later came to trial, and he diagnosed influenza. Two days later the patient was taken to hospital and died of meningitis. The general practitioner was held to have been negligent in not arranging admission at the time of the house visit. Clearly, he had underestimated the severity of the illness. The trial judge accepted the wife's evidence of the pattern of the symptoms, believing that the patient was:

> ... extremely ill and had been for some time. He was so ill that he had been unable to get out of bed to go the bathroom on several occasions. He was so ill that at one time he could not hold a glass of water and he was so ill that he was not answering the questions put to him by the doctor, such questions being answered by his wife.

The judge further remarked that:

> ... with such an ill and confused man I have come to the conclusion that Dr Munthali should have realised that this was something more than gastro-intestinal flu.

Dale v Munthali shows the importance of appreciating the severity of the illness in an emergency situation, even if there is no criticism of the doctor for failing to reach an exact diagnosis. By contrast, we now consider a case where a similar difficulty arose, but with symptoms that developed over an extended period of time. *Gordon v Wilson* (1991) is a useful illustration. In that case, a woman was seen several times by her general practitioners over an eight-month period. She had left-sided deafness and also suffered from giddiness. She later developed visual symptoms and later still complained of abnormal sensations on the left side of her face. She was eventually referred to a specialist for further investigation. She was found to be suffering from a benign meningioma on the surface of the brain and this had started to involve some of the cranial nerves to produce the symptoms. The court held that the practitioners had been negligent in not making earlier referral. They were criticised for failing to appreciate that the pattern of symptoms with which they were being presented was outside their field of expertise and was therefore not amenable to treatment by them.

(vii) Errors of judgment

In Chapter III we saw how the *Bolam* test is used to decide whether a doctor has fallen below an acceptable standard of practice or, in other words, whether he has been negligent. One of the general practitioner's tasks in the management of his patient is to make a clinical assessment of the illness. This is necessary before he can move on to a decision about what treatment is indicated. Part of the assessment process involves judging the importance to be attached to each symptom and physical sign. If, in so doing, the doctor makes a mistake we can say that he made an error of judgment. In addition to mishaps in reaching the diagnosis, errors of judgment can also occur in the treatment. The depth at which an intramuscular injection is given can be misjudged. Similarly, the length of a course of steroid tablets that would be best for the patient could be misjudged and damage could result from an unduly long course. The question will then arise of whether this error of judgment was negligent.

In *Whitehouse v Jordan* (1981), a senior registrar in obstetrics subjected a woman to the trial of delivery by forceps. After exerting traction several times and for a considerable duration he was unable to deliver the child and he proceeded to a Caesarian section. Proper respiration could not be established at birth and the child unfortunately suffered brain damage. When the case came to trial it was held, at first instance, that the obstetrician had been negligent because he had made an error of judgment in pulling too hard on the forceps, and that it was this that had caused the brain damage. The Court of Appeal reversed this finding. Lord Denning expressed the fear that if an error of judgment was equated with negligence:

> ... there would be a danger, in all cases of professional men, of their being made liable whenever something happens to go wrong.

The case then proceeded to the House of Lords, where it was observed that an 'error of judgment' is an ambiguous phrase as far as negligence is concerned. The error may be one that any competent and careful doctor could have made, and in that case it would not have been negligent. Conversely, it might have been an error which could have been avoided if proper care had been exercised, and it would then equate with negligence. The House held that, in this particular case, the obstetrician's error was of the type that could be associated with a proper standard of care and therefore held that the doctor had not been negligent.

It can therefore be seen that the expression 'an error of judgment' needs to be used with great care. When used without qualification it gives no indication about whether the mistake fell within the concept of negligence. It would be essential to know whether the error was within the *Bolam* concept. In other words, we would need to know whether or not it was an error that could have been made by a responsible body of medical opinion.

(viii) Assessing the magnitude of the clinical risk

All doctors take risks with their patients from time to time and it is an important part of the doctor's job to assess the magnitude of each risk. The doctor may become a target for criticism if he underestimates the gravity of a particular risk and cannot later justify subjecting his patient to it.

The concept of risk was considered in relation to consent on page 88. We saw how the doctor must assess the chances of the occurrence of a particular side effect when he considers whether it should be mentioned as part of securing the patient's consent to treatment. The more likely it is to occur, and the more serious it is likely to be, the greater will be the importance of informing the patient. If a serious side effect materialises that has not been mentioned, the patient may argue that his consent was not obtained.

In this section we consider the taking of risks at a later stage in the management of the patient's illness. No doctor can go every step of the way through diagnosis and treatment without taking a risk of some sort. The patient who presents with symptoms of a stomach upset may be in the early stages of gastric cancer but it would be unrealistic to refer every such case for endoscopy. Similarly, the feverish child with an apparent respiratory infection may be incubating meningitis but, again, it would be out of the question to have every such patient admitted to hospital for a lumbar puncture. When deciding to follow the course of action appropriate to a benign and likely clinical condition, rather than to a serious and unlikely one, the practitioner must consider two points:

- what the consequences will be for the patient if the more serious condition of the two turns out to be the cause of the illness; and

- what the cost will be, both in terms of suffering for the patient and resources for the NHS, of putting sufficient investigations in hand to rule out the serious condition.

If cheap, easy steps can be taken to ensure that the condition is innocent and if these will avoid exposing the patient to the risk of undiagnosed serious illness, it clearly follows that they should be taken.

In *Fellows v Thomas* (1994), this very dilemma arose although, in the event, it was not considered by the practitioner at the time of the illness. It was, however, considered by counsel for the plaintiff when the case reached trial. Mr Fellows, complaining of headaches, had been seen by his general practitioner. It was alleged on behalf of the plaintiff that the history was suggestive of a subarachnoid haemorrhage, but this was strongly resisted by the defence. The defending general practitioner, under cross-examination, insisted that he was given a history of the headaches being like a tight band around the head and, as such, would have been infinitely more suggestive of a virus infection, or even stress. Counsel for Mr Fellows put it to the doctor that the consequences of failing to diagnose a subarachnoid haemorrhage would have been catastrophic, and yet the price of excluding the possibility was relatively low. Attendance at hospital for a brain scan would be all that was required, with the possible addition of a lumbar puncture. Counsel put it that this was a small price to pay to avoid possible death or serious disability.

As increasingly sophisticated tests become available to detect serious disease, doctors may find themselves under ever more pressure to order the appropriate investigations. Against this, however, we have to bear in mind that the tests are becoming more expensive and that every pound spent in excluding a potential illness is a pound that becomes unavailable for the treatment of actual illness.

(ix)   The failure to reassess the diagnosis

Many patients seen by general practitioners are suffering from ailments of a fairly trivial nature. Of those who are suffering from more serious conditions, the majority can be investigated and treated by the general practitioner himself. This leaves an even smaller number who will need specialist referral by way of hospital admission or out-patient appointment.

Many serious conditions mimic trivial ones in their early stages. The presenting symptoms of a patient with lung cancer might be nothing more than an irritating cough which is indistinguishable from one caused by an innocent respiratory infection. The patient may appear fairly well at this stage and the chest may be clear on examination. The doctor therefore treats the matter as being infective, partly at least on the basis that this is a much commoner explanation for the symptoms. Provided the doctor had taken a proper history and carried out a proper examination, no one could blame him for that. It would be out of the question to refer every patient with a cough for an X-ray or clinic appointment when the symptoms had only been present for a day or two and there was nothing else to suggest sinister disease.

197

General practitioners are in a unique position to observe their patients over a period of time. The proximity of the surgery office to the patient's house, and the flexibility of the arrangements for seeing patients by appointment or as an emergency, make it much easier to keep a patient under close review than is the case with a hospital outpatient system. The general practitioner can easily arrange to revisit the house later or ask the patient to re-attend the surgery the next day.

If the patient with the apparently innocent respiratory infection starts to cough up blood, to become hoarse or to lose weight, the competent general practitioner will immediately suspect underlying disease and arrange for further investigation or specialist referral. The difficulty tends to arise when the patient fails to improve in the anticipated period of time and yet the symptoms do not change or become any more extensive such as to make the doctor suspect that the original diagnosis might not have been correct.

Clearly, a patient whose symptoms continue longer than expected should be reassessed at appropriate intervals. In one case, a teenage boy was seen with mild abdominal pain and vomiting which had started the previous evening. When the doctor visited he found no abnormality on detailed examination and diagnosed gastric flu. Over the next two days, the patient's mother telephoned the surgery three more times about continuing symptoms but, under pressure from the doctor, admitted that no new features had developed as far as she could tell. She was forced to be content with reassurance. When she telephoned again at the weekend, the trainee doctor visited and found that the boy had marked abdominal tenderness, a rapid pulse and a furred tongue. He suspected appendicitis and arranged immediate admission. At operation, the diagnosis was confirmed, but the organ had unfortunately perforated. Evidence for the plaintiff showed that, if he had been seen for assessment following one of the telephone calls, sufficient abdominal tenderness would probably have been found to have prompted a suspicion of appendicitis and that admission would therefore have been arranged early enough to have avoided the perforation.

The doctor must also be on his guard to reconsider the diagnosis with the passage of time even if no new features appear by way of either points in the history or physical signs on examination. In *Langley v Campbell* (1975), a man was seen by his general practitioner after having been unwell since the previous day. Influenza was diagnosed on the basis that his symptoms amounted to fever, headache, sweating and shivering. The symptoms failed to improve over the next few days and the doctor was called again on the fourth, the sixth and the eighth days of the illness. He persisted with the same diagnosis and reassured the patient accordingly. On the day after the general practitioner's last visit, the family called another doctor who arranged hospital admission. Malaria was diagnosed, but the patient unfortunately died two days later. At trial, evidence of fact showed that the family had told the general practitioner that the patient had recently returned from Uganda, and also that he had had malaria in the past. The plaintiff advanced the case on the basis that, in the absence of complications, a patient with influenza can be expected to start making a recovery in three or four days. The court held that the doctor was negligent in failing to realise that the illness might amount to some as-yet-undiagnosed disease more serious than influenza. He was not negligent in failing to diagnose malaria, but he was negligent in not being suspicious of serious disease when the pattern of his patient's history deviated markedly from that of the initial diagnosis.

We have seen how doctors must keep the diagnosis under review with the passage of time. Plaintiffs suing their doctors in general practice often have great difficulty demonstrating negligence in the early stages. This is because the diagnosis of a trivial illness is often perfectly reasonable when the symptoms have only been present for a short time. The plaintiff's case is likely to become stronger at each successive visit by the doctor, because the physical signs will probably have become more marked and the history will be of longer duration. Both of these points will militate against the initial diagnosis and will tend to suggest that the failure to revise it was negligent. Clearly, if the plaintiff can show that abnormal signs were probably present at a certain point it will be easier for him to demonstrate liability if the doctor failed to examine him. However, *Langley v Campbell* has shown that the mere persistence of symptoms, without abnormal physical signs, may be enough to show negligence.

It can be tempting for a doctor to allow himself to be reassured by a lack of physical signs when deciding whether a patient should be recalled for review at a later date. In the majority of cases in general practice the diagnosis is relatively trivial, there are no signs and the patient merely wants reassurance. However, the need to reassess the diagnosis is not dictated by the nature of the physical signs alone. The history is of the utmost importance and this was well illustrated in *Bova v Spring* (1990), where the only sign present was interpreted as being caused by a relatively innocent condition.

In *Bova's* case, a man was seen by his general practitioner complaining of chest pains, breathlessness and a cold. The only abnormal sign was tenderness of the chest wall and this was attributed to his having strained that part of the body when lifting a concrete block a week previously. The lungs were clear and the doctor therefore felt that no reassessment was necessary. Unfortunately, two days later the patient collapsed and died of suppurative lobar pneumonia. After hearing expert evidence for the plaintiff the judge found that tenderness of the chest wall was compatible with pleurisy. This point, coupled with the history, should have made the doctor realise the possibility of impending pneumonia, even though the lungs were clear at that stage. The judge held that the practitioner had been negligent in not visiting the patient the next day to reassess the diagnosis. He added that if review had been undertaken the chest signs would probably have developed by then and that prompt treatment would probably have saved the patient's life.

(x) Acquiescing with the diagnosis suggested by the patient

The general practitioner sees many cases where the patient already has a fair idea of what is wrong with him. He may have suffered from the condition before, or may have spoken to others who have had similar symptoms in the past. Indeed, the patient may have experienced some incident which fixes the explanation for the symptoms in his mind. For instance, an injury may have been followed by pain or he may have been in contact with an infectious disease that affected some other person in the same way.

Any of these points can lead the patient to offer the doctor an explanation. This can be prompted by a genuine desire to help the doctor with his assessment, but there may be a subconscious motive as well. The diagnosis offered by the patient is usually a fairly benign one, and the patient hopes that the doctor will confirm it, thereby eliminating the patient's fear of something worse.

The patient with persistent headaches and who fears cancer may suggest to the doctor that she needs help with her migraine. The doctor carries out a detailed examination, finds nothing abnormal and acquiesces with the diagnosis. He then issues repeat prescriptions for relevant medication over a period of time. If the symptoms had been unremitting and were accompanied by a persistent visual defect, the question would arise of whether the general practitioner should have challenged the patient's diagnosis, suspected a cerebral tumour and kept her under review.

Heart disease is another area where patients very often have their own preconceived diagnosis. They attribute the pain in the upper abdomen, as it spreads up towards the chest and throat, to indigestion. Indeed, they have every reason to hope that this is the correct explanation, because it will be easy for the doctor to treat and it will not pose any undue threat to their health in the long term. All general practitioners know that this pattern of symptoms can be suggestive of ischaemic heart disease, and good practice dictates that, in certain circumstances, the patient's explanation should not be accepted without question, and referral to a cardiologist should be made.

In one case, an elderly man had strained his chest while struggling to loosen the inaccessible sump plug on his boat engine. He had also felt sick and he complained to his doctor of acid in the stomach. The doctor found little abnormal on examination and acquiesced with this diagnosis. Two days later the supposed indigestion became much worse and the patient had to be admitted to hospital. Investigation showed that he was suffering from angina and the question then arose of whether the doctor should have been less ready to accept the explanation that he was offered.

In *Bova v Spring* (1990), this very situation arose, and the case reached trial. It was concerned with respiratory disease rather than heart disease, but the same principle applies. A man in his forties found that he had to strain to lift a concrete block and he developed chest pains. A week later he called the doctor because he was no better. He had also developed breathlessness with a cold and he had felt shivery. The general practitioner found tenderness in the chest wall at the site of the supposed strain, but noted that the lungs were clear. This led him to agree with the patient's explanation for the pain, and he assumed that a virus infection had caused the additional symptoms. No review or further investigation were thought to be necessary, but unfortunately the patient collapsed and died two days later. A post-mortem showed that suppurative lobar pneumonia had been the underlying illness.

Peter Bova's widow sued the doctor successfully on the basis that the pattern of symptoms, even without abnormal signs in the lungs, should have been sufficient to have made him suspect that the patient's own explanation of a muscular strain might not have been correct. He should have reviewed her husband's condition the next day, in case pneumonia was the true explanation. The judge was able to add that if such a review had been undertaken there would probably have been detectable signs in the chest at that later stage and that prompt treatment would probably have saved the man's life.

The judgment in *Bova v Spring* neatly summarised the danger for doctors who acquiesce with their patients' ideas in terms that:

> The fact that patients tended to ascribe their problem to something which they themselves can identify was further reason for caution on Dr Spring's part. The impression from his evidence was that he was very ready to put the chest pain down to the cause suggested by the patient.

As if to emphasise the point the judge added that:

> Accordingly, it was incumbent upon Dr Spring to be more circumspect than he was in eliminating other possible causes of the chest condition.

(xi) Reliance on specialist advice

All professional men have to work in collaboration with specialist colleagues, and the medical profession is no exception. The general practitioner refers some of his patients to hospital consultants, and the specialists themselves refer their patients to consultants in related specialities. The analogy readily comes to mind of the solicitor who sends a client's papers for counsel's opinion.

We are here concerned with the difficulty that arises when the specialist's advice is negligent but the professional who made the referral relied on it.[34]

It is reasonable to assume that there must be a strong presumption in favour of reliance. The system of referral would otherwise be unworkable and would undermine confidence between colleagues. Indeed, the very reason for the referral is that the person requesting the advice has good reason to believe that the specialist has superior knowledge in that particular area. This means that it would be difficult to challenge the opinion given, and an aggrieved patient will only be able to say that the reliance was negligent in exceptional circumstances.

Two cases illustrate this difficulty very well. One concerned a general practitioner who sent his patient for a chest X-ray to exclude serious disease when her attacks of bronchitis seemed to be unduly frequent. The report was negative, but the woman was later found to have developed lung cancer. Expert radiological opinion for the plaintiff showed that the film had been reported negligently and the question arose of whether the general practitioner was negligent to rely on it.

In the other case, a hockey player was taken to an accident and emergency department after a head injury on the field. He was considered to be suffering from concussion and was discharged, with a note to that effect, to his family doctor. Again, the general practitioner relied on the reassuring report when he

---

[34] For an example of a general dental practitioner who relied on the advice of a consultant and who was sued for negligently following the specialist's advice, see Ryan in *J Med Def Union* 1993, no 4 (pp 86-87).

was called to the house later that evening. Two days later the patient lapsed into unconsciousness and the family called an ambulance. An X-ray on hospital admission revealed a fracture on the base of the skull and the patient survived for only a matter of hours. Although the case was advanced primarily against the hospital, the statement of claim asserted that the general practitioner had placed undue reliance on the negligent accident and emergency report.

Having seen how there must be a presumption in favour of reliance, it would be as well to make an attempt at defining the categories into which a case must fall before that presumption can be rebutted. We can put it in terms of the family doctor who will have difficulty in justifying his reliance where:

(a) there is some obvious mistake or omission in the hospital report; or

(b) the patient gives a history of some new or exaggerated symptom since the report was made; or

(c) the practitioner himself finds some new or exaggerated sign on examination which shows that the suspected underlying disease process may be changing; or

(d) the report is so old that the practitioner, bearing in mind the known natural history of the suspected disease process, should realise that he can no longer rely on the report.

(xii) The importance of proper communications

No doctor in the UK can work in isolation. He has to co-operate with colleagues over the management of some of his patients. In general practice this is seen in its most obvious form when the doctor refers a case to a hospital consultant for a specialist opinion. Frequently this is arranged by way of out-patient clinic appointment or hospital admission. Good practice dictates that a referral letter should be written to ensure that the specialist is put in possession of all the relevant facts. It is inadequate to leave the patient with the task of conveying the information. If the patient is incapable of giving any history to the specialist, for instance because he is unconscious, the referral letter becomes particularly important. Nevertheless, it is important to attend to the matter of communication even with a coherent and conscious patient because the family doctor may know of some relevant point about which the specialist is unlikely to inquire. Additionally, the results of tests taken by the general practitioner may have become available and these will put the specialist to a distinct advantage when he first meets the patient.

A referral letter will assume even greater importance and be of more value to the specialist if the patient has been under the general practitioner's supervision for some time. That doctor should be able to put the specialist in a favourable position to take over the patient's care by giving a good account of how the illness has developed so far and what treatment has already been given.

Communications between doctors can be by way of letter or telephone call, but the latter is usually supported by the former. The question of whether or not the substance of the letter conforms to an acceptable standard would be decided according to the *Bolam* principle, which is discussed on pages 19-24.

If a form of communication is found to be negligent, for instance by the failure to include certain material facts, the question of causation will arise. This will concern how likely it is that the harm the patient suffered would have occurred if those points had not been omitted. The patient's advisers will want to know whether the hospital treatment would have been different, and would have had a better outcome, if the family doctor had written a proper letter and put the hospital staff on notice of everything that was relevant.

In *Coles v Reading and District HMC* (1963) a man with a finger injury attended a cottage hospital and had the injury dressed by the nurse. He was told that he should attend at another hospital for further treatment later the same day. For some reason, he did not follow this advice but instead attended his general practitioner's surgery some days later. The general practitioner had no letter or other communication from the cottage hospital. He did not ask the patient about details of his earlier treatment and merely renewed the dressing. Not long afterwards the patient died of tetanus infection which had entered the wound at the time of the injury. His father sued the cottage hospital and the general practitioner. It was held that the staff at the cottage hospital had been negligent in not providing the patient with a letter to the second hospital explaining what they had done and that the tetanus immunisation had not been given. Had they done so, the patient would probably have attended the second hospital and received the immunisation there. Alternatively, his general practitioner would probably have given him the injection when the patient visited the surgery. In either event, the patient would probably have survived.

The need for proper communications between different doctors working on the same case was also well illustrated in *Chapman v Rix* (1960). In that case, a butcher suffered an accidental knife wound to the abdomen when the point slipped off a joint of meat in the shop. He was treated initially by one Dr Rix at a cottage hospital, who thought that the wound was 'superficial'. He gave the patient a description of the injury in these terms and asked him to convey this information to Dr Mohr, his own general practitioner. Dr Mohr was understandably reassured by the patient's verbal account. Continuing symptoms of abdominal pain caused Dr Mohr to arrange readmission only after the patient's condition had markedly deteriorated two days later. At laparotomy the bowel was found to have been punctured by the original knife wound, and the patient unfortunately died a week later.

The case came to trial and at first instance Dr Rix was held to have been negligent in failing to write a letter to, or otherwise to communicate directly with, Dr Mohr so as to put him in possession of all the relevant facts. The Court of Appeal reversed this finding, and the case then came before the House of Lords. One of their Lordships considered what the outcome would have been if the patient had been under the care of either Dr Rix or of Dr Mohr throughout the whole period of time. He observed that:

> The fact is that Chapman fell between two stools and that this was due chiefly to failure of communication.

In the event, the House of Lords upheld the Court of Appeal's decision to exonerate Dr Rix despite the latter's reliance on the patient to convey the information. It was Lord Denning, dissenting, who focused on the very important distinction between what the first doctor sees fit to tell the patient and what he considers the second doctor needs to know. The patient may well need some reassurance and it will, in any case, be quite inappropriate to burden him with technical explanations. The second doctor, on the other hand, needs full details of the first one's management of the case so that he can take over the treatment and avoid lapses of the kind that occurred in *Coles* and in *Chapman*.

The alleged negligence in *Chapman* occurred nearly 40 years ago but it is probably even more important now for doctors to be assiduous in writing letters to colleagues. The plethora of technical investigations and sophisticated treatments currently available mean that there is even more opportunity for the patient to suffer as a result of poor communication between doctors.

(xiii) Contributory negligence

Until recently this concept was, and many would say still is, irrelevant to medical negligence. However, with patients expecting to play at least some part in the management of their health care, the question naturally arises of whether they can be held liable for part of their own damage. This will be of particular interest to a defending doctor who feels that his patient has not co-operated with the treatment. This could take the form of non-compliance with a course of medication, refusal to consent to investigation or failure to attend for follow-up.

Contributory negligence is a well-established rule of law (Law Reform (Contributory Negligence) Act 1945), whereby a victim of negligence will have any damages proportionately reduced if it is considered that he was partly to blame. In *Froom v Butcher* (1976), a motorist sued another driver successfully for being 100% to blame for causing an accident, but had his compensation reduced to 75% because he was held to be 25% responsible for his injuries by not wearing a seat belt. In this case, both drivers had contributed, in their different ways, to the injury. One driver had made his contribution by failing to drive carefully, and the other had made his contribution by failing to wear his seat belt.

In a medical context, this duty of care is traditionally considered to have been one-sided. The doctor owes it to the patient, but the latter cannot be expected to contribute to decisions regarding his treatment. The distinction between these two situations is that all motorists should be aware of danger on the road but patients, unlike doctors, cannot be expected to know the dangers involved in the mismanagement of health care. For this reason, the defence of contributory negligence has not generally been available to doctors in Britain who are being sued by patients.

In Canada, however, this defence has been tried twice, once with success and once without. In the successful case, *Bernier v Sisters of Service (St John's Hospital, Edson)* (1948), an anaesthetised patient, following an operation for the removal of her appendix, suffered severe burns to her feet from hot water bottles placed there by a nurse. The hospital argued that the burns were partly the patient's own fault because she had failed to notify the staff, on admission, that she suffered from impaired sensation of the feet. The judge disallowed this defence because she could not have been expected to foresee that this failure on her part would result in any harm to her when the reason for her admission had been to have her appendix removed.

By contrast, in *Crossman v Stewart* (1977), a patient went almost blind from chloroquine retinopathy when the drug had been prescribed for a skin disorder. The patient had her damages reduced by one-third because she obtained some of her supplies from a source unknown to the doctor, and the judge considered that she should have realised that this might be putting her own health at risk.

As a general rule at the time of writing, therefore, it would seem that any doctor who wishes to invoke the doctrine of contributory negligence to reduce the damages payable to his patient must not only show that the patient failed to look after herself, but also that she ought to have realised that this failure might result in harm.

A more recent UK case which settled in the plaintiff's favour provides us with a useful illustration. A man consulted his general practitioner several times with a history of headaches, low backache and recurrent fevers. Eventually he was referred to a hospital clinic where an acute prolapsed intervertebral disc was diagnosed, some tests were taken, and follow up was arranged for several weeks later. The patient was dissatisfied with the visit and failed to re-attend. At the time of his intended follow-up, his notes were filed away without it being noticed by the clinician that the earlier tests had shown abnormalities on blood testing and on X-ray. Some time later the patient returned to his general practitioner to declare his dissatisfaction and to complain of continuing symptoms. He was eventually referred to another hospital and was then diagnosed as suffering from tuberculosis of the lumbar spine. He sought to sue the first hospital on the basis that he should have been notified of the abnormalities which had been found, and that, if he had been so notified, treatment could have been started earlier and that he would have been more likely to have achieved a cure. The hospital argued that the patient had been contributorily negligent because he had failed to heed their advice to re-attend the clinic for his results, and that if he had done so the abnormalities would have been followed up at that stage. The patient countered this argument on the basis that, although he had failed to re-attend, he could not have foreseen the harm because the hospital doctor had reassured him that he only had a slipped disc.

In another case, an elderly man was admitted to hospital for abdominal surgery. The operation was followed by emboli in the arteries to one leg and steps were taken to deal with the matter. The patient was then discharged from hospital but later had to be readmitted with severe ischaemic symptoms in the limb. Further investigation showed that amputation below the knee was unavoidable, and the patient sued the hospital for negligence in allowing the emboli to have occurred at the time of the original operation. When a defence was served on the plaintiff it pleaded contributory negligence and pointed to the plaintiff's history of heavy smoking. It was argued that he had been advised frequently in the past to stop smoking and that he knew of the dangers. The defendant's case was that the blood vessels of the lower limbs would have been less severely affected by arteriosclerosis if the patient had heeded the advice to stop smoking, and that the emboli would have been less likely to have occurred.

Most patients who are advised by their doctor to see a specialist are only too keen to pursue the recommendation. In *Richardson v Kitching* (1995), there was an entry in the general practitioner's notes to the effect that the patient, who later died, was to be referred to an ear, nose and throat specialist to investigate deafness. In the event, the referral was not arranged until much later and the family asserted that the delay had been caused by the doctor forgetting to write the letter. This was resisted by the defendant, on the basis that the patient had refused the referral and that there had therefore been been no negligence in failing to arrange a hospital appointment. Counsel for the defendant referred to an earlier note in the records from which it was possible to infer that the deceased was a very ambitious man whose livelihood depended on being able to drive tens of thousands of miles each year. He used this entry to suggest that the fear of losing his driving licence, especially when the hearing loss was later found to be coupled with giddiness, meant that the deceased probably had refused the referral.

(xiv) Consent

When used in a medical context, the word 'consent' has a more precise meaning than in ordinary English usage. A patient must do more than merely agree to proceed with the treatment, she must agree to run the risks of its adverse effects. The failure to warn the patient about a side effect which later materialises is a common cause of complaint. Patients now feel they should be given all information relevant to their illnesses, to enable them to decide whether to go ahead with the treatment. In days gone by patients were usually content to leave all the decision-making to the doctor, as they felt that he was much better placed than them to advise.

All medical treatments are associated with the risk of a side effect, however trivial and however rare. Even an aspirin tablet can induce a minute amount of gastric bleeding. Cytotoxic drugs, used in the treatment of cancer and related conditions, can cause hair loss, and vomiting of the most unpleasant proportions.

There are all sorts of reasons why doctors sometimes fail to tell patients as much as they think they should be told. Probably the commonest reason is the sheer pressure of time, and there is more to the task than merely mentioning it. It needs an explanation to put it in perspective and it may raise other issues about which the patient wants to enter into a prolonged discussion.

Whenever a treatment is proposed, the question always arises of how much information the patient should be given. On the one hand, if she is told too little, she may agree to treatment to which she would otherwise not have submitted herself. In this case, she may have a case against the doctor for failure to obtain her consent. On the other hand, if she is told too much and warned of every side effect that has been known to occur, she may be too frightened to accept the treatment when, in reality, it would have been in her best interests to accept a minimal risk. Thus a balance has to be struck between the two.

This dilemma was considered in *Sidaway v Board of Governors of Bethlem Royal Hospital and the Maudsley Hospital* (1985). In that case, a woman underwent an operation to relieve pressure on a spinal nerve root in the neck which was causing pain in the arm. Unfortunately, some damage to her spinal cord occurred, and this was followed by a disability. She had no case against the surgeon for negligence in his operative technique, but she sued him on the basis that he had failed to warn her that this damage might occur. The evidence of the expert witnesses for the defence showed that the chances of this particular type of damage occurring were very rare and that it was generally accepted practice not to alarm patients about it. In *Sidaway*, it was held that a doctor should give warnings about all risks which would be disclosed by a responsible body of medical opinion, but that he need go no further than this. It was emphasised that the criteria for informed consent were in line with the principle enunciated in *Bolam v Friern Hospital Management Committee* (1957). In that case the standard of care as regards treatment itself had to be such as would be approved by a responsible body of medical opinion to avoid a finding of negligence.

The implication of the test in *Sidaway* and the alternative tests used in the American cases of *Canterbury v Spence* (1972) and in the Australian case of *Rogers v Whitaker* (1992) are discussed in some detail in Chapter XVI.

(xv)   The risk of side effects

We saw in the previous section that a complaint can arise when a patient suffers from a side effect of which she has not been warned, and of which she thinks she should have been advised. We also considered the rules used in deciding whether a warning should be given.

We are here concerned with the question of whether, quite apart from consent, the doctor should expose his patient to the risk at all. The concept of risk was discussed in *Bolton v Stone* (1951). That was a games case rather than a medical negligence case. The defendant, a cricket batsman, had hit the ball over a high fence at the edge of the ground and it struck the plaintiff, causing injury. Counsel for the defence gave various reasons why the taking of the risk was reasonable. One was that a ball had only been hit out of the ground six times in the preceding 20 years and another was that the ground had a perimeter fence seven feet high. These points helped the defendant's case that the risk of any harm occurring was so low that he was justified in taking it.

In medical treatment, the two main criteria to be considered when exposing the patient to a risk are:

(a) how likely is the side effect to occur?

(b) if it does occur, how serious will it be?

Clearly, the risk is at its most acceptable when the side effect is rare and trivial, and is at its least acceptable when it is common and serious. The difficulty tends to arise when it is common and trivial, or when it is rare and serious. Doubtless, the side effect in *Sidaway* was thought to fall into the last category, although that case was concerned with consent in relation to risk.

Before leaving the question of whether a risk should be taken, it is worth mentioning that an otherwise unacceptable risk may be justified if the patient is given sufficient information to be able to prevent it from materialising. For example, a woman has a suspected deep vein thrombosis and the doctor decides that she should be treated with anticoagulants to prevent a recurrence. The diagnosis is uncertain and the side effects are potentially very serious, in that the treatment could cause a brain haemorrhage.

The doctor warns the woman that bleeding is a sign of overdose, and that one of the first signs is blood-stained urine, which is relatively harmless. This makes the risk much more acceptable because it gives the patient the opportunity of avoiding the damage by reducing the dose of anticoagulant in good time.

XX   LAPSE OF FOLLOW UP

SUMMARY

(i)   Introduction

All general practitioners are concerned with making proper arrangements for the follow-up of potentially serious conditions.

Examples abound of alleged negligent follow-up in general practice, but we can cite the woman with the apparently innocent breast lump who is advised to return a fortnight later, fails to do so, and then arrives a year after that with an obvious cancer. We are not concerned in this discussion with liability for failure to refer the patient to a specialist when she originally attended or even for failure to invite her to return. Rather, we are concerned with liability for failing to recall her when she later forgets the original invitation. The difficulty, of course, is to decide in which cases it is the doctor's fault for not recalling the patient, and in which cases it is the patient's fault for forgetting the doctor's original advice.

There are many reasons why patients fail to re-attend after the allotted interval. It may be nothing more than forgetfulness. Alternatively, it may be the fear that the doctor will confirm their worst suspicions. Yet again, it may be that they think the original symptom has improved and they do not want to waste the doctor's (or their own) time.

We can now consider the general practitioner's duty for follow-up in relation to symptoms with which he is presented and in relation to the screening of apparently healthy individuals.

(ii)   Screening of healthy individuals

Organised screening of asymptomatic men and women has been with us for many years, but it received fresh impetus from the introduction of Kenneth Clarke's New Contract in April 1990. This gave doctors additional remuneration for carrying out the programmes or, put another way, they were penalised if they failed to reach their targets. This penalty was accentuated by, for example, a small lump sum payment for taking cervical smears from 50% of the eligible practice population, and a much larger payment (three times as great) for reaching the 80% level. This contrasted with the earlier 'item or service' system, by which a fee was payable for every smear taken.

If a patient feels perfectly well, attends for a smear test and then hears nothing more, there is a great temptation for her to assume that 'no news is good news'. However, this is one area of follow-up where we can be quite definite that it is the doctor's duty to take reasonable steps to inform the patient of an adverse result. It is not sufficient to file the result away and hope that the patient will remember to ask. The usual procedure is for the doctor, or his staff, to write to the patient or telephone her about it if she fails to make contact. Until recently, this meant meticulous and tedious record keeping, but it should now be relatively easy in computerised offices.

The next difficulty is when the patient fails to respond because, for example, the doctor's recall letter went astray in the post, or because the patient had moved to a different address and the letter was never forwarded. Virtually all doctors would accept that it is reasonable to make a second attempt at contacting the patient, but if even this fails it becomes increasingly difficult to show that the general practitioner has been negligent if he makes no further effort. Nevertheless, allowance would have to be made for the severity of the lesion. For example, a smear reported as 'dyskaryosis, suggest repeat in one year' would not demand such exhaustive efforts at recall as one which was reported as 'carcinoma in situ'.

So far, we have considered follow-up duty in relation to cancer smears, but the same general remarks apply to other screening. Thus, if a man is found to have a raised cholesterol on blood testing, it is the doctor's duty to inform him of the result and call him if he forgets to attend to the matter himself. There should be no difficulty in coming to terms with this from a legal point of view because it is foreseeable that the patient's failure to re-attend, and his lack of subsequent treatment, might have an adverse effect on his health. Indeed, this is the reason for the screening itself.

(iii)   Symptomatic patients

We now come to the more difficult situation, when a patient attends for reassurance about, for example, a painless lump. The doctor thinks that it is probably innocent but wants to check it again a month later because of the remote possibility of malignancy. The doctor may see fit not to tell the patient the full implications of failure to re-attend because it will only cause anxiety in the meantime. Clearly, this will depend very much on the patient and how much the doctor thinks it is wise to say. There can be no doubt that many patients, if told that there is the remotest chance of cancer, will insist on immediate specialist referral.

At risk of making a controversial and arbitrary distinction, we can suggest that a fair division of the onus for follow-up by doctor or patient can be made as follows:

(a) The responsibility lies with the doctor for recalling a patient who fails to re-attend if the doctor has, for some good reason, not told the patient that the condition may be serious and that harm could result if the matter is not followed up. This would occur typically in the patient who attends with influenza and is found to have a rather high erythrocyte sedimentation rate (a general screening test for a wide range of illnesses) on blood testing. The doctor thinks it is probably no more than a manifestation of the illness that has already been diagnosed, but is aware of the possibility that it might signify underlying malignancy. The doctor will probably advise repeating the ESR in a fortnight 'to be on the safe side', which leaves the patient with the impression that it is being done for no reason other than to ensure that the flu has cleared. It is suggested that in this type of case the onus is on the doctor to make a forward note to call the patient if he defaults.

(b) Conversely, the responsibility for ensuring that a follow-up appointment is made lies with the patient if she has been told that failure to attend could have serious consequences. This would occur typically where a diabetic patient attended with a potentially gangrenous toe. If he has been told that the lesion should be treated carefully to avoid risking loss of the digit, and he fails to re-attend, it is difficult to attach blame to the doctor for not recalling him. There may well be a 'policy argument' here, on the basis that it is unrealistic to expect doctors to have an active recall system for every patient whom they need to see again. Additionally, patients must take at least some responsibility for their own health.

(iv) Comparison between follow-up expectations in screening and in the investigation of illness

We have seen how the duty expected of a doctor to follow up an adverse screening result in an asymptomatic patient can be very much more onerous than when he is dealing with an ill patient. This naturally leads us to the question as to why there should be any difference.

There are at least three reasons for expecting the doctor to play a more active part in the former category:

(a) a patient who has merely been screened has no symptoms to remind him of the need to return for the result;

(b) a screened patient is far less likely to have an adverse result because he is drawn from a large pool of healthy people, who are likely to have normal results;

(c) a screened patient is likely to have to wait a relatively long time for his test to need repeating and he may well forget in the meantime. Conversely, a sick patient knows he is likely to need further investigation or referral quite soon, and this gives him less opportunity to forget.

These points show that the clinical background against which the test is ordered is of the utmost importance in deciding whether the onus of follow-up falls on the doctor or the patient.

(v) The question of identifying the doctor responsible for follow-up

We are here concerned with the situation where a patient attends a hospital clinic which orders a test, asks for a copy to be sent to the general practitioner, and invites the patient to re-attend for follow-up. The result of the test is abnormal, the patient defaults on his hospital appointment and no further action is taken. Here, the hospital may seek to blame the general practitioner on the basis that he had been notified about the abnormality and it was easier for him to trace the patient. This can also happen during screening, for example when a family planning clinic takes a smear, obtains an abnormal result and the patient then fails to telephone for it. It is virtually standard practice for these clinics to have results sent to the general practitioner who is then sometimes blamed for not acting on it.

The rule for resolving this kind of difficulty is based on the generally-accepted premise that the responsibility for the follow-up of a test falls on the person who orders it.

If, for some reason, the doctor who orders the test is unable to act on the result (for instance, because he is going on holiday) he must take positive action to shift the onus. For example, a general practitioner who takes a blood sample on a Friday must tell his partner to review the result the following week if the first general practitioner will be absent. Needless to say, the patient should also be told of the arrangement so that he knows whom to contact.

(vi) The implications for causation

So far, we have considered negligence in terms of whether a lapse of follow-up is the responsibility of the doctor who orders the test, of some other doctor, or even of the patient himself.

However, an assessment of causation will also be needed. How much difference would it have made if the lapse had been avoided? To this author's knowledge, there is no decided case on the point but reliance will probably be placed on the principle in *Hotson v E Berks HA* (1987), where the plaintiff was faced with admitting that, even if his hip had been X-rayed, he would have had no better than a 25% chance of recovery.

The medical experts will therefore have to estimate what the patient's outlook would have been if the abnormal result had been followed up promptly compared to the outlook which, with the delayed follow-up, the patient in fact had. If we look back to the example cited at the beginning of this section, we will be concerned with comparing the woman's outlook with early referral for a suspicious breast lump compared to the outcome of referral a year later. To formulate the claim, counsel will want the experts to consider two aspects. First, the question will arise of whether prompt attention would have altered the treatment in the short term. In our example, would such matters as an operation, radiotherapy and chemotherapy still have been necessary? Secondly, there will be the question of prognosis. If the patient had received prompt attention, would her prognosis have been better? On the basis of *Hotson* would she have stood a 51% chance of surviving for more than a certain length of time?

(vii) Summary

We have considered negligence and causation in cases where an intended follow-up has lapsed. To assess the merits of the case, and to enable the statement of claim to be drafted, the plaintiff's advisers will have to take into account the amount of information that was imparted to her when the test was taken and the clinical background to the case generally. They will then have to estimate the difference in outcome for both treatment and prognosis between the management that should have been instituted promptly and that which was actually given too late.

XXI THE SOURCES OF EVIDENCE OF FACT

(i) Introduction

All cases are dependent on the weight of their evidence for a successful outcome. A patient has to do more than merely show that the course of treatment the doctor is alleged to have followed was of a poor standard. The patient has to convince the court that her version of events is correct. If that version makes it difficult for the doctor to defend his position with regard to the care he gave, he may be able to overcome the difficulty by showing that the patient's version of the story is erroneous, and that the doctor's version is the correct one.

We must remind ourselves that in civil, as opposed to criminal, cases the rules of evidence are such that the patient has the burden of proof and that the case will be decided on the balance of probabilities. This means that the patient's advisers will want to assess whether their client is capable of sustaining the burden of proof, and they will also want to assess the chances of the court accepting it as probably being correct. Let us now consider these two points in more detail.

223

(ii)   The burden of proof

All medical negligence cases concern various questions of fact. They are concerned with points such as whether the patient was visited by the doctor on the day in question, what history the patient gave, what examination was carried out and what tests were ordered. When we say that the patient bears the burden of proof we mean that she has the task of convincing the court that her version of the relevant facts is the correct one. The converse does not apply. Thus the doctor does not have to produce an acceptable alternative to defend himself although to do so would clearly strengthen his case. The doctor need do no more than to undermine his opponent's version sufficiently to prevent it from being accepted.

Let us consider a case to illustrate the point. Suppose that a man died from asphyxia caused by laryngeal obstruction three hours after an antibiotic had been prescribed over the telephone by the general practitioner. The widow wants to sue the doctor on the basis that her husband had complained of having difficulty in breathing, of having difficulty in swallowing, of having a sore throat and of being unable to speak. She argues that with this history the doctor should have visited the patient, and that if he had so visited he would have arranged hospital admission. She will find it relatively easy to show that, if her husband had been admitted, a tracheotomy would have been performed and that his life would have been saved. This version of events makes it difficult for the doctor to defend his position on the standard of care he gave. He therefore has two options:

(a) he can produce his own evidence that the patient complained of nothing more than a sore throat, for instance, by showing that his detailed notes made at the time of the telephone conversation recorded the absence of the other symptoms;

(b) alternatively, he can ask the court not to believe the widow's story about the difficulty in breathing. If the events had taken place many years previously and if he can show that the widow has a poor memory he might well succeed in showing that there was little chance of the widow's version being true.

In summary, the onus is on the patient to present a credible story that is favourable to her case, or her action will fail. The doctor does not have to produce an alternative explanation to be able to defend himself.

(iii) The standard of proof

The expression 'beyond reasonable doubt' will be familiar to lay people as representing the standard of proof required in the evidence before an accused can be convicted and punished for committing a crime. Put another way, this means that the evidence must be sufficiently convincing to make it virtually certain that the subject really *is* guilty. In criminal cases, the dispute is between the whole State (in name 'the Queen') and the individual.

Conversely, in a medical negligence case, the two parties are individuals, doctor and patient, competing on more even terms. One or the other will win the case. They cannot both be right. Against this background a different standard of proof is adopted. It is on a 'balance of probabilities'. This means that each party is competing against the other on a 50:50 basis with their evidence. In other words, the court will have to decide whose version of events is most likely to be the correct one. We saw earlier how the burden of proof is on the patient. This has the effect that if both versions are equally likely to be correct, the patient will not succeed. The patient must surpass the 50% likelihood that his version is true. Lawyers sometimes refer to a plaintiff as having to show that her story is at least 51% likely to be the correct one.

A case which recently came to trial will suffice to show the difficulty this can present for a patient. In *Pleydell v Aubyn* (1993), a two-year-old girl was alleged to have been seen by her general practitioner several times during the course of a week in 1966 with abdominal pain and vomiting. At the end of the week she was admitted to hospital with appendicitis and by then the organ had perforated. This resulted in adhesions and infertility which were not discovered until some time after the girl had got married over 20 years later. Clearly, the patient herself was much too young at the time to be able to remember the events. She was therefore dependent on her mother and other family friends as witnesses. The doctor had long since died and the notes, if he ever made any, had disappeared. It might seem that the plaintiff would have a relatively easy task in building up a story about the doctor's visits and the symptoms which were presented. Unfortunately for her, the judge decided, on the basis that the mother was not a convincing witness and did not have a particularly reliable memory, that her story fell short of the required 51% likelihood of being correct. Judgment was given for the defending doctor even though he had no convincing story with which to counter that of the plaintiff.

(iv) Civil and criminal standards of proof

The difference between the civil and the criminal standard of proof was particularly well illustrated in the case of a woman who alleged that she had been assaulted by her doctor. She gave a history of upper abdominal pains which, she later asserted, were suggestive of a gastric disorder. For some reason the doctor seemed inclined to interpret them as having a gynaecological cause. Accordingly, he examined the abdomen and then proceeded to an internal examination.

The woman and her husband were both very upset and reported the matter to the police. The case was pursued in the Crown Court, but the doctor was acquitted despite the evidence against him being quite strong. The lack of a witness to the event that gave rise to the complaint meant that the prosecution could not achieve the required level of certainty to secure a conviction.

The aggrieved patient then initiated civil proceedings for negligence. She found herself in a much better position because the criminal trial had shown that the evidence probably amounted to a true version of the events, although it had fallen short of the required level of certainty. The first trial had therefore been a convenient proving ground and had helped her to know that she was more likely to succeed in an arena that required a lower standard of proof.

(v)   Methods the patient uses to support her evidence

The burden of proof is on the patient to convince the court that his story is likely, on the balance of probabilities, to be an accurate description of the events surrounding the circumstances of the alleged negligence.

The patient may well not have become concerned about the treatment, or even know of any possible damage which resulted, until a long time afterwards.

We have seen how, in *Pleydell v Aubyn* (1993), the patient's mother had a relatively poor recollection of the events of 25 years previously and that she was unable to convince the court that her version was probably correct. This is typical of the difficulties a patient can face with his evidence.

Unlike general practitioners, patients hardly ever keep notes of their visits to the doctor, and so have to rely on other methods for asserting that their version of events is likely to be correct. Let us now consider some of these methods.

(a) The patient's memory

Pleydell v Aubyn demonstrates how difficult it can be for a patient to remember the events of many years previously. Quite apart from a claim that certain symptoms were mentioned, there may even be a dispute about the dates of the incident, especially if no entry at all appears in what otherwise appeared to be fairly complete notes. A set of records which is neatly written, contains much clinical detail and covers the whole of the relevant time span strongly suggests that no other visits were made.

The patient may seek to argue that a vital entry is missing because the doctor did not have the file with him on an out-of-hours call. This will reduce the evidence that the visit took place to a dispute between the doctor's memory and that of the patient. The doctor is unlikely to have any recollection at all of the incident, but the patient may be able to make her version more credible by linking it to other unrelated but contemporaneous events.

If the patient can show that the visit to the doctor was on the morning of her grandmother's funeral, and that she distinctly remembers the delay in the waiting room making her late at the crematorium, the judge may be more inclined to believe her, especially if she gives the impression of being a credible and reliable witness. Similarly, if the patient's illness started while she was away on holiday and she claims that she particularly remembers seeing the doctor on the day she returned, she is more likely to be believed. In this kind of example, she may be able to support her case by producing copies of the air travel tickets for the relevant dates and linking them to a report from the air hostess that she complained of being unwell on that particular flight.

The Canadian case of Dale v Munthali (1977) provides a good illustration of how a judge may prefer the evidence of the plaintiff's memory to the evidence of the doctor. In that case, a man died of meningitis three days after being seen by his general practitioner. The doctor had underestimated the severity of the illness at the time of his visit and had dismissed it as influenza partly, it seems, because he did not seem to take into account the whole pattern of symptoms that had been explained by the wife. Inevitably, the doctor's notes reflected the less serious pattern of symptoms such that, when the case came to trial, he asserted that:

... the patient looked tired and ill but not very ill ... the examination results were normal.

One of the difficulties for the doctor with his evidence was that he was not notified of the patient's death until some months later and the judge observed that:

... it is unfortunate that Dr Munthali did not make careful notes. This was a routine house call to him.

Conversely, the wife argued that her husband had been extremely ill, unable to get out of bed and unable to answer the doctor's questions. The judge, preferring the evidence of the wife's memory, remarked that:

Mrs Dale's memory of the events leading up to her husband's death would, of course, be sharpened by the impact of his death. In retrospect this was not just a routine house call to her and I think she would tend to remember every detail of what occurred.

In view of this, he went on to:

... accept the evidence of Mrs Dale as to what occurred and where there is a conflict I reject the evidence of Dr Munthali.

(b) Diaries

Very few patients keep diaries about their visits to the doctor. They are unlikely to have a written record of the dates let alone the symptoms that were mentioned. This contrasts with the doctor's notes.

In *Richardson v Kitching* (1995), the deceased's wife produced a diary that contained details of her late husband's appointments with the general practitioner in 1983. She naturally felt this would help to corroborate her version of events. The entries in the diary, however, only referred to the date and the times of the appointments, there being no mention of the complaints. Counsel for the defending doctor was quick to challenge the plaintiff in terms that, particularly so many years ago, she was unlikely to be able to remember which symptoms related to each visit.

Another case involving reliance on a diary settled in the plaintiff's favour, but her entries were more detailed than those of Mrs Richardson. A woman made several visits to her doctor about a lump in the breast which she had found. The doctor initially reassured the patient, but later referred her to a specialist, whereupon the lump was found to be cancerous. The doctor's notes were scanty, to say the least. It so happened the patient's mother was dying of cancer at the time and she was seeing her quite often. She kept a diary of her mother's last illness and she also wrote down all her visits to the surgery and the symptoms she mentioned, together with the doctor's response to them. The diary was very helpful to the patient in advancing her case.

(c) Friends and relatives as witnesses

In addition to her own memory, the patient may seek to strengthen her evidence by relying on that of her family and friends. She may ask her husband to testify that he sat in the consulting room with her while the doctor took the history.

In one case, a mother took her child to the doctor's surgery with a sore throat and the receptionist told her to attend for an appointment the next day. When the mother woke up the next morning the child had died of asphyxia in the night. A post-mortem showed that the child's airway had become obstructed by grossly enlarged tonsils. The mother advanced the case on the basis that if the receptionist had let the child see the doctor he would have examined the throat and would have prescribed an antibiotic. From this point, she argued that the death would probably have been avoided. To support her evidence, she called the friend who had accompanied her on the fateful visit to the doctor's receptionist. The friend was able to testify what symptoms the mother had described and what reply the receptionist had given. She was also able to give a description of the distress in which the child was alleged to have been. Her evidence was of great assistance to the plaintiff in advancing her case.

(d) Ambulance records

Records kept by an ambulance control centre may help to corroborate a patient's evidence.

If a patient maintains that the doctor summoned an ambulance with insufficient urgency, and that the delay contributed to her damage, she may be able to support her case by producing the ambulance documentation. Those records will confirm the time at which the call was received, and when the vehicle eventually arrived. There may also be details of the instructions which the doctor gave. This will help to counter any suggestion by the doctor that the delay was caused by the ambulance staff rather than by him.

(e) The district nurse's notes

Many elderly patients are treated in their own homes by district nurses in collaboration with a general practitioner. A common example is dressings for an ulcer on an ischaemic leg. All doctors know of the alarming rapidity with which these lesions can progress to gangrene, especially in diabetic patients. The patient may want to rely on the district nurse's notes as evidence of the state of the limb at the time in question.

In one case, an elderly man had suffered from a black area on one toe for several weeks. His general practitioner asked the district nurse to visit regularly for the application of dressings and he himself visited from time to time to prescribe antibiotics and pain-killing tablets as required. Some time later, the doctor was on a routine visit when he was alarmed to find that the whole foot had turned black and he arranged immediate hospital admission for gangrene. Unfortunately, the leg had to be amputated. The patient's daughter produced the district nurse's notes to support her allegation that additional areas of the foot had turned black several days beforehand, and that the nurse had contacted the surgery to request a doctor's visit but that it had not been forthcoming.

(f) The medical records

Medical records, although primarily the concern of the defending doctor, will be of considerable interest and assistance to the patient. He may want to use the records of the general practitioner, of an admitting hospital doctor on the ward, or even of an accident and emergency department. The general practitioner's notes will be evidence that the patient was seen on certain dates, but previous entries may help to discredit the skill that the doctor exercised on a particular day. For instance, if the doctor is alleged to have failed to examine the abdomen of a patient who is complaining of vomiting, and an entry by another doctor on the previous day shows tenderness to have been present, it strongly suggests that the tenderness would have also been found on the day in question.

An admitting hospital doctor's notes may help to corroborate the patient's version and to show that the general practitioner's notes are incomplete. One man was admitted to hospital by his general practitioner, whose notes indicated the symptoms to have been little more than vomiting, but the daughter alleged that her father had complained several times of bringing up blood. The hospital entry 'haematemesis 4 days' strongly supported the plaintiff's evidence. It was made all the more cogent because no referral letter had been written, and this meant that the hospital doctor's entry was likely to be a true reflection of the history he received from the patient, uninfluenced by any written information from the general practitioner.

It is common for patients who think they have had no satisfaction from their general practitioner to attend their local accident and emergency department. The plaintiff may want to use those notes to support her evidence. As an example, we can cite the patient who attends an accident and emergency department one evening and the note documents a history of chest pains, coughing up blood and a swollen leg since that morning. These symptoms suggest the possibility of a thrombosis in one of the leg veins, and a blood clot in the lung. If the A & E note also mentions that the patient was seen by her general practitioner at midday it will make it very difficult for the general practitioner to refute this, especially if his notes are incomplete.

As a final example of medical records in support of a plaintiff's evidence, we can mention those of the optician. One patient attended an optician with what was described as blurred vision in one eye and the optician's notes recorded a marked reduction in visual acuity in that eye, together with obvious restriction of the visual fields. The optician sent the patient straight to his general practitioner and posted the letter. The patient attended the doctor later the same day, without the letter, and complained of blurred vision. The doctor failed to assess the visual acuity or the fields and merely prescribed some eye drops. When the patient was seen at hospital the next day with a detached retina it was relatively easy for the plaintiff to show that, if the doctor had carried out a proper examination, he would have suspected the diagnosis and made immediate referral, which would have led to a better outcome.

(g) Employment records

Many illnesses cause patients to be absent from work for a period of time. Brief spells of sickness often cause little concern for an employer, but more prolonged absences may raise two areas of concern. The first, of course, relates to the employer's understandable anxiety to keep the firm's financial loss to a minimum. However, there may also be concern about the fitness of the individual to return to his usual job. The illness may be such as to make him a danger to himself or to others. This would apply particularly to jobs involving the use of machinery or the driving of buses or trains. To assess an employee's safety at work, the employer may have had him medically examined for the purpose. That doctor's report may be available at a later date and lend credence to the plaintiff's claims about the severity of his symptoms.

A young widower advanced a case against his late wife's general practitioner on the basis that she had given him a history of breathlessness on several occasions, but that he had ignored it. Certainly, there was no evidence to support this symptom in the general practitioner's contemporaneous notes. It so happened that the woman had a full-time job at a well-known supermarket where she had to help other personnel to move heavy items from the warehouse to the display area. She had a poor sickness record and the employer had her examined by the company doctor. When those notes were obtained by the plaintiff's solicitor there was hardly any reference to difficulty in breathing, and a detailed examination had revealed nothing abnormal on repeated occasions. This did nothing to assist the aggrieved husband in his assertions that the general practitioner had been negligent in terms of history taking. Conversely, it would have helped the defending doctor to support the validity of his own notes.

A bus driver's widow was more fortunate with her case, when the general practitioner's notes failed to mention the angina from which she alleged her husband had been suffering during the months prior to his death from ischaemic heart disease. The bus company had arranged for their driver to be examined to ensure that he did not represent a danger to the public and he had also had a recent examination by yet another doctor for renewal of his public service vehicle licence. These other records all tended to confirm the widow's allegations and this strengthened her evidence considerably.

(h) The post-mortem report

Post-mortem findings can also help to support a plaintiff's evidence after the patient in question has died.

A young man paid several visits to his general practitioner complaining of headaches, vomiting and visual disturbances. The matter was dismissed as being migraine, but the day after his last visit to the doctor, he collapsed and died. A post-mortem showed that he was suffering from a cerebral tumour which was exerting pressure on his optic chiasma. The widow argued that this post-mortem finding strongly suggested that physical signs, such as papilloedema, would have been present during life if the doctor had carried out a proper examination. She further argued that if the general practitioner had examined the fundi he would have found the papilloedema, would have referred his patient urgently to a neurologist and that treatment would have been given which would have saved her husband's life.

(vi) Methods the doctor uses to support his evidence

We have seen how the burden of proof is on the patient to convince the court that his story is 51% likely to be a true reflection of the state of affairs at the time of the alleged negligence.

In defending, the doctor will want to produce a different version which is 50% likely to be correct. Alternatively, he may want to discredit the patient's evidence to prevent the judge from believing it to be 51% likely to be the real version.

To succeed with either of these tasks, the doctor will rely on various materials. By far the most reliable material in his favour is likely to be his contemporaneous notes, but there are other methods available to him as well. Let us therefore consider these in detail.

(a) The contemporaneous notes

Notes made at the time of the alleged negligence are probably the most valuable aid a doctor can have to defend his position. To fulfil this role they must, of course, be contemporaneous, but they must also be legible and complete in all relevant detail.

Notes made at the time of the incident are more likely to be accepted as a true record than those written days or weeks later, because they are not influenced by lapses of the doctor's memory. Clearly, the longer the interval between the incident in question and the making of the notes the less reliable they will be.

An example of a record made later than the contemporaneous note on the Lloyd George card, the A4 sheet or the computerised print-out, is the letter that a doctor may write to the Family Health Services Authority when a complaint is made against him. With a time limit of only 13 weeks, compared to the limitation period of three years for litigation, it is common to see these letters dated a relatively short time after the incident. If the case later proceeds to litigation that letter may be of considerable help to the doctor.

A further advantage of the contemporaneous note from the doctor's point of view is that it is almost certainly unbiased. This means that it has not been written under the threat of impending litigation, assuming that the patient made no obvious complaint at the time. Notes written after even a verbal complaint has been made are open to bias and the doctor may have difficulty in convincing a court that the language used in a note or letter was not at least partly designed to protect his position.[35]

No doctor can be expected to record every single detail of a consultation or house visit. It is not only unnecessary, it is a waste of the doctor's valuable time. However, a certain basic level of note-keeping is expected. In general terms, this usually involves a record of all relevant symptoms, all positive examination findings and any relevant negative points in either the history or the examination. If the doctor has failed to record an important point it may give him a difficulty with his evidence.

Suppose that a patient refers himself to an accident and emergency department one hour after seeing his general practitioner with chest pains and is found to have high blood pressure. If the doctor has made no record of the blood pressure it will be difficult for him to convince the court that he did take it and it was normal. On the other hand, if the disputed point involves some aspect of the examination which would not normally be recorded it will be much easier for the doctor to

---

[35] For a discussion about medical notes which can be regarded as 'self-serving statements', see pp 251–54.

argue that no abnormality was present at the time, on the basis that he would otherwise have written it down.

Finally, notes must be legible, at least to the doctor himself and to his partners and office colleagues. A court is less likely to accept an illegible note as purporting to record what the defending doctor claims.

(b) Notes relating to other family members

In the recent case of *Richardson v Kitching* (1995), the plaintiff, who was the deceased's wife, asserted that she had seen the doctor with her daughter on a particular day and had reminded him to write a specialist referral letter for her husband. The defendant was able to resist this allegation by producing the daughter's notes for the day in question and showing that the entry was not in his handwriting. Furthermore, he was able to show from his appointments book that he was not in the habit of holding surgery sessions on that particular day of the week.

(c) Hospital letters to and from the general practitioner

Apart from his own contemporaneous notes, the general practitioner often has other material in his file with which to defend himself. There may be a copy of a referral letter he wrote at, or just after, the time of the alleged negligence. If no copy was taken, the hospital may be able to produce the original. The doctor may also have a discharge summary or an out-patient clinic letter which gives a version of events that is favourable to his case. He may be able to persuade the court to accept the document as true because it was made by another doctor who was not a party to the proceedings and, in any case, no complaint or litigation had arisen at that early stage.

(d) The hospital notes

The general practitioner may want access to the hospital case notes. Thus, a note made by an admitting hospital doctor or by a clinic doctor in the out-patient department may give a version of the patient's symptoms that is favourable to the doctor's case.

This may help to make good deficiencies in his own notes which have fallen short of proper standards and are making it difficult for him to show that his patient's version of events is probably wrong.

As an example, we can cite the woman who alleges that she complained to her doctor about a breast lump and that he did not examine her. The patient is then seen in a hospital clinic a week later for follow-up of asthma, and routine examination of the chest is recorded as showing no breast abnormalities. This will make it much easier for the doctor to show that, even if he had examined the breasts on the earlier occasion, he would not have detected a lump and would not have pursued the matter any further.

(e) The receptionist and the appointment book

Appointment books can be of assistance in support of evidence for both the doctor and the patient.

The doctor may be able to resist an allegation that a patient attended on a certain day by producing the relevant appointment sheet, and showing that the patient's name does not appear. Alternatively, the doctor may be able to show that an appointment had been booked but that the receptionist had written 'did not attend' against it. If the rest of the appointment book appears complete and carefully kept, it would suggest that the patient did not attend on that particular day.

Recent case law has provided us with a convenient example. In *Fellows v Thomas* (1994), the judge, when finding for the plaintiff, observed that a disputed date in the doctor's notes was corroborated by the office appointment book, and the judge preferred this evidence to that of Mrs Fellows' memory.

(f) The office staff

Secretaries and receptionists can be called to give evidence on a doctor's behalf.

This arises especially where a patient telephones the office and speaks to the receptionist, asking for the doctor to call, and later alleges that symptoms were described which warranted an urgent

237

house visit. The message is relayed to the doctor, who visits quite some time later, claiming that no sense of urgency had been expressed. The doctor may call his receptionist to give evidence testifying to what the patient really said.

(g) Nursing home cases

Many general practitioners attend residential nursing homes on a regular basis as part of their practice, and deficiencies in a doctor's own evidence can sometimes be made good by relying on the notes made by the nursing staff in attendance.

If an elderly resident is transferred from the nursing home to a hospital and has a gangrenous leg amputated, the doctor may be in a difficult position if he has not recorded details of circulation problems at an earlier visit. He may be helped by the nursing notes if they record a healthy appearance of the limb. This may suggest that a carefully-performed examination would not have prompted admission at that earlier stage.

(h) The doctor's memory

The doctor's memory may, or may not, be better than that of his patient. The difficulty for the doctor who tries to rely on his memory is that he has seen many other patients in the meantime, and the incident would probably have been of a fairly routine nature to him. Conversely, the patient, unless she is an unduly frequent attender at doctors' surgeries and hospitals, may have had hardly any medical dealings since then. Additionally, the matter is of a far from routine nature for the patient because it concerns her own health. Indeed, the whole affair may well be a source of high anxiety for her.

When considering the advantage that a patient may derive from his memory of the doctor's visit (see page 228), we referred to the Canadian case of *Dale v Munthali* (1977). In that case, we saw how the judge decided to:

> ... accept the evidence of Mrs Dale as to what occurred and where there is a conflict I reject the evidence of Dr Munthali.

The judge had earlier remarked that:

... it is unfortunate that Dr Munthali did not make careful notes. This was a routine house call to him ...

This case shows how the patient is, generally speaking, much more able than the doctor to rely on the evidence of his memory. On the other hand, if the doctor has made detailed notes, these may well carry more weight than the patient's memory. Furthermore, an extensive record is more likely than a scanty note to prompt the doctor's memory. Indeed, the judge may attach more weight to the doctor's memory if the judge can see that it has been prompted by a written record.

(i) 'Invariable practice'

In a defence served by the doctor in response to the plaintiff's statement of claim, it is common to see an assertion that a particular procedure was carried out, even though no note was made about it. This is supported by the claim that it was the doctor's 'invariable practice'. In other words, the doctor feels he is in a position to say that, for instance, an examination point did receive his attention even though he made no notes and cannot remember it. As an example, we can cite the doctor who has recorded his patient's blood pressure but is alleged not to have taken the pulse. It is further alleged that, if he had done so, he would have found it to be irregular or unduly rapid. He will counter this by arguing that it was his invariable practice to take the pulse before moving on to the blood pressure and the fact that he has not recorded it means that it must have been normal.

(j) The post-mortem report

We have already considered the post-mortem report as an aid to the patient's evidence (see pages 233–34), and we saw how the pathologist's findings can sometimes help to show that a certain physical sign would have been present during life if the doctor had examined the patient more carefully. However, the converse can also apply, and the doctor may find that the post-mortem report helps to show that no such signs would have been present.

In one case, a man was admitted to hospital with a short history of abdominal pain and, at operation, was found to have a

Part B: The Conduct of the Litigation

perforation in the small intestine. Unfortunately, he did not make the rapid recovery that had been anticipated following such a procedure, and he died a few days later. At post-mortem it was found that his liver, although not unduly enlarged, was severely affected by secondary cancer deposits. The pathologist naturally searched the rest of the body for signs of a primary growth but was unable to find any evidence of one. He could do no more than to speculate that the malignancy might have arisen from a minute primary cancer of the lung.

After the patient's death, the wife sued the general practitioner on the basis that her husband had seen him on numerous occasions during the preceding few months. She asserted that the finding of the cancerous liver was strongly suggestive of the proposition that more careful examination would have revealed an abnormality which would have prompted investigation, and earlier treatment of the malignancy. In this case, the doctor's case was strengthened by the fact that the pathologist could find no evidence of a primary growth and this suggested that the primary itself was not only undetectable clinically but was also unlikely to have given rise to any symptoms.

(vii) The use of medical tests in litigation

We normally think of medical investigations, such as blood tests and X-rays, as methods a doctor uses to improve his accuracy of diagnosis. The results of tests that were ordered at the time of the alleged negligence will be subjected to the scrutiny of advisers on both sides to make an assessment of the true state of affairs at the relevant time. The results will form a very important part of the evidence, and each side will be trying to identify data that supports its side of the case.

Investigations can, however, very occasionally be undertaken for the specific purpose of the litigation. This would normally be restricted to non-invasive tests such as X-rays. These are sometimes ordered to demonstrate the extent of the harm the plaintiff has sustained. This will help to assess the prognosis and it will also assist in quantifying the damages with greater accuracy. Alternatively, the result may assist either the plaintiff or the defendant with his case on causation.

In one such case, a woman alleged delay in the treatment of a vascular abnormality. Unfortunately, she suffered some degree of brain damage from blood clots which escaped into the cerebral circulation. Her legal advisers wanted a scan carried out, in the hope that the result would bolster their assertions that the impaired intellectual function had been caused by the release of emboli and not by some unrelated and naturally occurring disease process for which the defendant could not be blamed.

In another case, it was the defendants who wanted support from a medical test. It was alleged on behalf of a brain-damaged child that the disability had been caused by the negligence of the obstetrician. A scan was ordered by the defence. It showed that there was an excess of fluid in the child's brain and that this could only have been caused by factors operating *in utero*. This result put the obstetrician, whose treatment had been the subject of some valid criticism by the plaintiff's experts, in a good position to defend himself because the plaintiff's case had failed on causation.

XXII THE CREDIBILITY OF EVIDENCE OF FACT

SUMMARY

 (i) Introduction...243

 (ii) The credibility of the doctor's notes...244

 (iii) The credibility of the defendant's memory...246

 (iv) The use of medical notes to support the defendant's memory.................................247

 (v) The credibility of the plaintiff's memory...248

 (vi) Self-serving statements................................251

(i) Introduction

For a plaintiff or defendant to win his case, he must convince the judge of the accuracy of his version of events and, if the facts are disputed, this can present considerable difficulties for either side. In the previous chapter we considered some of the sources of evidence upon which the two sides may rely. The defendant's principal source is usually his contemporaneous notes, although these may be supplemented by other items. The plaintiff, on the other hand, may well be reduced to little more than her memory, although she can rely on other sources including, of course, the doctor's notes.

It is worth noting that most of the dispute in a medical negligence case is usually about evidence of fact rather than about evidence of opinion. A convenient example is the case of *Fellows v Thomas* (1994), where, although there was general agreement between the two sides about the proper management of a patient with an undoubted diagnosis of a subarachnoid haemorrhage, there was considerable dispute about the evidence of the symptoms, as well as about the evidence of whether or not an examination was done. The techniques that counsel will use to support the evidence of his own side and to undermine that of his opponent can be a source of considerable interest, and an understanding of these approaches can go a long way towards assessing the merits of any particular case in which litigation arises.

In this chapter we shall consider the credibility of that evidence. We shall see how each side will attempt to buttress the strength of its own evidence and to undermine that of its opponent.

(ii) The credibility of the doctor's notes

We saw (on pages 234-36) how the doctor's contemporaneous notes can be one of his most valuable assets when he has to defend an action by an aggrieved patient. Perhaps the main reason for their worth is that the judge will be inclined to believe the notes as they were made at the time of the alleged negligence and were not subject to lapse of memory. They were also, almost certainly, made without bias from fear of litigation, and the wording was composed by a professional person well versed in accurate recording of clinical matters. All these factors taken together mean that good notes carry very high credibility with a judge.

If the content of the notes is adverse to the plaintiff's case, she will want to undermine that credibility. She will want to make the judge think that he cannot rely on them, and that her story is more likely to be the true version of events. There are various ways in which the plaintiff can attempt to do this, and *McGrath v Cole* (1994) provides a useful illustration. This was a case in which a young woman alleged negligence by her general practitioner because he treated her for a urinary tract infection when she was in the early stages of pelvic inflammatory disease that later rendered her sterile. Mrs McGrath had been discharged from hospital shortly after dilatation and curettage for an incomplete miscarriage. At trial she alleged that she had complained to her

244

doctor of abdominal pain and urinary symptoms. The doctor had recorded in his notes that she had had sexual intercourse just three days after the operation. Counsel for the plaintiff, on examination of the general practice expert and the gynaecology expert, attempted to show that a woman was highly unlikely to have had intercourse at such a time. He asked questions designed to show that she would not have been in a fit state physically or emotionally. Having undermined the reliability of the notes on this particular point, counsel was then able to use that to advantage in showing that the notes as a whole may well have been influenced by erroneous history taking or incomplete record keeping. This was used to strengthen the argument that the severity of the symptoms had been understated in the notes, or even that some visits to the surgery had never been recorded.

Counsel for the general practitioner, Dr Cole, countered these attacks to restore the credibility of his client's notes. He resorted to various lines of argument. He pointed out that the records as a whole made mention of several minor complaints such as toothache and this suggested that the doctor was a painstaking note keeper. He also emphasised that the expression 'did not attend' appeared from time to time in the sequence. If he had kept a note of failed attendances it was difficult for the plaintiff to argue that there really had been visits that were not recorded. Counsel for Dr Cole was even able to show that the handwriting of one particular entry was that of a different doctor from the doctor whom Mrs McGrath earlier asserted she had seen. The demonstration of such an error by the plaintiff was designed to cast doubt on the worth of her attacks on the notes.

The lack of a clear record of a particular symptom, or indeed of its absence, is something that may be used by the defendant to show that it was unlikely to have been present. In *Fellows v Thomas* (1994), a man was seen twice by his general practitioner with headaches of sudden onset, and which were later found to have been caused by a subarachnoid haemorrhage. The plaintiff alleged that vomiting had been an additional symptom, but there was no mention of it in the notes. The defending general practitioner relied on this to suggest that the patient had not complained of vomiting, and he attempted to support this point further by emphasising that he had not prescribed an anti-emetic.

The absence of a definite record can be as relevant to a physical sign as it can to a symptom and this also arose in the case of *Fellows*. No examination had been recorded, and the defendant sought to show that this indicated that nothing abnormal had been found when he carried out the examination as part of his invariable practice.

For many years, good medical practice has dictated that a note should be made of relevant negative findings as well as positive ones. For the defendant in *Fellows* to make his case he had to dispute this point and justify a lack of negative record. He argued that general practitioners were less concerned about detailed notes in 1987, the time of the alleged negligence, than they were when the case came to trial in 1994. Counsel for the plaintiff countered this by showing that there were several entries in the records between 1982 and 1985 where negative symptoms and signs had been recorded.

(iii)   The credibility of the defendant's memory

The doctor's notes are usually his most valuable evidential asset but he may well find that a detailed entry prompts his memory at a later date. A scanty entry will be less helpful to him in this respect and he will be more vulnerable to having the accuracy of his version undermined by his opponent.

In one case, the patient seized upon the apparent unreliability of the doctor's memory to discredit the rest of his evidence. The defendant disclosed a written statement to the plaintiff's advisers and this referred to events that had taken place on a home visit which had been the subject of a complaint. The general practitioner had his written notes to remind him of the clinical details, but he relied on his memory for the rest of the circumstances. He claimed that he had made a telephone call to a hospital from the house next door and that the neighbour had been an elderly widower. The plaintiff was able to show that she had a telephone in her own house, and that her neighbours were a young married couple who had been on holiday at the time.

We have seen how, in some cases at least, a plaintiff has had great difficulty in convincing the court that he can remember the details of events which took place several years previously. In *Pleydell v Aubyn* (1993), this was certainly the case, but *Dale v Munthali* (1977) provided a contrast, where the wife's memory proved more persuasive than the doctor's note. Doctors usually have more difficulty than patients when they have to rely on memory alone, because they have usually seen numerous other similar cases both before and after the events in question. In *Fellows v Thomas* (1994), the general practitioner was faced with this difficulty because his note was so scanty and he did not become concerned about the possibility of a complaint until he received the letter before action nearly two years later. In response to that letter he gave a wealth of detail about the consultations, and claimed to be able to do so without the notes because the patient had moved to another practice in the meantime. His ability to recall such detail in this way was designed to support his memory at trial, but this was challenged severely when counsel for the plaintiff pointed out that the words in his letter bore a striking similarity to the content of the notes. This suggested that he must have had access to the notes when responding to the letter before action, and doubt was then cast upon his honesty.

(iv) The use of medical notes to support the defendant's memory

The doctor's notes can help him in two ways. The facts that they record are extremely persuasive to the judge, but they can help in another way too. The mere sight of a note that a doctor made at the time may prompt his subsequent memory of other details that were not recorded. The effectiveness of the note in this way will be influenced by two factors. The first is the amount of detail it contains (this is discussed on page 235). The second point concerns the length of the interval between the writing of the note and the moment that the author looked at it with concern at the prospect of a complaint. Clearly, the longer the interval, the less effective will the note be in terms of refreshing his memory.

There are two cases which illustrate this point very conveniently. In *Dale v Munthali* (1977), the doctor had made a very scanty note and he had a further difficulty in that he did not hear about the death of the patient until several months later. His note was of little assistance to him and, when the case reached trial, the judge was more inclined to believe Mrs Dale's memory. A much more recent case, *Fellows v Thomas* (1994) provides us with a contrast. Mr Fellows' subarachnoid haemorrhage and stroke occurred only a few days after the general practitioner had last seen him, and the notes that were made, despite being criticised by the plaintiff's expert as being inadequate, at least served as a recent reminder of the incident and assisted the credibility of his factual recall.

(v) The credibility of the plaintiff's memory

Just as the doctor's most persuasive evidence comes usually from his contemporaneous notes, so the patient's usual source is her memory. There is enormous variation from case to case in the credibility of the plaintiff's memory as far as the judge is concerned. In *Pleydell v Aubyn* (1993), the judge refused to accept the patient's mother's assertions about events 25 years previously, even though there were no medical notes in existence on which the defending doctor could rely. Conversely, in *Dale v Munthali* (1977) there was a note, albeit a rather scanty one, and yet the judge was minded to say that he would:

> ... accept the evidence of Mrs Dale as to what occurred and where there is a conflict I reject the evidence of Dr Munthali.

We saw how counsel for the plaintiff in *McGrath v Cole* (1994) attempted to undermine the credibility of the doctor's notes, but it is usually easier for his opponent to demonstrate unreliability of the patient's memory. This can be done in several ways, and some of them were used in the *McGrath* case to discredit the patient's evidence of fact.

Perhaps the most immediate obstacle to be overcome by one who relies on memory is to show that it has not faded with the passage of time. *Pleydell* demonstrated this very forcibly, as the alleged negligence had occurred a quarter of a century earlier. Defence counsel may attempt to reinforce any doubts of this kind by cross-examining the plaintiff on her written statement, which will have been disclosed before the trial, to see if she can be made to contradict herself. For example, the plaintiff may insist that she saw the doctor on a particular day of the week. Counsel may then be able to show that the doctor's dated note was written on one of the other six days.

A careful search of the medical records may reveal similar illnesses, or even recurrences of the same illness, both before and after the time in question. Skilled cross-examination can sometimes capitalise on these other events to show that the patient is confused about which symptoms occurred on each occasion. In *McGrath* it was alleged by the plaintiff that she had been in very severe pain when she saw the doctor on one particular appointment. The note for that date showed that a certain pain-killer had been prescribed. The defence relied on a British National Formulary entry for this drug to show that it was indicated in pain of 'mild to moderate' severity. This made it difficult for the plaintiff to insist that her pain had been unduly severe.

The illness of the child in *Pleydell* had been 25 years before the case reached trial, and Mrs McGrath's symptoms had been the subject of investigation 12 years before trial. In *Fellows v Thomas* (1994), the alleged negligence had occurred more recently, but the delay was still in excess of seven years and this meant that the plaintiff's memory was still vulnerable to having doubt cast upon it. In anticipation of this difficulty, counsel for the plaintiff, in his opening speech, took the opportunity of bolstering the credibility of both Mr and Mrs Fellows' evidence in two ways. He started by emphasising that the patient himself, John Fellows, had been an intelligent and articulate man and would therefore have been likely to have given a clear account of his symptoms when he saw the doctor. Counsel then went on to point out that Mrs Fellows was a nurse and that, both in her dealings with the hospital immediately after the time of the alleged negligence and in her subsequent statement to her legal advisers, she would have given a reliable account of the events. In cross-examination, counsel for the defence attempted to counter this last point by putting it to Mrs Fellows that, because she was a nurse, she knew the symptoms of a subarachnoid haemorrhage and therefore gave what amounted to an artificial account of the illness, distorted to fit the diagnosis that was ultimately reached, rather than giving a genuine account.

One of the difficulties facing the plaintiff at trial in *Fellows* was that Mr Fellows himself had suffered considerable brain damage from the undiagnosed subarachnoid haemorrhage such that, when the case reached trial, there was some difficulty in using him as a witness. However, the plaintiff's team were anxious to secure his evidence, and so the court adjourned to the hospital where Mr Fellows was receiving treatment, and his evidence was taken in a side room off the main ward. He had considerable difficulty in getting his words out clearly but, under examination-in-chief, he referred to the headache which was the subject of the litigation as 'a pain like you would never know you had in your life' and he clasped his hands to the back of his head in the most dramatic and convincing way. He went on to add that he had never experienced anything like this in his life before. As if in anticipation of evidence from a brain damaged person being seen as unreliable, counsel continued his examination-in-chief by asking Mr Fellows if he could remember the name of a shop that he had used on a few occasions at the time of the alleged negligence seven years previously. In the event, Mr Fellows gave some convincing details. He was also able to say, without any prompting, that he had seen the doctor on three occasions and this provided very convincing support for the proposition that the doctor's notes, which only recorded two visits, were incomplete.

We saw earlier how defence counsel in *McGrath*'s case tried to show that the pain had not been as severe as alleged, by pointing out that the pain-killer prescribed was not unduly strong. In *Fellows*' case, defence counsel took a different approach. It was an undisputed fact that Mr Fellows' headache had started on a Saturday night and it was accepted that he did not see the doctor until the Monday, or possibly even the Tuesday. Why, counsel asked, did he not call the doctor on the Saturday night or on the Sunday if the pain was as bad as claimed? Mrs Fellows was able to resist this suggestion to some extent by explaining that her husband was a stoical man and, in any case, he had been used to illness in the past and was not in the habit of calling the doctor out lightly. Another difficulty for the plaintiff in *Fellows*' case arose when counsel for the general practitioner produced supermarket till receipts to show that he had been able to drive a round trip of ten miles and load £150 worth of provisions into a car within a very short time of seeing the doctor. This was in an attempt to show that the symptoms and disabilities were not as severe as alleged. Despite this approach, the neurological expert for the plaintiff said that activity of that kind was perfectly compatible with the illness the general practitioner had earlier failed to diagnose.

The credibility of the plaintiff's memory was also severely challenged in *Richardson v Kitching* (1995). In that case, the deceased's wife was adamant that she had discussed her late husband's case with the doctor when she visited the surgery with her young daughter about an unrelated matter. When the case reached trial, the defending general practitioner was able to produce a copy of the girl's notes to show that, at the time in question, the entry was not in his handwriting. He was even able to add that on that particular day of the week he did not hold surgery sessions. The daughter's notes were of considerable assistance to the defendant in undermining the credibility of the plaintiff's memory.

(vi)   Self-serving statements

A self-serving statement is one which is considered to have been made with the intention of protecting the author's position in the event of subsequent criticism or complaint. This tends to make it unreliable as a description of the true state of affairs at the time, because it introduces the possibility of bias.

Both the plaintiff and the defendant have to produce evidence of fact to support their cases at trial. Understandably, each will do his best to produce a version that is favourable to his own arguments.

The word 'statement' in this sense normally refers to a written document prepared for the litigation and which is used in evidence at court. It will, of course, have been disclosed to the other side considerably earlier. There are, however, other items of evidence and we saw (on page 234-36) how the doctor's notes can be a considerable asset to him. We also saw how these notes are only likely to be persuasive to the judge if they are contemporaneous. However, it has to be acknowledged that it is unrealistic to expect all notes to be strictly contemporaneous every time. Now and again they will have to be written shortly after the event. The file may not have been available on a night visit and there may have been no spare card or 'sticker' in the doctor's bag. Notes will then be written the next morning or after a weekend of duty.

Suppose that a clinical note is used at trial which was written after the event and which is adverse to the patient's case. It will be in the patient's interest to show that the note is in some way inaccurate. Put another way, she will want to show that it is not a true reflection of the state of affairs at the time of the alleged negligence. The patient may want to undermine the doctor's evidence as regards the history or the extent of the examination.

Quite apart from showing that the doctor's memory may have lapsed a little by the time the note was eventually written, there is another way that the patient may be able to discredit it. That is by showing that the note is 'self-serving'. In other words, the note was expressed in such a way as to assist the writer's case if at some later date he was sued and had to produce his records. Even though litigation can take an extended period of time to get underway, the doctor may start to fear the possibility within just a day or so of the incident if the patient takes a turn for the worse in the meantime. Naturally, the doctor will want to counter the suggestion that his note was self-serving and will assert that the possibility of a complaint never entered his mind.

Two examples will suffice to demonstrate the difference between sets of notes, one of which was thought to be self-serving, and the other considered to be entirely innocent.

In the first case, a man called the doctor to his house on a Friday night because he was worried that his wife had symptoms of meningitis. The doctor duly visited, asked a few questions and made a cursory examination. He reassured the couple along the lines that he had seen several other cases of influenza earlier in the week and he left the house without making any notes. Throughout the Saturday the patient's condition steadily deteriorated, and on the Sunday morning the husband called another partner from the surgery who was on duty for the weekend. This doctor found clear signs of meningitis and arranged immediate hospital admission. Unfortunately, the woman had by this stage sustained considerable brain damage. When the first doctor heard the news on his arrival at the surgery on the Monday morning, he thought it would be prudent to write some notes while the matter was still fairly fresh in his mind. He dated the note to coincide with the visit on the Friday rather than the time of writing on the Monday. When the patient later wanted to complain, the solicitor wrote a letter before action to the practitioner to secure disclosure of the notes. The plaintiff was surprised at the amount of detail they contained and their manifestly favourable slant. She remembered no notes being written at the time of the house call on the Friday night, and she also thought it likely that the doctor would hear of the unfavourable outcome as soon as he returned to the office on the Monday morning. This made the plaintiff and her solicitor suspect that the content of the note had been tainted with the adverse knowledge. In other words, the note was 'self-serving' or, as her solicitor rather succinctly put it, was 'exculpatory'.

The other case provides a useful contrast. One Christmas Eve, a general practitioner was asked to see a woman, at her house, with headaches and various other symptoms which he dismissed as migraine. He had received the request while having lunch at his own house and did not have the records with him. He therefore dictated a note in the car immediately afterwards and this was typed when the office opened the day after Boxing Day. It so happened that the patient's condition did not improve over the two-day holiday period and another partner was called. The partner diagnosed a small stroke and sought specialist advice. The consultant was critical of the management on the first visit, and the patient later sued. She attempted to show that the note that had been formally written on the day after Boxing Day was self-serving and that it was done with the knowledge of the adverse outcome and of the specialist's criticism. In the event, the doctor was able to show that his usual practice on out-of-hours calls was to dictate notes in the car at the time, and that they were never typed until the secretary returned to work, perhaps a couple of days later. Additionally, he was able to show that he was unaware of any damage sustained or of any criticism until the consultant's letter arrived in the office after New Year.

Having considered these two examples, we can see how a self-serving statement is one in which the factual content or the general tone suggests that the writer's principal aim was to protect himself from a subsequent complaint rather than to make a genuine record.

XXIII DAMAGES

(i)   Methods of assessing damages

The term 'damages' refers to the amount of money that the defendant is ordered to pay to the plaintiff following a successful negligence action.

There are two methods of assessing damages, and the traditional approach, particularly in the UK, is to confine the calculations to a matter of compensation for the victim. There is, however, an alternative, known as punitive damages, where the assessment is higher because it goes beyond being merely compensatory and takes other factors into account.

(ii) Compensatory damages

The assessment of damages is an integral part of any medical negligence action, and will be of the utmost concern to both

255

plaintiff and defendant. The figure will become a reality if the plaintiff is successful with his case on both negligence and causation.

The object of a damages award is to put the plaintiff, as far as possible, into the position that he would have occupied if the wrong had not occurred, and it can only be expressed in financial terms. In some spheres of law, such as breach of contract, this is entirely appropriate, because money is capable of restoring the plaintiff's position. Inevitably, this does not apply in medical negligence, because no amount of money can restore a life or a limb. The most that can be achieved is compensation, and in many cases this is felt by the plaintiff to be woefully inadequate. For example, it is readily acknowledged that no amount of money can compensate for the loss of a child.

The question will therefore arise of how damages are quantified. Each side builds up its own idea of what the case is worth. Counsel for the plaintiff will draft the Statement of Claim to which a schedule of damages is attached. A figure will be calculated which is the sum of general damages and special damages.

General damages are claimed for 'pain, suffering and loss of amenity' which cannot have a precise financial value put on them. They also cover physical defects and disabilities such as the loss of a hand, the loss of the sight of an eye, the loss of the ability to walk, or the presence of a scar from an unnecessary operation. In addition to present losses, general damages may take future suffering into account. A reduction in fertility from a failed diagnosis of pelvic inflammatory disease, and an increased chance of arthritis in a failed diagnosis of congenital dislocation of the hip, serve as convenient examples.

Special damages allow for losses which can readily be quantified in terms of money and which have been suffered during the time leading up to the trial. Perhaps the commonest area here is loss of earnings but there may be other expenses, such as taxi fares to attend for physiotherapy sessions, that would not have been necessary but for the negligence. Loss of earnings will first relate to the period between the alleged negligence and the time that the Statement of Claim is served. The plaintiff will also be anxious to recover future losses as well but these, in view of the inevitable difficulty that can arise in their quantification, are placed under the heading of general damages. Reference can also be made to them by way of future pecuniary loss. The Statement of Claim may refer to this in terms that the plaintiff is 'seriously handicapped in the labour market'. A young widow whose husband was earning a good salary that was likely to increase with his seniority may have a very large claim for future losses. The special damages claim may even extend to the cost of special equipment or house alterations which become necessary as a result of the plaintiff's disability.

'Kemp and Kemp'[36] is the lawyer's guide to the assessment of general damages. A comprehensive work running to three volumes and regularly updated, it provides reports on the 'quantum of damages' in decided cases of personal injury. Most of the cases are of a criminal, motor or industrial injury nature. However, the figures are relevant to medical negligence litigation because the compensation for the loss of a limb will be the same regardless of whether it was caused by an employer's negligence or a doctor's negligence. The book has sections devoted to various parts of the body and includes other matters such as the psychological damage caused by a scar on the face.

Having chosen a particular damages figure as a starting point, it is of the utmost importance to take the circumstances of the plaintiff into account. For example, a little finger would be of particularly high value to a concert pianist. A thumb would be of similar importance to a surgeon and a great toe to a seaman. A decision will then have to be taken on the other variables such as how many more years of employment the plaintiff could have expected, and whether pension rights will have been lost.

In this way, each side will reach a figure for what it thinks the damages should be. If the case settles out of court, the final figure may be somewhere between the two. However, if the case goes to trial the judge will make the final decision.

Judicial decisions on damages have been the norm in the UK for nearly three decades. *Ward v James* (1965) was the last jury trial in a civil case in this country other than defamation, and they had

---

[36] For further remarks about this reference work, see p 296.

been getting rarer for some years before that. Jury trials in medical negligence cases are still held in the USA, but they have been the subject of criticism in the UK. The fear is often voiced that a jury will award unduly large damages because it sympathises with a disabled plaintiff in a witness box, and it couples this with the knowledge that the award is being financed from the defendant's insurance company.

The size of the estimated damages figure has some influence on the court in which the case will be held, and even whether it will reach court at all. A defendant facing a plaintiff with a strong case is more likely to make an offer out of court if the damages are small rather than risk an expensive fight. In this case, the defendant will expect to be given a 'discount', as the plaintiff has been able to avoid the risk of losing the case in court. Indeed, a defendant may even make an offer of settlement if the plaintiff does not have a particularly good case but is legally aided. The defendant's difficulty here is that, even if he wins, he will be unable to recover his defence costs from the Legal Aid Board and this may amount to considerably more than the offer he may be able to persuade the plaintiff to accept. Until recently, medical negligence actions have been heard in the High Court, but cases where the damages are likely to be less than £50,000 are now downgraded to the county court unless the case is considered to be unduly complicated.

The figure a plaintiff can expect to receive in damages is related strictly to the harm he has sustained as a result of the negligence. In a personal injury case it is likely to reflect the whole departure from full health. In a medical case, however, it will be calculated from the difference between the smaller amount of harm that would have been caused by the illness, properly treated, and the larger amount that was actually caused. We can thus think in terms of 'layers of damage'. A woman who sees her general practitioner with a cancerous breast lump and is referred promptly to a specialist may have a 50% chance of surviving for eight years. If there is a negligent delay in referral she may have a 50% chance of surviving for two years. The damages figure to be claimed by her dependants will relate to the lost six years that was caused by the negligence.

With English law in its present state, damages are awarded on an 'all or none' basis. This means that the plaintiff will receive a full award if he can show that it is more than 50% likely that the negligence caused the damage. Conversely, the plaintiff will receive nothing if he cannot discharge that burden of proof. This was laid down by the House of Lords in *Hotson v East Berkshire HA* (1987) and was fully discussed in Chapter VII.

(iii) Punitive damages

We saw in Chapter XIV on criminal negligence, particularly section (iii) 'gross negligence as a crime', that the legal system hardly ever deals with negligent medical treatment as if it was a crime. We also saw how the focus of attention in tortious liability is confined to the harm that results. Indeed, if the harm is negligible, the plaintiff's case will fail on causation. This contrasts with crime, where the court's attention is spread on a wider front. The state of mind of the defendant is considered to be highly relevant and is taken into account in addition to the harm suffered by the victim. This can be seen in a dramatic form when a defendant has been convicted of murder and is facing a heavy sentence. This will be reduced if the offence is downgraded to manslaughter because the prosecution cannot prove the necessary intent. Compensatory damages in tort provides a stark contrast in that the defendant's state of mind is irrelevant to the amount he must pay.

It is exceptional for a medical negligence case to qualify as a crime. It has to be very extreme indeed in some particular respect. There may, however, be a reference to some aspect of the doctor's attitude to the treatment of his patient. In *R v Bateman* (1925) the judge told the jury that the doctor could only be convicted of manslaughter if:

> ... the negligence of the accused went beyond a mere matter of compensation between subjects and showed such disregard for the life and safety of others as to amount to a crime against the State and conduct deserving punishment.

Despite the apparent great gulf fixed between tort and crime in medical negligence cases there is, so to speak, a 'half-way house'. It takes the form of punitive damages. This method of assessment has been used from time to time in parts of Europe and the USA but judges in the UK have generally found it to be an unattractive notion.[37]

Punitive damages are higher than compensatory damages because they include an allowance for additional factors over and above compensation. An award of punitive damages must not, however, be confused with the imposition of a punishment in a case of criminal negligence. The word 'punitive' refers to the method of damages assessment and not to the nature of the act.

Punitive damages are, in a sense, a form of punishment, and they are divided into an 'aggravated' and an 'exemplary' variety. In the former type, the main focus of attention is on the plaintiff, whereas in the latter it is on the defendant. Some patients will bring a case mainly to see the doctor punished rather than to gain a financial settlement. This type of plaintiff wants his day in court and will be most disappointed if counsel settles the case on the morning of the trial. If the judge thinks that the doctor's attitude is sufficiently blameworthy he may raise the compensatory figure to an exemplary one to reflect his disapproval of the defendant's behaviour. Some other patients have been left smarting with indignation when their compensatory award is very low. They feel the award should reflect the sense of upset they have suffered from the way in which their case was handled by the doctor. If the judge makes an allowance of this kind it will be termed 'aggravated damages'.

It can thus be seen that exemplary damages are designed to make an example of the doctor, whereas aggravated damages reflect the greater degree of disturbance to which the doctor is considered to have subjected his patient.

(iv) The effect of the damages figure on the conduct of the claim

A discussion about damages in a particular case usually centres around the financial worth of the claim. This means that there will

---

[37] For a fuller discussion of punitive damages, with particular reference to the disadvantages they are considered to have as far as medical negligence is concerned, see *J Med Def Union*, 1994, no 1, pp 7-8.

be an assessment of the combined figure for general and special damages that the plaintiff hopes to receive when his case reaches a conclusion in his favour. However, it is important to realise that the figure itself may well have a profound influence on the conduct of the litigation from a very early stage.

Let us consider the effect of this on a range of cases that fall into the following groups of increasing value.

(a) Cases where the value is zero

This means that there has been no quantifiable damage and the case therefore cannot proceed. Even if the case is strong on negligence it will fail on causation in the fullest sense.

(b) Cases where the value is more than zero but is still minimal

These cases may receive detailed initial consideration but are doomed to failure at some stage because the *de minimis* principle (see below) will mean that the damage did not qualify as being 'material'.

(c) Cases where the value is more than minimal but is still fairly low

If the damages figure is likely to be less than the cost of advancing the case it is unlikely to proceed on legal aid. Only a privately-funded plaintiff who is determined to 'have his day in court', and is unconcerned about what most people would regard as prohibitive costs, will ask his advisers to move this kind of case forward.

(d) Cases where the value is moderate or high

In these cases, the cost of advancing the case easily justifies the expected damages award and, if strong on negligence and causation, they are likely to receive full support from the Legal Aid Board or a private client.

(v)   The *de minimis* principle in damages

In the preceding section we saw how a case with minimal damages will fail at an early stage. The *de minimis* principle was discussed under 'material contribution causation' (page 63). It was pointed out that the law does not recognise minutiae and that, for a case to succeed, the contribution made by the negligence must be sufficiently great to qualify for the adjective 'material'. Inevitably, this remark also applies to the figure for damages because this, in money terms, is what has been caused by the doctor's negligence.

In one case, a woman took her elderly mother to the general practitioner with a septic toe. The mother was given an antibiotic and was about to leave the consulting room when she asked for a bottle of linctus for a cough that had been troubling her for some time. The doctor had replaced the notes in the Lloyd-George envelope by this stage and failed to notice that the patient was an insulin-dependent diabetic. He wrote a prescription for ordinary cough linctus and the patient went home. Within an hour of the first dose the patient felt most unwell and the daughter took her back to the surgery. It was found that the sugar in the linctus had caused a temporary increase in the patient's blood sugar level, but this rapidly settled. The plaintiff had little difficulty in showing that the doctor had been negligent in prescribing that particular kind of linctus for her and she had equally little difficulty in showing that the negligence had caused the harm. However, she had to concede that the damage amounted to no more than a very short period of feeling unwell and that her case was therefore likely to fall within the *de minimis* principle.

(vi)   Comparison between English and American attitudes to punitive damages

Judicial attitudes to punitive damages are very different on the two sides of the Atlantic. We mentioned earlier in this chapter that judges in the UK are not attracted to the idea.

Nevertheless, the notion has been subject to judicial comment in recent years. In *Kralj v McGrath* (1986), a mother brought a case against her obstetrician after the death of a second twin. She made unduly serious allegations about the way she had been handled and the child's birth had been managed. Despite the treatment being described by the experts for the plaintiff as 'totally unacceptable' and 'horrific', the judge was minded to say that:

> It is my view that it will be wholly inappropriate to introduce into claims of this sort ... the concept of aggravated damages.

And he added that:

> Such a result seems to me to be wholly inconsistent with the general approach to damages in this area, which is to compensate the plaintiff for the loss that she has actually suffered, so far as it is possible to do so, by the award of monetary compensation and not to treat those damages as being a matter which reflects the degree of negligence or breach of duty of the defendant.

To see how this English attitude contrasts with the American approach we need look no further than a recent personal injury case in New Mexico.[38] An 81 year old woman was a passenger in a car when she wanted to drink a cup of coffee which had just been bought at a branch of McDonalds, the hamburger chain, and she placed the cup between her legs while she removed the top. Unfortunately, some of the hot coffee was spilt and she received burns to her legs, groin and buttocks. She was awarded damages of 2.9 million dollars (£1.9 million) and one of the jurors said that they wanted to send a message to the fast-food industry in terms that 'the coffee is too hot out there'. Although this was not a medical negligence case it shows only too clearly that the jury was prepared to attach significance to the conduct of the defendant in the very way that was disapproved in *Kralj v McGrath*.

---

[38] See *The Times*, 20 August 1994.

(vii) The classification of damages

We have referred to a range of sanctions that can be brought against a negligent doctor. If we leave aside those which can be imposed following quasi-judicial hearings by such bodies as the General Medical Council and Family Health Services Authorities, we can provide a convenient classification as shown in the figure below:

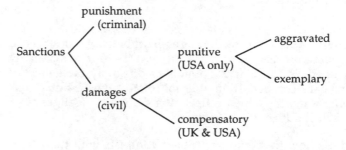

(viii) Speculation about future business prospects

In various parts of this book we have considered the difficulties that can face a plaintiff in showing that, but for the doctor's negligence, he would have avoided the damage to his health or, put another way, he would have achieved certain cure. The rule in *Hotson v East Berks HA* (1987) dictates that an 'all or none' approach must be taken when calculating the sum of general and special damages. Many injured plaintiffs are, however, concerned about business prospects which may no longer be open to them in their reduced state of health. It goes without saying that no business prospect is certain to yield a benefit. In *Fellows v Thomas* (1994), the plaintiff attempted to make a claim of this kind as part of his damages award. In the early part of his life he had been a hospital porter, but had subsequently progressed to become the manager of a nursing home. Shortly before his illness he had been having a discussion with the owner of the home about the possibility of entering into a partnership agreement which would have involved setting up an additional home that might have generated substantial profits. He asserted that the illness had deprived him of this advantageous prospect. Unfortunately, he met with a difficulty because defence counsel was able to show that the prospect was extremely speculative. No suitable property for the proposed additional home had even been identified, and no investment or mortgage inquiries had been made. In reality, the plan had been little more than a discussion during the course of a short car journey.

If a plaintiff can go further than this in demonstrating the reality of future prospects, the judge is unlikely to rely on the rule in *Hotson* to give an 'all or none' figure for damages, nor will the judge rely on *Chaplin v Hicks* (1911) to choose a proportional amount to reflect the lost chance. Rather, he is likely to choose a rounded figure as a compensatory amount in recognition of the loss in general terms.

XXIV THE ROLE OF THE EXPERT

Summary

(i)   Introduction

Every medical negligence case stands or falls by the evidence that can be called to support it. This evidence, however, is of two separate and quite distinct kinds. First, there is evidence of fact, and secondly, there is evidence of opinion. The expert has an important role to play in both of these spheres, as litigation may well arise from a dispute in one, the other, or both. In other words, he may be asked to advise on the likelihood of whether something did happen as well as on the question of whether it should have happened.

In this chapter we shall consider what is expected of the expert from the time that his instruction letter first arrives to the stage when the case reaches trial.

(ii)   The expert's acceptance of the case

When an expert is approached by a plaintiff's solicitor or by a defence organisation there is far more to taking the case than simply writing a letter accepting it and saying that the report will be done when time permits. The expert's first task when he receives such an inquiry is to ensure that he can deal with the matter properly. Perhaps the most important point is to establish that the case is in the right field of medicine for the expert's speciality. He may have been approached in the mistaken belief that he was from a different background and the expert must make at least a brief assessment of the case before agreeing to accept it.

The length of time it takes before the report is ready is another factor to be considered. Busy experts can find it difficult to prepare reports within the schedule imposed by their clinical duties, and undue delay can cause great difficulty for the solicitor. The solicitor has deadlines to meet for the service of documents but may not want to instruct counsel until he has the expert's report to hand. Even if the solicitor does approach counsel at an early stage the latter may be unable to draft the pleadings without the report being available. Furthermore, a plaintiff's solicitor may have been approached by his client when limitation is already approaching, and this means that time will be short even when the expert's instruction letter first arrives.

Case papers are sometimes sent with the instruction letter and sometimes they arrive later. Additionally, they may all be dispatched at the same time, or they may be sent in separate batches as they become available from their original sources. Whichever method is used it is very important for the expert to check the papers carefully. Medical notes may, of course, be incomplete and this can be an important point in the litigation. The expert must ensure that he has been sent everything that he is meant to see. It is very irritating for a solicitor to be told, after waiting several months for a report, that an important item is missing from the bundle when the solicitor should have been informed of this at the outset.

Experts who take cases from both sides have to be particularly careful to keep their work properly organised, and we can give an example of the sort of difficulty that can arise when they do not do so. One expert accepted a case and told the solicitor the report would take two months. Four months later it was still not available. When the solicitor started to press the matter after six months he was told that the expert would be unable to do it because he was already acting for the other side. He had known this when originally instructed, but had not checked his office records carefully enough at the time to notice this. Not only had the solicitor lost six precious months but he had, unwittingly, disclosed a good deal of privileged material which could have been prejudicial to his case. The only solution was for the expert to discontinue his services for both sides and drop the case altogether. This had the effect that both parties in the litigation had to find new experts, with all the delays that were bound to be involved.

(iii) Engaging an expert

Before embarking on the role of the expert in detail we should consider various preliminary matters such as how the expert comes to be engaged on the case, and what sort of background he should have. Both parties in the litigation need expert witnesses. Indeed, they may each need several such persons, perhaps one to deal with negligence and one to deal with causation. Furthermore, the parties may need to approach several different experts for each of these topics. The first opinion may not have been supportive, and a second opinion may therefore be wanted. Even if the first one is supportive it may be felt desirable, particularly if the case is likely to reach trial, to have a second expert to buttress the opinion of the first one.

This brings us to the question of how each side finds its experts. In passing, it is worth mentioning that although some experts are in the habit of working for either plaintiffs or defendants, there is certainly no rule about this and it is not even particularly desirable. It can be quite valuable for an expert to take cases from both sides from time to time as it tends to make him more adept at anticipating the stance that his opponent will probably take.

Plaintiff and defendant organisations tend to have different methods of engaging their experts. Solicitors acting for plaintiffs probably place most reliance on the experience of experts whom they have used previously and with whom they are satisfied. If they are faced with a case involving a field of medical practice with which they have not previously been involved they may make enquiries of outside agencies who maintain up-to-date lists of experts in various specialities. Assistance of this kind can be made available by Action for Victims of Medical Accidents, the Law Society, The Association of Personal Injury Lawyers, and the British Academy of Experts. A solicitor may be attracted to an expert by reading a journal article or a book written by him or the solicitor may have attended a lecture given by the expert. It is not unknown for an expert to be approached because the solicitor has been impressed by his performance at trial on the other side in an earlier case.

Some of these sources are, for obvious reasons, not particularly likely to be used by defendants. Most defence organisations find that the bulk of their work involves medical litigation, and they tend to have their own comprehensive lists of experts upon whom they call regularly. This is certainly the case with the Medical Defence Union and the Medical Protection Society as far as general practitioner cases are concerned, but it probably applies in much the same way to solicitors acting for health authorities under the Crown indemnity scheme covering hospital negligence.

It goes without saying that an expert should have the right background, qualifications and experience. A deficiency in any of these areas is likely to reduce his credibility. This could cause particular difficulty if the case reaches trial, because counsel for the other side will lose no opportunity in exposing these areas of weakness. This will be in an effort to show the judge that the opinion being given should not be regarded as being unduly authoritative. When considering the expert's role in negligence and causation (see pages 273-77) we shall see how the type of person needed will vary from case to case, and how a suitable choice can be made.

(iv)   Evidence of fact

We are here concerned with the facts of the case. This involves the task of establishing what did, or did not, happen at each of the various stages in the doctor's treatment of the patient.[39]

In Chapter XXI we saw how each side relies on documents and other materials to support its version of the facts of the case. In some instances, however, notes have been lost, or they may never have been made, and there will therefore be no contemporaneous evidence available to throw light on what probably happened at the time in question. In this situation the expert may be able to make inferences from later material.

For example, a woman alleges that she attended her general practitioner with a lump in her breast, and that he carried out no examination. She therefore refers herself to a surgeon privately the next day. The surgeon's notes document her dissatisfaction with the general practitioner the previous day and record clinical details of the lump. His operation notes of the following day state that a sizeable malignant tumour was identified. The difficulty for the plaintiff in suing the general practitioner is that the latter's notes, and his receptionist's appointment book, contain no record of the consultation at all. Alternatively, notes may have been made, but mention nothing more than 'mastitis' on examination. In this type of case, the expert for the plaintiff will be able to locate the surgeon's notes in the bundle. He will then be able to infer that if a tumour of the dimensions recorded by the surgeon was present on a particular day it is extremely likely that it would

---

[39]   The sources of evidence of fact are described in Chapter XXI and its credibility is discussed in Chapter XXII.

have been equally apparent to the general practitioner a day or two earlier.

It is convenient to think of this approach to the establishment of facts in terms of 'inferential evidence'. Leaving aside the possibility that the woman may have lied to the surgeon about her alleged visit to the general practitioner, those notes imply that she really did attend and that the lump really was present. If the general practitioner has no record of her attendance this will make it difficult for him to defend himself.

Many lawyers, especially those with relatively little experience of medical negligence cases, have considerable difficulty in interpreting the notes. Quite apart from the question of illegible handwriting, there is the significance of various tests that may have been ordered. The expert will be able to help the lawyer make sense of much of this material, and thus build up a picture of the case. The expert will also have to take into account the patient's version, and the significance of any discrepancies. In this way the expert will be able to say what he thinks is most likely to be the correct version of what history was given, what examination was carried out and what tests were ordered.

It must be remembered that there is no need for certainty. The plaintiff merely has to show that his version is more likely than not to be correct (51% likely). Conversely, the defendant has two options, and both of them often cause him less difficulty than that facing the patient. He can produce a different version of his own which is equally likely to be correct (50% likely). Alternatively, he can produce evidence that contradicts that of his opponent, to reduce the likelihood of the plaintiff's version being correct to 50% or less.

(v) Evidence of opinion

We have seen how a study of the evidence of fact involves establishing what probably happened. If there is a dispute in this area the matter will be settled ultimately by the judge when the case comes to trial. Thus, the judge's task is no more than to balance the likelihoods of fact. If the plaintiff cannot persuade the judge that her version is probably correct, her case will fail.

However, if the plaintiff can succeed on this point, she will next have to show that the treatment she received fell below an acceptable standard or, in other words, was negligent.

Medical practice is not an exact science. Although scientific principles do feature, and very important they are too, it must be considered an art as well. Thus the study of therapeutics involves much more than a knowledge of drugs and their side effects. It includes the giving of explanations, the provision of reassurance where appropriate, the extension of conventional courtesies at consultations, and even comforting of the bereaved. Few of these matters have been described in textbooks, let alone subjected to the rigours of scientific analysis, and so it is not surprising that there is ample scope for disagreement about the proper way to practise medicine.

A negligence action can only be advanced successfully if it can be shown that the treatment fell below an acceptable standard. In other words, it will involve a question of whether it fell outside the *Bolam* principle (this is discussed in detail in Chapter III). It will also be necessary to show that the doctor's shortcoming caused, or at least made a material contribution to, the alleged damage (this is discussed in Chapter IV).

It is apparent that, as regards evidence of opinion, the expert in a case has to advise in two distinct areas: that of negligence and that of causation. We can now consider each of these two separate roles.

(vi) The expert's role in negligence

When establishing negligence, the expert's opinion is of paramount importance. He must be able to tell his instructing solicitor and the client what treatment the patient had a right to expect against the background of facts they have been able to establish. If the expert thinks it fell short of that standard, he must be able to identify the shortcomings and explain what should have been done. If alternative treatments would have been acceptable the expert must identify them as well, and explain what difference it would have made if they had been pursued. It is fruitless to advance a case on the basis that some other course of action should have been pursued if the eventual outcome would have been the same.

If the expert is confident that the treatment fell short of proper standards, he must advise the plaintiff. If the case later comes to trial he must be prepared to say so in court but he may find his opponent's expert is of a different opinion. It is here that the expert evidence will be considerably strengthened if he can support it by references. These can take the form of textbooks, journals or similar matter. Some materials are much more persuasive than others. If a particular examination or treatment is recommended in a basic text, it implies that every doctor should follow that course and the failure to do so is negligent. For example, any student textbook of otorhinolaryngology makes it clear that when a patient complains to his general practitioner of hoarseness of more than three weeks' duration, referral to an ear, nose and throat specialist for laryngoscopy is mandatory, to rule out the possibility of throat cancer. If such a patient is given repeated courses of antibiotics for a prolonged period of time without referral it will be relatively easy for the plaintiff to show that this course of action fell outside the *Bolam* principle. Conversely, if some abstruse physical sign is only mentioned in an advanced specialist textbook, it will be much more difficult to show that the general practitioner should have known about it.

In addition to the desirability of a reference being at a basic level, it is also important that it should be contemporaneous with the time of the alleged negligence. This is particularly relevant if the incident that gave rise to the complaint occurred some years previously. In the benzodiazepine litigation, many cases were advanced against general practitioners who issued repeat prescriptions in the 1960s and 1970s on the basis that they gave insufficient supervision to their patients with regard to initiation, monitoring, and withdrawal of the drugs. Many of these cases collapsed when the defendants showed that the data sheets that the manufacturers had issued before the mid-1980s made no mention of the dangers of addiction.

In some cases, the doctor may have been labouring under adverse conditions. We are all familiar with the junior hospital doctor who is called from his bed in the early hours of the morning. The general practitioner can also find himself under pressure on being asked to see an extra case at the end of his morning appointment session when he is trying to avoid delay in attending an urgent house call. Although some of these difficulties do not fall strictly within the concept of negligence, they are all part of the reality of the situation and no potential litigant can afford to ignore them. The expert should be well placed to assess their significance because in his own practice he will have encountered similar situations on many occasions.

Before concluding our discussion about the expert's role in negligence, it cannot be emphasised too strongly that he must have had extensive firsthand experience in the field of medical practice that is the subject of the criticism. Additionally, it is desirable that he was in practice at the time that the event under consideration occurred. In other words, he must be able to make his assessment of the incident from exactly the same standpoint as the defendant who was presented with the illness that is the subject of the litigation. Thus, it is inappropriate to ask a cardiologist to assess the care given by a general practitioner who visits a patient with chest pain and tells him it is indigestion. It is equally inappropriate to ask a 30 year old general practitioner to comment on the standard of note-keeping of his peers of a generation earlier.

Unfortunately, this counsel of perfection occasionally has to be tempered with realism in cases where, for instance, it is impossible to find an expert of the right age and type who is willing to give evidence. This difficulty is most likely to arise in cases where the alleged negligence occurred many years ago and was in an esoteric field of medicine. The risk of engaging an unsuitable expert is that it paves the way for opposing counsel to discredit the evidence by showing that it was not supported by extensive personal experience.

(vii) The expert's role in causation

We have seen how the expert on negligence must come from a background that is intimately involved with the field of medical practice from which the complaint arose. If the case reaches trial, the judge then has the task of deciding which side's expert has produced the more convincing evidence. Probably the main factor in the decision will be the degree of documented support given to the opinion, but there will be other less clearly defined factors such as the general demeanour of the witness and how resistant he is to being discredited by counsel for the other side.

The expert on causation is in a different position altogether. He may well have no experience at all of the field in which the complaint arose, and he may not even have been qualified at the time. We saw how important it is not to use hindsight when assessing liability. Conversely, when assessing causation, it is not just permissible, it is highly desirable, to use more modern information and opinions if they help to explain the outcome of the case more clearly.

Let us revert to our example of a moment ago, in which a general practitioner visited a patient with chest pains and told him it was indigestion. We can extend the case to say that it occurred many years ago, and the patient was later admitted to hospital with coronary artery disease and died. Causation will concern how likely it is that the patient would have survived the acute attack if he had been admitted promptly. It will also concern an assessment of his subsequent life expectancy. The expert in this case will be entitled to rely on the post-mortem findings which would not, of course, have been known to the general practitioner at the time. He will also rely on the latest research studies for an indication of the percentage chance of survival of that type of patient for various periods of time regardless of whether those studies were conducted long after the supposed negligence. Thus his task is to make as accurate an assessment as possible of the likely outcome of the case if the general practitioner concerned had acted differently at the time. Needless to say, he cannot use material that relies on treatments which were not available at the time. For example, he can use later mortality and morbidity studies in patients treated conservatively but he cannot take into account figures for patients being considered for coronary artery by-pass grafting if it was not available at the relevant time.

Just as the expert on negligence must come from a similar background to the defendant, the expert on causation must have experience in the pathology or the treatment of the illness in

276

question. The choice may not be very easy. For instance, an inexperienced solicitor wants to advance a case against a general practitioner who has failed to admit a patient complaining of low back pain and inability to pass urine, which is later found to have been caused by cauda equina compression. The solicitor finds it difficult to know whether to instruct a neurologist or a neurosurgeon. The expert himself may well not appreciate this important point, or, worse, he may agree to take the case to avoid losing the fee. In this case, the expert will be more vulnerable to cross-examination by opposing counsel who will be supported by an expert able to give more persuasive evidence on causation.

It can be seen that, for the proper assessment, and advancement, of the case there is usually a need for more than one expert. Very often two will be needed, one for negligence and one for causation. Additionally, if the case is likely to reach trial it may be thought desirable to have more than one for each field so as to provide mutual support. It is by no means unusual to have four experts supporting one side and the number may be even higher. The more experts involved in the case, the more important it becomes to ensure that they collaborate with each other and understand exactly the arguments on which their colleagues rely. The solicitor will circulate their various letters and reports to ensure a cohesive approach as the case progresses, but the ultimate meeting of the minds is likely to be reached at the conference with counsel (pages 283-84).

(viii) The preparation of the expert's report

When a solicitor for plaintiff or defendant asks an expert to prepare a report on negligence he is, in effect, asking the doctor to give his own opinion as to whether or not the treatment was of an acceptable standard. The fact remains, however, that the lawyers for the plaintiff are doing all they can to support their client and have an interest in obtaining a 'positive' report. In the same way the other side wants a 'negative' report to protect the doctor's position. We must add here the point that many experts, particularly the less experienced ones, need help and guidance in the preparation of their reports.

Taken together, these points raise the question of how much a doctor should allow himself to be influenced by the instructing solicitor when deciding how to phrase his report. There may well be plenty of room for manoeuvre here, such as by shifting the emphasis a little, or perhaps by omitting various points which the lawyers consider to be hardly relevant. A dilemma arises because, on the one hand, the lawyer is instructing and paying the expert but, on the other hand, the expert's prime duty is to give an unbiased opinion to the court.

This difficulty was considered by Lord Denning in the Court of Appeal in *Whitehouse v Jordan* (1981). An expert's report on behalf of the plaintiff was criticised by Lord Denning on the basis that:

> It was the result of long conferences between the two professors and counsel in London and it was actually 'settled' by counsel. In short, it wears the collar of special pleading rather than an impartial report. Whenever counsel 'settle' a document, we know how it goes. 'We had better put this in', 'we had better leave this out', and so forth. A striking instance is the way in which Professor Tizard's report was 'doctored'. The lawyers blacked out a couple of lines in which he agreed with Professor Strang that there was no negligence.

When *Whitehouse v Jordan* reached the House of Lords' attention was again focused on the matter in terms that there was:

> ... some concern as to the manner in which part of the expert evidence called for the plaintiff came to be organised. This matter was discussed in the Court of Appeal and commented on by Lord Denning MR. While some degree of consultation between experts and legal advisers is entirely proper, it is necessary that expert evidence presented to the court should be, and should be seen to be, the independent product of the expert, uninfluenced as to form or content by the exigencies of litigation. To the extent that it is not, the evidence is likely to be not only incorrect but self defeating.

(ix) The loyalties of the expert

When an expert is commissioned by a solicitor for either side he is, if one could put it this way, working for that side rather than the other one. He is being given material by that side, and being paid by that side, so his whole attention is focused on doing what he can to assist that side. Similar comments, of course, apply to the solicitor and to counsel in terms of their loyalty to the litigant. As in any professional relationship, it is essential that the client is confident that all members of the team are loyal to her.

When we come to discuss the expert's role in court (see pages 284-87) we shall see that his task alters a little in that he must adopt an independent position and the client must be made aware of this, so that he does not think that for some reason the expert has become a hostile witness for the patient's side. In passing, we can mention that plaintiffs, if they receive negative reports on their cases, seem to think that the expert has been hostile from the outset. They think that they know better than the expert because they were there at the time of the alleged negligence, and a negative report is seen merely as doctors 'closing ranks'. These cases can give plaintiffs' solicitors considerable difficulty in terms of trying to persuade their client to accept the negative opinion.

A recent case will help to show how easy it can be for the solicitor's choice of expert to sap the confidence of the prospective litigant at an early stage. A woman alleged negligence by an orthopaedic specialist and consulted a local solicitor. It would clearly have been out of the question to enlist the help of a local orthopaedic expert on the question of negligence, but it was felt that a nearby doctor could do the report on condition and prognosis as this would not involve criticism of a known colleague. However, the plaintiff had only been sitting at that expert's desk for a few minutes when it became apparent from the conversation that he was a colleague and a friend of the defendant. The client immediately felt uncomfortable about the nature of the relationship and thought it would be difficult to give her trust entirely to that particular expert. She feared he would be in a position of divided loyalties and her solicitor then had to find another expert.

(x)   Checking the documents

At several points we have seen how a case can stand or fall by the documents available to support each side's version of the facts.

We have also seen how medical notes may be lost with the passage of time, or may never have been made in the first place. It is therefore of the utmost importance to ensure that all relevant documents are made available for study as evidence of fact. Lapses here are particularly likely to arise when there are several defendants, such as a general practitioner, ambulance staff and a hospital. One of these may have written a letter to another without keeping a copy. Alternatively, it may have been written to an agency involved in the treatment but which is not party to the litigation.

The expert is ideally placed to identify documents that may have been misfiled in the bundle with which he has been supplied. He should also be able to tell his instructing solicitor if anything is missing. For example, a case arises of a general practitioner who allegedly incurs delay in sending for an ambulance. No notes were made in the rush at the time, but the expert will know that there is a strong likelihood that the clinical findings were recorded in the letter which the general practitioner sent to the hospital with the patient. The defending doctor's solicitor is almost certain to know this, but an inexperienced solicitor for a plaintiff may not realise it, and it is the expert's job to point it out.

We can also cite the example of a general practitioner who sees a woman with gynaecological symptoms. He takes a smear and records this in his notes but fails to arrange follow-up. She is later found to be suffering from cancer of the cervix and she wishes to sue for negligent follow-up and failure to refer. Her expert searches the general practitioner's notes and finds no evidence that the report was ever returned from the laboratory. He will then advise the solicitor that discovery is needed of the hospital records to show what report would have been available if the defending general practitioner had pursued the matter at the time. If the report was never posted but was negative in any event it will make the case impossible to advance because it shows that the malignant change started after the time of the alleged negligence. In other words, no matter how diligent the general practitioner had been in ensuring that he had sight of the report, he would still have made no gynaecological referral at that time. Alternatively, if the smear was reported as negative and the next one, which was positive, was taken only a very short time later, it raises the possibility of negligent reporting of the first one. In this case, the litigation would then expand on a new front, against the cytologist.

(xi) Studying the other side's reports

As the litigation progresses, the experts for each side will be building up their versions of the case with particular regard to the standard of care and causation. The solicitors for each side will consider these expert opinions and take a view on the case. If the plaintiff's solicitors think that the case in either of these areas is weak they may withdraw their allegations. Similarly, if the defendant's solicitors feel they are in a weak position, they may recommend an offer of settlement.

However, if both sides are confident that they are in a strong position the case will proceed, and the experts' reports will be disclosed to the other side. This now occurs by 'mutual exchange' and has the effect that it prevents each side from moulding its case deliberately in such a way as to undermine its opponent. In a recent case, a defendant's failure to perform his part of the exchange caused consternation initially in the plaintiff's team. They thought they were on strong ground and that the case would proceed for trial on the basis that the defendants were equally confident. Their suspicion that this failure was a tacit admission of liability was soon confirmed when they received a quite generous offer of settlement.

Historically, the system of mutual exchange has not always been the case. Expert medical reports are, by their very nature, prepared for the purpose of litigation. This therefore makes them subject to 'privilege' (see pages 164-65) and traditionally they were not disclosed. This principle was held to apply in *Rahman v Kirklees AHA* (1980) and it typified the old-style 'trial by ambush'. In *Lee v SW Thames* (1985) the Master of the Rolls, Sir John Donaldson, granted privilege to the employer of an ambulance service 'with undisguised reluctance'. Finally, in *Naylor v Preston* (1987) he considered that 'a duty of candour' was owed by the defendants. This change of policy has given rise to the present system of 'cards on the table' litigation, which is generally considered to be in the interest of fairness and to facilitate the early settlement of cases, one way or the other.

Following mutual exchange, the experts will be faced with the task of studying the opposing report. The expert on liability will have to review the approach his opposite number has taken with regard to evidence of fact and evidence of opinion. The defendant's reports may well propose a very different sequence of events to that asserted by the plaintiff's expert, and the latter will have to assess the likelihood of his side's story being accepted by the judge. This assessment will also fall to counsel who, in court, will have the task of persuading the judge of its accuracy. As regards evidence of opinion, the plaintiff's expert will have to assess the merits of the alternative treatment regimes which the defendant holds were perfectly reasonable in the circumstances. Thus the plaintiff may assert that her husband, who was seen with chest pains at lunchtime one day by his general practitioner should have been admitted to hospital immediately. Conversely, the defendant may hold that it would have been equally reasonable for the general practitioner to ask a cardiologist to make a domiciliary visit on his way home that evening. If the patient was found dead in his bed at teatime, the plaintiff's case will fail if she cannot show that the latter course was unreasonable. The important point here is that the judge cannot 'prefer' one form of treatment to another, in the same way that he can 'prefer' one set of facts to another.

The expert who assesses the other side's report on causation may also find himself meeting some arguments that are hard to resist. The expert may find that his opposite number has managed to locate a morbidity study of which he was hitherto unaware and which indicates that the patient's chances, without the negligence, were not nearly so favourable. If faced with this difficulty, the expert may be able to circumvent the argument by showing that wrong inferences had been drawn from the statistics. Alternatively, he may be able to argue that the cohort of patients in the study was not closely matched with the age and sex of the plaintiff. This will help to invalidate a comparison between negligent and proper treatment. The expert may even be able to show that the original research methods were flawed and that this gave rise to biased results.

(xii) The conference with counsel

The conference with counsel is a meeting between all those people who are taking part in the advancement, or the defence, of the case. It will include the litigant herself, her solicitor, counsel and the experts. It is usually held at counsel's chambers but this is not invariable. For reasons of convenience, it may be held at the solicitor's office. It may even be held at the patient's bedside if she is dying and the case is subsequently to be taken over by the relatives on behalf of the deceased's estate.

Traditionally, the client was not always invited to attend. This was on the basis that she was probably incapable of understanding the issues, and any contribution from her would amount to little more than interference. However, it is usual now for the client to be included and her contributions to, for example, evidence of fact are regarded as being invaluable. Conversely, the client's attendance may not be considered so appropriate at a conference which is primarily concerned with issues of causation, as this is likely to be an entirely technical discussion.

In one case, a plaintiff was asked to leave the room when the question of causation was to be discussed. Counsel was aware of the poor prognosis of the litigating patient and rightly felt that to hear the discussion at first hand would be depressing for him and would tend to reduce his sense of well-being in what little time he had left.

Sometimes those attending will include other people as well; for example, the plaintiff may be going to rely on the evidence of a neighbour who witnessed the doctor's house visit. Alternatively, a general practitioner may wish to call his receptionist as witness to remarks that were allegedly made by the patient when he called at the office or made a telephone request for help. Attendance by such other people at the conference gives counsel the opportunity of assessing how convincing their evidence will be if the case comes to trial.

There is no conventional stage in the proceedings at which a conference is generally called. It can occur at any time and there may even be more than one conference. However, it is usual to accomplish as much as possible by letter and written report first. This is partly in the interests of economy and it has to be added that many plaintiff cases fall away as soon as the first expert's report is available. This has some advantage, in that the case reaches a conclusion with the least possible expenditure.

Counsel may see fit to draft the pleadings before or after the conference, but in many cases the latter course is considered preferable. He will have studied the various reports and statements earlier, but the conference gives him the opportunity of interviewing the client and experts at first hand. It will help counsel to see how well those on his side will respond to his examination-in-chief, and how they will hold up against cross-examination by the other side.

When counsel has drafted the statement of claim, or the defence, it is usual for the solicitor to send a copy to the experts for their approval before it is served. This ensures that the statement is sufficiently precise and complete to avoid it being unduly vulnerable to a request for further and better particulars from the opposing side. A claim that is drafted in wide or vague terms gives the defence more scope to ask awkward questions of the plaintiff's advisers.

(xiii) In court

Appearance in court represents the ultimate point of focus for the expert. He must be aware that every case on which he accepts instructions might reach that pinnacle and he should only agree to become involved on this basis. The would-be expert who responds to an initial enquiry by saying he will assist 'as long as I do not have to stand up in court' is of no help to a solicitor acting for either side.

The statistics, however, show the reality of the situation. In this author's experience, the proportion of initial plaintiffs' instructions that come to trial amount to considerably less than 1%. Many cases fall away at an early stage and this suggests that complaints are often prompted by factors that do not fall within the concept of negligence. Examples of this include inadequate explanations, poor communications, and just plain lack of courtesy. Others will fall by the wayside at a later stage because, although strong on negligence, they prove to be weaker than originally expected on causation.

Throughout these relatively early phases some worthwhile plaintiff cases collapse because the litigant is funded privately and is daunted by the financial prospects of continuing. Alternatively, the plaintiff may be tempted to accept a derisory offer in settlement as it at least relieves her of the anxiety of continuing the litigation. It also gives her the feeling that, psychologically at least, she has won the case. Remortgaging the house to finance the case is not an attractive plan for a litigant who cannot be sure of success. The proportion of cases in this category may well increase as the contraction in legal aid which came into force in 1993 takes its toll.

In the earlier part of this chapter we saw how the expert engaged in a case, whether for plaintiff or defendant, has a duty to assist the litigant. In passing, it should be mentioned that for a plaintiff's expert this does not mean working to advance and win the case regardless of the circumstances. A properly set out report explaining that the treatment was not negligent can go a long way towards helping a patient come to terms with an unfavourable outcome. This can be a valuable form of assistance, and plaintiffs' solicitors who suspect all along that their client has no worthwhile case are only too glad to receive such a report, because it brings the matter to a conclusion.

At trial, the expert has a slightly different task. Although he is representing one particular side his prime duty is to the court. This means that he has to help the judge decide the outcome of the case. He may find it difficult to remember this point when he feels sympathetic towards his client and is facing aggressive cross-examination by opposing counsel. It is at times like this that the expert must remember that short, simple, direct answers to questions will be much more persuasive to the judge than long, complicated responses which drag in material that is not strictly relevant to the question. The latter course of action merely serves to confuse the judge on a matter he may well have difficulty in understanding in any event. This risks making him unsympathetic and could contribute towards losing the case.

An expert who seems unable to answer a question in court can be a source of irritation for the judge, and a liability to his own side. Perhaps two of the commonest reasons for an expert's apparent failure to give a proper answer are:

- that he does not understand the question;

- that the answer he knows he must give is adverse to his side of the case.

On the first of these points, it has to be said that no expert should feel embarrassed or ashamed at having to respond by saying he is not clear about the meaning of the question. He should not hesitate to ask counsel to make it clearer. He can take some comfort from the thought that the judge may not fully have understood its implications either. On the second point, any expert in court must realise that he has very little hope of being able to give a favourable answer to every single question. This, of course, especially applies when he is under cross-examination, but he must remember that a competent barrister may try to capitalise on an evasive answer, with the result that even more damage is suffered.

The task of the expert in the witness box is, in a sense, very simple. It is to give direct answers to the questions that are put to him. It does not extend any further than this. In particular, he must resist the temptation to give the court a medical lecture as if he were talking to students on a ward round. Additionally, he must not express opinions on topics about which he has not been asked. To venture down either of these paths is asking for trouble. The expert might annoy and confuse the judge by doing so, and it may give the other side an unexpected opportunity to make matters even more awkward for him.

The expert who has never appeared in court may well be filled with fear and trepidation at the prospect. This feeling is likely to become enhanced as the date approaches and the effort of both sides at settling the dispute seem to come to nought. The expert has visions of opposing counsel making it look as if his evidence of fact is completely unreliable, and his evidence of opinion is not worth the paper on which it was written. The wise course of action for any expert in a case approaching trial is to ensure that he is familiar not only with the evidence of himself and his colleagues, but also with that of his opponents. We saw earlier how, at mutual exchange of reports, the expert will have had the opportunity of studying the other side's evidence. From this he should be able to foresee the arguments that might be put forward against him and to anticipate many of the awkward questions. In other words, he can do no more than familiarise himself thoroughly with the implications of all the papers on which reliance will be placed at trial.

The role of the expert in court has received judicial comment in *National Justice Compania Naviera SA v Prudential Assurance Company Ltd (Ikarian Reefer)* (1993).[40] This was a shipping case, but the judge's remarks are equally relevant to medical negligence litigation. They were as follows:

1. Expert evidence presented to the court should be, and should be seen to be, the independent product of the expert uninfluenced as to form or content by the exigencies of litigation.

2. Independent assistance should be provided to the court by way of objective unbiased opinion regarding matters within the expertise of the expert witness. An expert witness in the High Court should never assume the role of advocate.

3. Facts or assumptions upon which the opinion was based should be stated together with material facts which could detract from the concluded opinion.

4. An expert witness should make it clear when a question or issue falls outside his expertise.

5. If the opinion is not properly researched because it was considered that insufficient data was available, then that has to be stated with an indication that the opinion was provisional. If the witness cannot assert that the report contained the truth, the whole truth and nothing but the truth then that qualification should be stated on the report.

6. If, after exchange of reports, an expert witness changes his mind on a material matter then the change of view should be communicated to the other side through legal representatives without delay and when appropriate to the court.

7. Photographs, plans, survey reports and other documents referred to in the expert evidence have to be provided to the other side at the same time as the exchange of reports.

---

40 *The Times*, 5 March 1993. Discused in *Personal Injury and Medical Law Letter*. May 1993 p 29.

(xiv) The expert's immunity from suit

It goes without saying that a medical practitioner can be sued if he gives negligent treatment to his patient. It is equally apparent that he can be sued if he gives negligent advice to a patient. The question therefore arises of whether the practitioner can be sued when he is giving expert advice to a client on a case involving alleged negligence by another doctor.

Solicitors can be sued for mismanaging their clients' affairs at any stage, but barristers are immune in respect of their conduct of a case in court. This rule was made long ago to ensure that counsel could fulfil his duty to the court without fear of external pressure or threats. Barristers are, however, liable for negligent advice or other conduct of the case unrelated to the court hearing. We have seen how the prime duty of the expert at trial is to give an unbiased and independent opinion to the court and he is therefore immune in the same way.[41] The question of the extent to which an expert can claim immunity outside the court was considered by the House of Lords in *Saif Ali* to include:

> ... pre-trial work so intimately connected with the conduct of the case in court that it could fairly be said to be a preliminary decision affecting the way that the case was to be conducted when it came to a hearing.[42]

Although this was not a medical negligence case the same principle was very recently applied to a medical expert.[43] The expert's position is therefore that he can indeed be sued if he is negligent in his advice to a solicitor or client before court proceedings have been started. It is perhaps convenient to think of advice given at this level as being equivalent to that the expert will give to a patient who is ill, or which a solicitor will give to a client who is contemplating litigation.

---

[41] For a more detailed discussion of the immunity of the expert witness, see Stone in *J Med Def Union* vol 11, no 1 (January 1995), pp 8 and 9.

[42] *Saif Ali v Sydney Mitchell & Co* [1980] AC 198.

[43] *Landall v Dennis Faulkner & Alsop & Others* [1994] 5 Med LR 26.

PART C

THE CASE LAW

XXV INTRODUCTION TO CASE LAW

(i)   General background

It is important to realise that case law is not merely a catalogue of decisions judges have made over a period of time. Some 'case books' may give this impression when opened by the casual reader, who finds little more than an alphabetical list of cases between the two covers. Although the decision in an individual case that reaches court is, so to speak, carved in stone, it must be appreciated that case law is a living and flexible subject. As well as being a record of the past it is, at least within limits, a predictor of the future. Conclusions can be drawn from past cases which help to assess the likely outcome of those of the future.

As we shall see in a moment, negligence in clinical practice is what we call a common law subject. This means that it is based on the case law that makes up the common law. The decided cases which appear in this part of the book are mostly concerned with negligence alleged in medical cases, and the majority of them have been selected from the realms of general practice. However, a few non-medical cases have also been included, and some of these are taken from the field of industrial injury. The reason for this is that the legal reasoning used by the judge in reaching his decision is also relevant to medical cases. For example, in the case law section on causation, the decision in the industrial case of *Bonnington Castings v Wardlaw* (1956) helps us to see the approach a judge would be likely to take when faced with a case of a patient damaged by a prolonged course of tablets and only part of the course had been prescribed negligently.

The status of the court giving the decision in any particular case has a profound influence on the question of whether or not it is 'binding' on another court in a later case. When a civil case, such as one of alleged negligence, reaches trial it is heard in the county court. However, if the damages award is likely to exceed £50,000, or if the case is unduly complicated, it will be heard in the High Court. If an appeal against the court of first instance is allowed it will be heard by the Civil Division of the Court of Appeal. If the appeal goes still further, the case will be heard by the House of Lords. Thus, when we come to the cases on causation, we shall see how, in *Hotson v East Berkshire HA* (1987), a proportionate approach was taken by the court of first instance when assessing damages for a boy who was deprived of the opportunity of cure of his fractured hip by a hospital's negligence. The defendants appealed, only to find that the Court of Appeal upheld the trial judge's decision. They then appealed to the House of Lords, which overruled the decision, and held that an 'all or none' approach should be used. This meant that the boy, instead of being awarded 25% of full damages to cover his loss of a 1 in 4 opportunity of cure, received nothing. The House held that he had to prove he was more likely than not to have been cured if he had been given proper treatment, and this, even if it was well short of certain cure, would have entitled him to receive full damages. The rule in *Hotson*, as it was a House of Lords decision, is therefore binding on all lower courts, and they are now bound to follow it.

Courts of first instance are assisted by the decisions of other courts of their own status. To some extent, these other decisions predict what the Court of Appeal would be likely to find in the case in question. The Court of Appeal itself is bound by its own decisions. Conversely, the House of Lords can go behind its earlier decisions, and will do so in rare cases. It thus has a freer hand in influencing the evolution of case law. Nevertheless, all courts, including the House of Lords, recognise the importance of certainty in the law and earlier decisions will only be overruled when there has been some important social change.

(ii)   Statute law

One of the features of the English legal system is the co-existence of statute law and common law, sitting one alongside the other. Although it is the common law with which medical negligence is mostly concerned, it is as well to spend a moment on the meaning of statute law, so as to see the matter in perspective, especially as it is extremely relevant to the administrative aspects of the National Health Service.

A statute is an Act of Parliament. It is drafted by specialists called Parliamentary Counsel, and in its early stages is known as a Bill. It then goes forward for the approval of both Houses of Parliament where, in theory at least, it is considered by a democratically-elected body representative of the majority of the adult population of the UK. If so approved, a Bill will then go on to receive the Royal Assent, after which it is known as an Act and it then becomes law.

Two simple examples will suffice. Various Road Traffic Acts have provided that a motorist shall not exceed a certain speed on a motorway or drive with more than a certain level of alcohol in the blood. Similarly, the National Health Service Act 1946 provided that hospitals be set up to employ medical and nursing staff. It also provided that general practitioners shall maintain lists of their patients and be paid by the State as independent contractors.

Statute law has been in existence for centuries, but in early times there were relatively few Acts of Parliament and most of these made little impact on the everyday life of the citizen. However, with the advent of the Industrial Revolution there was a marked increase in legislation of this kind. Doubtless this was in response to the need to regularise various aspects of trade. The Factory Acts were aimed at protecting employees in hazardous manufacturing operations and may have been prompted by those who thought they had been exploited by unscrupulous employers. Similarly, the Sale of Goods Acts have sought to regularise the relationship between buyer and seller, and to prevent one taking unfair advantage of the other. Since the beginning of the 20th century the volume of statute law has increased inexorably. It has outstripped Parliament's ability to produce it, and the system of delegated legislation has played an ever-increasing role in its development.

Delegated legislation is a system by which an Act of Parliament gives power to a Minister to make regulations so that the law can be extended without alteration of the primary legislation. These enabling Acts allow Statutory Instruments to be drawn up and in Chapter II we saw an example of such a document. Statutory Instrument 1992 No 635 was the National Health Service (General Medical Services) Regulations 1992. Part of that document (paragraph 12 of Schedule 2, the 'Terms of Service' for doctors) defines the duties expected of a general practitioner when he is included in the medical list of a Family Health Services Authority. Indeed, enabling Acts and their resulting statutory instruments have had a profound influence on the development of the administrative aspects of the National Health Service.

Part of the reason for delegation of legislation by Statutory Instrument is that it gives an opportunity for the Minister concerned to consult those people who will be most affected. Additionally, it allows the Minister to consult suitable experts in the field who will be far better placed than a Member of Parliament to ensure that it is appropriately drawn up. The Statutory Instrument is 'laid on the table' of both Houses, and can be challenged by Parliament.

It can be seen that the growth of statute law has meant that our everyday lives are now very much more regulated than those of our predecessors a couple of centuries ago. Naturally, this applies to the whole population, but it applies with even greater force to the doctor.

(iii)   Common law

In the 12th century a system developed whereby judges went 'on circuit' to different parts of Britain. The arguments put forward by the two sides in the case were based on the long-established custom of the land. Over a period of time, the threads of these customs became interwoven into a system of law. At the end of their tour the judges returned to Westminster and discussed cases with their colleagues who, as likely as not, would have been trying similar cases on their circuits. In this way, judges were able to achieve some degree of uniformity in their decision-making processes. When they next went on circuit they were more likely to give judgments in line with those being given by their colleagues elsewhere. In this way, the judges developed what became known as the 'common law'. It represented a code which took into account the customs of the country and lent some degree of uniformity to all the courts in the land. In other words, it was 'common' to all courts. It was not ordained by Parliament and amounted to no more than a general consensus view of what was right and just in particular circumstances. Nevertheless, it commanded respect because the code had been distilled by the decisions of hundreds of cases and it provided a level of certainty for the future that had previously not been possible. Moreover, it allowed changing circumstances such as social factors to have some influence on the current state of the law. A judge could, within limits, depart from an earlier decision if it was felt that recent social developments called for a different decision.

Murder is an example of a common law offence. By this we mean that there is no statute, no Act of Parliament, which says that it is an offence to take another person's life. For centuries, however, the common law, through its earlier decisions, has laid down that anyone found guilty of murder will be punished.

The evolution of the common law covered all aspects of life and provided the backbone of the English legal system for centuries. With the coming of the Industrial Revolution and the need for statutory regulation of so many aspects of life, the common law gradually gave way to statute law and there has been an even more marked erosion of the former by the latter since the beginning of the 20th century. Many developments of the common law were integrated with earlier statutes and 'codified' into later statutes.

Medical negligence, however, is very much a common law subject. It was a common law decision that produced the *Bolam* test for the standard of care (see Chapter III) and there is no statute which tells a doctor what treatment to give in any particular case. Despite this, doctors on the medical lists of Family Health Service Authorities do have a limit to what can be expected of them enacted in paragraph 3 of their 'Terms of Service', as follows:

> ... a doctor shall not ... be expected to exercise a higher degree of skill, knowledge and care than ... that which general practitioners as a class may reasonably be expected to exercise.

An additional point to note is that, following a finding of negligence, the patient's remedy is 'common law damages'. No statute can restore the status quo after a medical accident. Even a monetary award, as compensation, is merely assessed on the basis of other similar cases. These provide a 'tariff' which judges can use as a starting point and to guide them in each particular case.

'Kemp and Kemp'[44] (see page 257) provides lawyers with a yardstick for damages by quoting figures that were reached in earlier decisions. It gives detailed circumstances of each case so as to allow a fair comparison. Indeed, it may even give the complete judgment, as no two cases are exactly alike, and this allows lawyers to see what parallels can be drawn.

Although many administrative aspects of the National Health Service are subject to statute law, medical negligence in clinical practice is little affected by it. It is to the common law that we must look in our study of this topic. We can now move on to consider how precedents are evolved from the wealth of case law which, over a period of time, has come to represent the common law. Before doing so, however, we must bear in mind that the claim itself is brought within the framework of statutory law which governs the procedure for advancing or defending the case. This concerns such matters as the limitation of actions by lapse of time, and this particular facet (and the legislation that governs it) is considered in some detail in Chapter IX.

(iv)   Precedent

We have seen how the system of common law produced a degree of consistency between cases with regard to the decision-making

---

44   *The Quantum of Damages,* by Kemp and Kemp.

process. This consistency was highly desirable. It helped the law to command respect because it was seen as being fair. It treated each case alike and prevented injustice. Another advantage was that it made the law predictable. A litigant could assess how likely he was to win if his case came to trial.

In this way, a system of precedent developed, with each case building on its predecessor. This process was not, however, an automatic and unthinking one. It took account of all the circumstances of the case. Many of the facts of the case in hand probably have been nearly identical to an earlier one, but the events may have happened some years later. The judge may therefore think that a different decision should be given so as to allow for more modern social circumstances. Similarly, in a medical case, it may well be that the current of lay and medical opinion has changed such that different standards are expected. In the chapter on consent (see pages 90-91) we saw how the law relating to consent was established in this country in *Sidaway v Board of Governors of Bethlem Royal Hospital and Maudsley Hospital* (1985). We went on to see how a different approach was taken in the American case of *Canterbury v Spence* (1972). However, that precedent would be unlikely to have any influence on a judge in the UK unless there was a House of Lords decision that overruled *Sidaway*. Among other things, the system of precedent is overwhelmingly concerned with certainty in the law. This helps the lawyer to advise his client with confidence about the likely outcome of the client's case.

Binding precedents are those that bind a court to follow an earlier decision. Courts are bound by decisions of superior courts, and usually follow decisions of those of their own status. They are not bound by inferior courts. Decisions by Commonwealth jurisdictions may be persuasive. Counsel may refer to them in support of his case, and will invite the judge to place some weight on them, although the judge will not be bound to do so.

If a judge is faced with a binding precedent he may nevertheless feel that justice in the case will not be well served by following it. If this happens, he may be able to circumvent the difficulty by 'distinguishing' the facts of the case in hand. He may find that there were enough inconsistencies in the facts of the two cases to justify ignoring the earlier one and dismissing it as irrelevant. If a disgruntled litigant feels he has been disadvantaged in this way he can appeal to a higher court for the decision to be reversed.

The system of precedent that has evolved from the development of the common law is of the utmost importance to the lawyer. When assessing the merits of a case the lawyer will study the case law on the subject, knowing that his opponent will be doing the same. If the case reaches trial, counsel will cite cases he regards as persuasive and he will invite the judge to place weight on those authorities. The judgment itself is likely to make reference to those cases which the judge considers are good authority for the decision he gives. It follows that the precedents upon which reliance is placed form the basis for the legal reasoning underlying the decision.

It is for this reason that the case law section of this book is important and we are now well placed to go through those cases and to see how the doctor's management of the illness, at the bedside or in the consulting room, can later give rise to a judicial decision and how this can influence a subsequent case.

XXVI TABLE OF CASES

Note:

The cases in this chapter have been grouped into sections according to the issue with which each one is mainly concerned. However, it must be appreciated that all relevant legal points have to be covered in the advancement of any negligence case. For example, in *Dale v Munthali* (1977) the plaintiff's principal task was to show that the doctor had fallen short of acceptable standards in failing to diagnose malaria, but the case is also a useful illustration of how the plaintiff's memory can be a source of very strong evidence when compared to inadequate medical notes.

The allocation of the cases into different sections in this chapter serves no purpose other than convenience and ease of reference.

(i)   Existence of a duty of care

(For a discussion of this subject see Chapter II)

Bolton v Stone, 1951
Donoghue v Stevenson, 1932
Haley v London Electricity Board, 1964

BOLTON v STONE [1951] 1 All ER 1078 House of Lords

The facts

A cricket ground was surrounded by a high fence which was intended to protect passers-by from balls that had been hit far and high. In one particular game, a batsman hit just such a ball, which cleared the fence and struck the plaintiff, causing injury. The plaintiff sued the batsman, on the basis that he should have realised that the ball might go over the fence and should have been more careful.

Matter for the court to decide

The first point the plaintiff had to establish was that a duty of care was owed to him by the batsman. In other words, he had to show that the batsman should have realised that a passer-by might be close to the other side of the fence and that there was a chance that a well-hit ball could cause injury.

Held

It was held that no duty of care was owed by the batsman to the plaintiff. Evidence showed that the ball had only been hit out of the ground half a dozen times during the previous three decades. Furthermore, the fence was seven feet high and sufficiently far away from the batsman's position for him quite reasonably to have believed it to be extremely unlikely that his ball would clear it.

☆ ☆ ☆

DONOGHUE v STEVENSON [1932] AC 562 House of Lords

The facts

Two girls were sitting at a table in a cafe in Paisley, near Glasgow. One of them had bought a bottle of ginger beer and had drunk part of it. As an act of kindness, she allowed her friend to finish the bottle. The friend poured the second part of the bottle into her own glass, but it contained a decomposed snail which had unfortunately been included in the bottle during the manufacturing process. She was unaware of this until she took it into her mouth, whereupon she spat it out and later sued the manufacturers.

Matter for the court to decide

The initial difficulty for the second girl was establishing that a duty of care existed. She had to establish this point before she could proceed to the questions of liability and causation. She had to overcome the traditional approach to the 'neighbour principle' which appears to have viewed a legal neighbour in narrow terms such that a duty could only be owed to people who could be seen, heard or were proximate in some other way. This girl's difficulty was that the act occurred hundreds of miles from the manufacturer's premises and the manufacturers had never heard of her.

Held

Lord Atkin, in his famous judgment which has defined the 'neighbour principle' in such clear terms that it is still in use today, posed the question, 'Who is my neighbour?' The answer he gave was:

> ... persons who are so closely and directly affected by my act that I ought reasonably to have had them in contemplation as being so affected when I am directing my mind to the acts or omissions which are called into question.

Having thus defined the required relationship between plaintiff and defendant, he held that the manufacturer did owe a duty of care to the girl. It was foreseeable that their manufacturing technique, and any faults associated with it, would affect whoever consumed the contents of their bottles.

☆ ☆ ☆

HALEY v LONDON ELECTRICITY BOARD [1964] 3 All ER 185
House of Lords

The facts

A partially-sighted man was walking along the pavement and was approaching the site where there was an excavation for electricity repairs. The Electricity Board were aware that fencing precautions had to be routinely undertaken, to prevent passers-by from being injured. As the plaintiff in this case was partially-sighted he did not notice the fencing in time, fell into the hole and was injured.

Matter for the court to decide

The court had to decide whether a duty of care was owed by the Electricity Board to the partially-sighted plaintiff. The important point here was to decide whether or not the defendants owed a duty of care to partially-sighted persons which was over and above that owed to fully-sighted persons.

Held

It was held that the proportion of partially-sighted persons walking along this particular pavement was sufficiently high to mean that the defendants should have taken care to fence the hole in a way that would allow for their disability.

☆ ☆ ☆

(ii)   Breach of the duty of care

(For a discussion of this subject see Chapter III)

* Denotes Commonwealth or American case

BATEMAN v DOIRON (1991) 8 CCLT 284

The medical facts

A man suffering from coronary artery disease was admitted to the accident and emergency department of a small urban hospital in New Brunswick, Canada, in 1986. This department was staffed by a local general practitioner who failed to diagnose the true nature of the patient's illness or to institute sufficiently prompt treatment. The man died, and the family sued both the doctor and the hospital who ran the department.

Matter for the court to decide

The court had to decide:

(a) whether the general practitioner fell short of acceptable standards by failing to diagnose the heart disease and to arrange proper treatment; and

(b) whether the hospital fell short of proper standards by only making a general practitioner available rather than a specialist skilled in accident and emergency medicine generally, or in cardiology in particular.

Held

(a) The court held that the general practitioner had not fallen short. The inability to diagnose the condition accurately was perfectly in keeping with the standards expected of a competent general practitioner. An additional point in the doctor's favour was that the patient had been assessed by a cardiologist just a few hours previously and no great concern had been expressed at that point.

(b) The hospital had not fallen short in merely providing a general practitioner for this kind of duty because this was a small urban hospital (in Moncton) and it was perfectly reasonable to staff the department with part-time general practitioners. This was distinguished from the requirement that would be expected of a large teaching hospital elsewhere in Canada.

☆ ☆ ☆

BOLAM v FRIERN HOSPITAL MANAGEMENT COMMITTEE [1957] 2 All ER 118

The medical facts

Mr Bolam was a patient who suffered from depressive illness. His general practitioner referred him to a consultant psychiatrist, who recommended electro-convulsive therapy. There was a school of thought which believed that muscle relaxant drugs should be used during the convulsion, with the intention of preventing the occurrence of fractures. However, the psychiatrist to whom Mr Bolam was referred belonged to a different school of thought which believed that there were side effects to the use of such drugs and that they outweighed the possible benefits. Mr Bolam duly underwent the treatment without the relaxants, but he unfortunately found that both his hips had been fractured in the process. He therefore sued the psychiatrist, together with the anaesthetist, for negligence in terms of failure to use the muscle relaxants.

Matter for the court to decide

The court had to decide whether the failure to use the muscle relaxants amounted to negligence. Put another way, it had to decide whether that failure amounted to a course of action of which no responsible body of medical opinion would approve.

Held

The plaintiff's action failed. McNair J was the trial judge and it is worth quoting the relevant part of his judgment:

> A doctor is not guilty of negligence if he has acted in accordance with the practice accepted as proper by a responsible body of medical men skilled in that particular art ... Putting it the other way round, a doctor is not negligent if he is acting in accordance with such a practice merely because there is a body of opinion that takes a contrary view.

McNair J recognised that there were two 'responsible bodies' of medical opinion. One of them believed it was good practice to give the muscle relaxants, and the other was of the view that it was good practice to withhold them.

BOVA v SPRING, 1990 [1994] 5 Med LR

The medical facts

A 44 year old man, Peter Bova, was attempting to move a slab of concrete and he developed persistent pains in the right side of his chest. A week later his wife called the doctor because he started to complain of diarrhoea, breathlessness and feeling shivery. Additionally, he felt the pains were worse on movement. On examination, the doctor found that there was 'exquisite tenderness' of the chest wall where the patient thought he had strained himself, but there were no abnormal sounds in the lungs. The practitioner confirmed the patient's suspicion of a muscular strain and attributed the other symptoms to a coincidental virus infection. No follow up for reassessment was arranged.

Two days later, Mr Bova collapsed and died. A post-mortem showed that the weight of the right lung was almost double that of the left one. The cause of death was given as suppurative lobar pneumonia.

Matter for the court to decide

There was no doubt that the doctor had accepted the patient's suggestion of a muscular strain in the chest wall and had dismissed the other symptoms as being unconnected and harmless. The doctor felt that he had eliminated more serious causes within the lungs because he could detect no abnormal sounds. Expert evidence for the plaintiff showed that, if the patient had been re-assessed the day after the initial diagnosis, an examination of the chest would probably have revealed signs of pneumonic consolidation and that urgent treatment would have been put in hand which would have saved the patient's life.

The court therefore had to decide whether the practitioner had afforded a proper standard of care in not arranging to visit the patient again on the following day for reassessment.

Held

The judge held that the doctor had been negligent in failing to arrange a follow-up visit. He conceded that:

Dr Spring was not guilty of elementary errors of examination, nor was he negligent in not referring Mr Bova to hospital ...

and he based his criticism on the premise that:

Dr Spring had erred ... in proceeding from the absence of confirmatory signs of pneumonia at the moment of examination to an unequivocal diagnosis of muscle strain to the right chest.

☆ ☆ ☆

CHAPMAN v RIX, 1960 [1994] 5 Med LR 239

The medical facts

A butcher, Edward Chapman, was boning meat at Sainsbury's on 18 October 1955. The knife slipped and caused an abdominal wound below and to the left of the umbilicus. The man was taken to a cottage hospital where Dr Rix, a general practitioner, examined and probed the wound. He found that it had penetrated the deep subcutaneous fascia but not the underlying muscle. He formed the opinion that it had almost certainly not penetrated the abdominal cavity. He therefore treated it with a suture and sent the patient home to be seen by his own doctor. He provided no letter for the patient to take but relied on the patient to give his own doctor a message to the effect that the wound was only 'superficial'.

Later that evening, the patient called his own general practitioner, Dr Mohr, who, although the pain had moved to the other (right) side of the abdomen, decided that there was nothing seriously wrong.

Two days later, on 20 October, Dr Mohr was called again, visited, found that the patient's condition had deteriorated and arranged immediate admission to a surgical unit. Peritonitis was diagnosed, resulting from the original knife wound. Despite an emergency operation the patient died on 26 October.

Matter for the court to decide

There were originally nine allegations of negligence, including Dr Rix's failure to reach the correct diagnosis and his failure to have the patient detained in hospital under surgical supervision. However, many of these fell away at an early stage and the case was ultimately narrowed down to just one point. That was Dr Rix's failure to provide a letter for, or otherwise communicate directly with, the deceased's own doctor in such a way as to put him in full possession of all the relevant facts.

Held

(a) At first instance

The trial judge held that Dr Rix had been negligent in failing to communicate with Mr Chapman's own doctor and imparting to him the exact nature of his findings when he examined the wound.

(b) Court of Appeal

On appeal by Dr Rix, the judgment was reversed, with a finding of no negligence in failing to provide a letter.

(c) House of Lords

The plaintiff appealed against the Court of Appeal's reversal of the trial judge's finding, but after what seems to have been a very considerable difference of opinion, the majority dismissed the appeal, finding in Dr Rix's favour.

When asked by his own barrister at the trial why he had not sent a letter, Dr Rix said:

> I could not put into a letter anything that the patient could not tell him himself or that Dr Mohr could not infer from my action.

In exonerating Dr Rix, Lord Goddard remarked that:

> ... it seems to me clear that in acting as he did Dr Rix was actuated firstly by the opinion he had formed that the wound

was superficial and also bearing in mind the minute possibility to which I have referred that it was necessary for the patient to be kept under observation. For what other reason had he been so insistent that the patient's own doctor should be called in and advised as to what had happened and what had been done?

later adding that:

True it is that Dr Rix did not communicate directly with Dr Mohr, but he had emphatically warned the patient to call in his own doctor, and he did, and to tell him exactly what had happened and what had taken place at the hospital, and this was done ...

and later still adding that

Dr Mohr must have known, or at least Dr Rix might assume that he would know, that he was called in for the purpose of keeping the patient under observation.

Interestingly, it was Lord Denning who dissented from this view and was critical of Dr Rix. He was sympathetic to the giving of a reassuring opinion to the patient himself but thought that he should have been more explicit as far as communicating with a medical colleague was concerned. He put it like this:

I can understand that a medical man may sometimes feel justified in giving misleading information to a patient so as not to worry him. But if he does so, he must be very careful to give the true information to his relatives and those about him, and most important of all, he must be careful to give the true information to his own doctor who has to treat him. It was the failure of Dr Rix to observe this rule, which I should regard as elementary, which was his mistake here. I realise that Dr Rix acted promptly and with the best intentions, and he deserves every credit for so doing, but at the critical point I fear that he failed.

COKER v DOLLAND (1993) (Unreported)

The medical facts

An 18 year old unmarried girl had a Caesarian section in the 36th week of pregnancy on the grounds of pre-eclampsia. She was observed to have had significantly raised blood pressure readings and protein in the urine during the time immediately preceding hospital admission. The readings settled quite quickly and the proteinuria disappeared soon after the birth. The consultant physician under whose care she had been in respect of the hypertensive control then wrote a letter to the general practitioner saying that he considered it reasonable to prescribe the contraceptive pill.

The general practitioner duly prescribed the Pill but it was alleged that the girl paid several visits to him, accompanied by her father, complaining of severe headaches, visual symptoms and difficulty in co-ordinating her limbs. It was also alleged that she asked the general practitioner to take her off the Pill in view of these symptoms but that he resisted the suggestion. Unfortunately, it was not long before she had a cerebral thrombosis and died, leaving the baby in the care of the grandparents.

Matter for the court to decide

The court was faced with conflicting expert evidence. On behalf of the plaintiff it was alleged that the pill should have been stopped when the general practitioner was being faced with repeated complaints of the type about which warnings are given in the British National Formulary (BNF) and in the Monthly Index of Medical Specialities (MIMS). Conversely, the defence argued that there was no good evidence that the girl had ever attended as often as was alleged or that, even if she had so attended, these complaints were ever voiced.

Held

The court found in the defendant's favour. One of the difficulties for the plaintiff's side was that the girl's father had died between the time of the alleged negligence and the trial, and therefore his opinions became nothing more than hearsay. Additionally, the general practitioner's notes contained no record of the alleged visual symptoms and the only entry which referred to headaches suggested that there were good grounds for thinking that the probable cause was sinusitis.

The important point here was that the diametrically opposed views of the experts for each side were based on different factual backgrounds. Once the court had decided, in the defendant's favour, on the probable circumstances of the case, the expert for the plaintiff could do no more than to fall in line with the view held by that of his opponent.

☆ ☆ ☆

COLES v READING AND DISTRICT HMC AND ANOTHER (1963) (Unreported)

The medical facts

A 21 year old man suffered a finger injury when a lump of coal fell on it. He attended a cottage hospital and the wound was dressed by the nurse. He was advised to go to a main hospital in Reading for further treatment which would have included a tetanus immunisation. For some reason he failed to follow this advice and instead he visited his general practitioner some days later. This doctor did not ask the patient what treatment he had been given up to that point and merely changed the dressing. Unfortunately, the patient died shortly afterwards from overwhelming tetanus infection. The man's father sued both the cottage hospital and the general practitioner.

Matter for the court to decide

There were two potential defendants. The plaintiff advanced a criticism of the cottage hospital on the basis of failure to write a letter to the second hospital, which, in the event, would have been read by the general practitioner. That letter would have put the general practitioner on notice of what treatment had been given so far, and that a tetanus immunisation was yet to be administered. The plaintiff also criticised the family doctor for not making more diligent inquiries about his patient's earlier treatment, especially as he had not been provided with a letter.

Held

The cottage hospital was held to have been negligent in failing to communicate properly with professional colleagues by way of a letter which should have provided the relevant information. Additionally, the general practitioner was held to have been negligent in not inquiring of the patient what treatment he had received from the cottage hospital, or in not communicating with its staff to ensure that the immunisation had already been given.

☆　☆　☆

DALE v MUNTHALI (1977) 78 DLR (3d) 588

The medical facts

One Thursday night a man became ill, complaining of aching all over and of having a high fever. During the Friday and the Saturday he developed vomiting and diarrhoea, and his wife noticed that he was having difficulty in hearing. The general practitioner was called on the Sunday morning and he diagnosed influenza. During the rest of the Sunday and throughout the Monday the patient's condition deteriorated and on the Tuesday he was taken to hospital. On admission, pneumococcal meningitis was diagnosed and he died the next day.

Matter for the court to decide

Expert evidence for the plaintiff showed that the patient was almost certainly suffering from meningitis at the time of the doctor's visit on the Sunday. The court therefore had to decide whether the general practitioner should have made that diagnosis or should have at least been suspicious that the patient was sufficiently ill to have justified immediate hospital admission.

Held

(a) At first instance

It was held that the general practitioner had been negligent in not arranging admission.

The judge acknowledged that headache and neck stiffness are the two classic signs of meningitis. It was further accepted that the doctor had not asked about the presence of headache and had not tested for neck stiffness. Thus far, it appeared that the presenting symptoms were consistent with influenza. However, the judge accepted the wife's version of events in preference to that of the doctor who had kept very scanty notes. The judge pointed out that the patient:

> ... was so ill that he had been unable to get out of bed to go to the bathroom on several occasions. He was so ill that at one time he could not hold a glass of water and he was so ill that he was not answering the questions put to him by the doctor, such questions being answered by his wife.

The judge went on to say that:

> With such an ill and confused man I have come to the conclusion that Dr Munthali should have realised that this was something more than gastro-intestinal flu. His examination should have been more thorough and in all the circumstances I have reached the conclusion that he should have arranged for Mr Dale to be admitted to hospital right away for further testing.

(b) On appeal

The general practitioner appealed. He seized upon the fact that the judge at first instance acknowledged that it was not negligent to fail to diagnose meningitis. At that trial, the doctor was only criticised for failing to suspect something serious. This led the doctor to appeal, on the basis that it was inconsistent to exonerate him for failing to reach the diagnosis and yet to criticise him for failing to arrange admission.

The Ontario Court of Appeal held that:

In our view there is no inconsistency between [the trial judge's] finding that the appellant was not negligent in failing to diagnose meningitis, and his further finding that he was negligent in failing to realise that Mr Dale was suffering from something more serious than gastroenteritis.

Evidential note

This case has been listed under 'breach of the duty of care' in the case law section of this book on the basis that the doctor fell short of proper standards by failing to arrange hospital admission. However, the case is also a good illustration of the evidential difficulty a defendant can face if he has kept inadequate notes. Although the patient died just three days after being seen by the doctor, the first the general practitioner heard of it was a notification that reached him some months later. At the time of the house visit, the case appeared to him to amount to nothing more than a routine visit for influenza and he therefore had virtually no recollection of it when the litigation started. He was therefore entirely reliant on his contemporaneous notes. In his defence he therefore argued that all the responses of the patient were appropriate and that there seemed to be no difficulty with the patient's hearing. Conversely, the wife asserted that difficulty in hearing was one of her husband's dominant symptoms at the time, and the judge preferred her version of events. He believed that the trauma of her husband's death would have sharpened the widow's memory of the time and that this would have left the history of events very clear in her mind for a long time afterwards. He said:

I accept the evidence of Mrs Dale as to what occurred and where there is a conflict I reject the evidence of Dr Munthali.

☆ ☆ ☆

DURRANT v BURKE (1989) [1993] 4 Med LR 258

The medical facts

On 6 December 1981 a seven month old boy, Marlo Durrant, became ill and began to vomit. His mother sent for a doctor, and a locum diagnosed gastroenteritis and gave her a note which was to be taken to the surgery the next morning. The boy's own general practitioner acted upon that note and, on 7 December, visited the baby for assessment. When he arrived he was able to confirm the locum doctor's original diagnosis and advised the giving of fluids at regular intervals. He said he expected that the condition would have improved by the next day. Unfortunately, the child's condition did not improve and he continued to vomit during the night so his mother then called the doctor again the next day. On this second visit, the general practitioner arranged for hospital admission. The hospital diagnosed hypernatraemic dehydration and the child was later found to be suffering from brain damage.

The mother alleged that the general practitioner should have realised, on his first visit, that the child was at risk of dehydration and should have arranged hospital admission at that stage. She also alleged that, having not so arranged, he should have visited the child early in the day of the second visit even though the mother had not requested him to do so.

Matter for the court to decide

The court was faced with the decision as to whether the general practitioner had fulfilled proper standards of practice in terms of the advice he gave to the mother about feeding the child and the doctor's arrangements for follow-up.

Held

The court held that the general practitioner had given proper advice to the mother in terms of maintaining an adequate fluid intake. Additionally, it was held that there was no additional duty on the general practitioner to check on the child on the morning of the second visit when there was no request to do so by the mother.

The judge pointed out that:

> ... it was Mother's understandable concern with the baby not eating which was the cause of the trouble. Had she been less concerned and merely carried out what the doctor had told her to do, namely to give a little fluid often, the condition of hypernatraemic dehydration would probably not have

315

developed as it did. By feeding the child cereal on the Monday and Tuesday she unwittingly masked the development of the condition and I have no doubt that she thought that Marlo was improving which is why she did not get in touch with the doctor on the Tuesday.

☆   ☆   ☆

FELLOWS v THOMAS (1994) (Unreported)

The medical facts

John Fellows was the manager of a private nursing home. He developed a headache which caused him to visit his family doctor. It was alleged on his behalf that the headache had started very suddenly, during intercourse, late one Saturday night. It was further alleged that it had been felt most severely at the back of the head, that is in the occipital region, and had been accompanied by vomiting. He paid at least one visit to the doctor, although was not until the Monday or the Tuesday, and it was also alleged that there were two more visits, only one of which was mentioned in the notes. The symptoms persisted to some extent, but a fortnight later Mrs Fellows found her husband sitting at the bottom of the stairs having had a stroke. He was admitted to hospital and diagnosed as suffering from a subarachnoid haemorrhage. His speech was very badly affected and he was partially paralysed down one side of the body.

Matter for the court to decide

Mr Fellows sued his general practitioner, Dr Thomas, in negligence. He asserted that the symptoms were very suggestive of a subarachnoid haemorrhage and should have prompted immediate referral to a neurosurgeon. The other part of the plaintiff's case was that, if he had been so referred, there would have been an operation to clip the aneurysm from which the haemorrhage had arisen and that this would have averted the stroke. Dr Thomas' note for the only visit at which there was a description of the illness mentioned 'viral symptoms'. It also referred to the headache as being 'sudden' but the defendant argued that this description was perfectly consistent with an onset lasting as much as 24 hours. He added that this was not in the least suggestive of a subarachnoid haemorrhage which, even the plaintiff had to concede, was an exceptionally rare condition in general practice. Under cross-examination, Dr Thomas clung firmly to this version of the history and indicated with his hand that the distribution of the headache had been described to him as being 'like a band' starting at the front of the head. This was in marked contrast to Mr Fellows. When the court was sitting at his bedside for the morning he was asked about the site of the pain and he clasped both of his hands to the back of his head in a most dramatic gesture.

Held

Mr Justice Owen held that the claim should fail. He considered the credibility of the plaintiff's version of events and said 'As to Mrs Fellows' evidence I find it impossible to accept it as reliable,' adding later in the judgment that:

> Mrs Fellows is clearly wrong in her memory, her error showing in dramatic form the difficulties caused by late presentation to the court of vital evidence.

The judge explained this on the basis that:

> The years and a desire to help her estranged husband have played their part in creating in the mind of Mrs Fellows an inaccurate picture of the events.

Mrs Fellows had been convinced that her husband, following the initial development of the headache on the Saturday night, had waited over the weekend and gone to the doctor on Monday. Her difficulty, of course, was that the general practitioner's entry was dated Tuesday. The judge accepted the date of the note as correct and remarked that it was corroborated by the office appointment book for that week. This delay by Mr Fellows in seeking treatment merely served to reduce the apparent severity of the symptoms that were being presented to the doctor, and this was very helpful to the defendant's case in terms of justifying his failure to arrange specialist referral.

☆ ☆ ☆

GORDON v WILSON (1991) [1992] 3 Med LR 401

The medical facts

A woman in Aberdeenshire saw her general practitioner on a number of occasions between January 1983 and August 1985 with symptoms of left-sided deafness and difficulties with balance. She also presented other symptoms, namely difficulties with vision, increasing abnormal sensations on the left side of the face, and difficulties with eating and swallowing. Additionally, there were some behavioural symptoms. At the end of the time in question she was referred for specialist investigation which resulted in her having a benign meningioma removed from part of the brain. By the time that the operation was carried out the tumour had involved several cranial nerves.

Matter for the court to decide

The pursuer advanced the case against the general practitioner on two fronts:

(a) that, with this combination of symptoms, she should have been referred at an earlier stage in the development of the symptoms; and

(b) that, when she was ultimately referred, the arrangements should have been put in hand with more urgency.

Held

On the first point, the court held that the general practitioners were negligent in terms of failure to refer at a sufficiently early stage in the development of the symptoms. It took the view that the combination of symptoms was sufficient to require investigation of a kind that would lie beyond the competence of a general practitioner to carry out fully.

As regards the second front on which the case was being advanced, the court held that the pursuer had not produced sufficient evidence to show that the referral was made with a less than adequate degree of urgency.

LANGLEY v CAMPBELL (1975) The Times, 6 November 1975

The medical facts

A man who lived in England had been employed by his firm to work in Uganda. He returned from that country on 1 July 1970 but nine days later he started to feel very unwell with headache, fever and alternate sweating and shivering. The general practitioner was called the next day and diagnosed influenza. However, the symptoms did not improve and the doctor was called three more times. He visited two days, four days and six days after his original assessment, but at none of these subsequent visits was there any evidence that the patient had developed a recognised complication of influenza.

The family were concerned that the failure of the supposed influenza to improve during the course of just a few days meant that the symptoms were being caused by malaria. In view of this fear, the family told the doctor that the patient had recently returned from Uganda and they also told him that the patient had suffered from malaria in the past. They therefore suggested that a blood test should be taken and that a second opinion should be sought. Despite the expression of these fears, the general practitioner reassured the family that the illness was being caused by nothing more than influenza. Additionally, he said that he had discussed the matter with a colleague who agreed that malaria was out of the question.

The day after the doctor had made his fourth visit, the family became so concerned that they called another doctor who arranged immediate hospital admission. The patient was seen by two Asian doctors who confirmed the illness as being malaria, but the patient died two days later.

Matter for the court to decide

The court accepted that malaria was an extremely rare condition in England. Indeed, this was the basis of the general practitioner's defence and he asserted that influenza was so much more common that it was a perfectly reasonable diagnosis. The court therefore had to decide whether the failure to diagnose malaria and to seek specialist advice was negligent.

Held

The plaintiff's action succeeded. Medical evidence on the widow's behalf showed that patients suffering from influenza nearly always start to improve after three or four days. The expectation of this pattern of recovery applies in the absence of complications such as a chest infection which would explain any lack of improvement or, indeed, any deterioration. In this particular case there had been no evidence of complications to explain the continuing ill health.

Evidence of opinion for the plaintiff also showed that any patient who fails to make the expected progress against the background of the provisional diagnosis should have that diagnosis reviewed for fear that there is some more serious underlying condition. An additional point was that evidence of fact confirmed that the family had told the doctor that the patient had just returned from Uganda and that he had suffered from malaria in the past.

The court therefore held that the general practitioner had been negligent in failing to suspect a more serious underlying condition than the originally diagnosed influenza, and in failing to seek specialist advice. It accepted that the doctor could not be expected to have made a specific diagnosis of malaria, but he should have realised that the absence of improvement after four days meant that the matter should have been taken more seriously.

The plaintiff also succeeded on causation in that she adduced evidence that if serious illness had been suspected on the third, or even the fourth, visit and hospital admission had been arranged, malaria would have been diagnosed and the resulting treatment probably would have saved the patient's life.

☆ ☆ ☆

MAYNARD v WEST MIDLANDS REGIONAL HEALTH AUTHORITY (1985) [1985] 1 All ER 635, [1984] 1 WLR 634

The medical facts

A woman was admitted to hospital for investigation of an illness that had been diagnosed provisionally diagnosed as tuberculosis. She was under the care of two specialists and they both agreed that the distribution of the enlarged glands within her chest cast an element of doubt on the diagnosis. They considered that this particular distribution was suggestive of Hodgkin's disease, and that further tests should be undertaken to exclude this possibility. The tests involved a biopsy of the glands and, in the process, the recurrent laryngeal nerve was damaged in its passage through the chest. The patient was rendered hoarse.

Matter for the court to decide

No negligence was alleged in relation to the technique used in the operation to take the biopsy. The patient advanced her case on the basis that the diagnosis of tuberculosis was so obvious that the operation itself was unnecessary, and if it had not been performed, the hoarseness would never have occurred.

The court then had to decide whether the mere decision to carry out the biopsy represented a falling short of proper standards.

Held

At first instance, the trial judge found for the plaintiff. The defendants appealed. The Court of Appeal reversed that decision and the House of Lords upheld this reversal. It was pointed out, on behalf of the defendants, that:

> ... it is not enough to show that there is a body of competent professional opinion which considers theirs as a wrong decision, if there also exists a body of professional opinion, equally competent, which supports the decision as reasonable in the circumstances.

The question was also raised of judges who prefer one opinion to another. On this point it was said by Lord Scarman that:

A judge's preference for one body of distinguished professional opinion to another also professionally distinguished is not sufficient to establish negligence in a practitioner whose actions have received the seal of approval of those whose opinions, truthfully expressed, honestly held, were not preferred. If this was the real reason for the judge's finding, he erred in law even though elsewhere in his judgment he stated the law correctly. For in the realm of diagnosis and treatment, negligence is not established by preferring one respectable body of professional opinion to another. Failing to exercise the ordinary skill of a doctor (in the appropriate speciality, if he be a specialist) is necessary.

☆ ☆ ☆

McGRATH v COLE (1994) (Unreported)

The medical facts

Betty McGrath was aged 18 in late 1982 when she saw her general practitioner with symptoms which were initially thought to have been caused by a urinary tract infection. Her condition soon deteriorated, however, and she was admitted to hospital with a diagnosis of an incomplete miscarriage. A dilatation and curettage was performed, and she was then discharged. Twelve days after the operation, she again had to be seen by the doctor and was once more diagnosed as suffering from a urinary infection. A tender cervix was found on examination, but this was attributed to the short period that had elapsed since the operation. Amoxil (penicillin-related antibiotic) was prescribed and the symptoms started to ease.

Four months later, Mrs McGrath went to the doctor with lower abdominal pains, spotting and painful intercourse. Examination revealed that the cervix was still tender. A mild pelvic infection was diagnosed and Amoxil was again prescribed.

As time passed, Mrs McGrath found herself unable to conceive and, on later investigation by a gynaecologist, was found to be suffering from blocked fallopian tubes which had almost certainly originated from the undiagnosed pelvic sepsis following the D & C for the miscarriage three years previously.

322

Matter for the court to decide

It was alleged by the plaintiff that the general practitioner had been negligent in diagnosing a urinary tract infection following the D & C. In the alternative, it was alleged that, even if the general practitioner had diagnosed pelvic sepsis, he should not have relied on treatment with Amoxil alone, but should have added a further antibiotic or, better still, referred his patient to a gynaecologist for more detailed investigation.

The defending general practitioner argued that the cervical tenderness in the initial stages was easily explained on the basis of the patient's recent D & C and, in any case, the use of Amoxil alone in pelvic inflammatory disease was perfectly acceptable treatment in 1982/83.

As a matter of evidence of fact in this case, the doctor's position was assisted considerably by the apparent ease with which counsel for the defence undermined the credibility of the plaintiff's memory of the severity of her symptoms. Twelve years had elapsed between the alleged negligence and the case reaching trial. Mrs McGrath found it difficult to remember the pattern of her symptoms with a convincing degree of precision, and counsel for Dr Cole invited the judge to place more reliance on the handwritten medical records.

Held

The plaintiff's claim failed.

No formal judgment was available when this book went to press.

☆ ☆ ☆

MORRISON v FORSYTH 1994 [1995] 6 MED LR 6

The medical facts

Edward Morrison was a 39 year old man who attended an accident and emergency department at 4.05 am one day with, it was later alleged by his widow, difficulty in breathing. The hospital staff diagnosed viral laryngitis as the cause of the

323

symptoms and recommended gargling with aspirin. By 4.30 pm he was worse and asked a neighbour to telephone the doctor. The symptoms in his throat meant that he was reduced to writing a description on a notepad so that a message could be relayed to the general practitioner.

The doctor diagnosed a throat infection and issued a prescription for an antibiotic without seeing the patient. Unfortunately, his condition deteriorated rapidly and at 7.30 pm an ambulance had to be called. On arrival at hospital he was pronounced dead. The pathologist who carried out the post-mortem observed that 'death in this case was the result of laryngeal obstruction due to an acute infection of the neck of the type described as acute synergistic gangrene. This is a most unusual condition which is characterised by the extreme rapidity of its development'.

Matter for the court to decide

The case was heard at the Court of Session in Edinburgh by Lord Clyde. It was alleged on behalf of the pursuers that, at the time of the telephone call to the general practitioner at 4.30 pm, four symptoms had been present. It was further alleged that they were all mentioned or, at the very least, enquiry should have been made about them. They were:
• sore throat
• hoarseness
• difficulty in swallowing
• difficulty in breathing.

Of these four, the last one was, of course, the most serious, and it was asserted that with this combination of symptoms the patient should have been seen for assessment and that he would then have been admitted to hospital for relief of airway obstruction.

The defender relied heavily on the detailed note she made of the telephone call and it is worth recording it here:

7.9.89 4.30pm   Phone call from patient's wife indicating patient has sore throat and pain on swallowing. Was seen last night at WIG (A & E) – no treatment suggested or given but told to contact GP if no better. Sounds infective. Patient's wife happy to accept prescription if phoned to Thistle Pharmacy – no visit requested. Rx Difflam Oral Spray (use qid) Trimethoprim 100mg x 20 (2 tab bd).

Held

The pursuers, namely the widow and her children, lost their case. It was held that the defender had put herself in a position to make a reasonable diagnosis of a relatively innocent throat infection and to prescribe an antibiotic without seeing the patient at first hand.

Evidential note

Doctors, particularly general practitioners, are often criticised for making diagnoses and for prescribing treatment over the telephone. They are also criticised for making inadequate notes or, worse still, no notes at all of advice that they give on the telephone. In this case, the defender's case was enormously strengthened by the note she made at the time. It was contemporaneous, legible and detailed. This made its credibility very strong indeed.

For a more detailed discussion of the credibility of the doctor's notes see pages 244-246.

PHILIPS v WHITELEY, 1938 [1938] 1 All ER 566

The facts

A woman wanted her ears pierced. She therefore visited a jeweller who undertook the operation and observed his usual precautions in doing so. Unfortunately, the operation was followed by sepsis and the woman sued the jeweller for undertaking the operation in a negligent manner.

Matter for the court to decide

The court had to decide whether the manner in which the jeweller undertook the ear piercing procedure was in accordance with acceptable practice.

325

Held

It was held that the woman's action should fail. She failed to show that the jeweller's standard of care fell short of that to be expected of jewellers in general. There was no justification in the argument that the sepsis would have been avoided if the jeweller had provided a level of care that equated with that of a surgeon. The standard by which the operation was to be judged was not that which would be given by surgeons in general but rather by jewellers in general.

☆ ☆ ☆

PLEYDELL v AUBYN (1993) (Unreported)

The medical facts

In August 1966, a two year old girl was unwell for about a week with vomiting and abdominal pains. She was seen several times by the general practitioner who apparently diagnosed gastroenteritis as being the cause. At the end of this time she was in more distress and was admitted to hospital where, at laparotomy, she was found to be suffering from an appendix abscess. She appeared to recover from the operation with no after-effects.

However, 22 years after the original illness, she found that she was unable to conceive and, on investigation by a gynaecologist, she was found to be suffering from obstruction of the fallopian tubes by adhesions from the original undiagnosed appendicitis. Despite tubal surgery, she was unable to conceive in the normal way, but after resorting to *in vitro* fertilisation she did conceive and a child was born.

Matter for the court to decide

The court had to decide whether the general practitioner had been negligent in not arranging hospital admission at one of the earlier visits during the week in August 1966, when the girl was unwell with undiagnosed abdominal pain.

Held

The court held that the general practitioner had given an acceptable standard of care. Expert evidence for the defence showed that the appendicitis probably did not start until the end of the week. That evidence supported the thesis that the condition really had been one of a viral illness, such as gastroenteritis, during the earlier visits at which no admission arrangements were made. It had only developed into appendicitis towards the end of the week and this coincided with the girl going into hospital.

☆ ☆ ☆

RICHARDSON v KITCHING (1995) (Unreported)

The medical facts

Mark Richardson was an energetic and ambitious salesman. He had been a little deaf in one ear since 1978. It was alleged on behalf of his widow, the plaintiff, that in September 1981 he had seen the doctor about it and had been told that he would be referred to an ear, nose and throat consultant. The note for this entry, however, only referred to an unrelated matter. The next entry was two years later, September 1983, which did mention a referral, but in the event no arrangement was made. A third entry a year later still, September 1994, recorded the additional symptom of giddiness, but still no referral was made. A letter was eventually written to a consultant after a further six weeks, but before the appointment materialised the patient had to be admitted to hospital and was found to be suffering from an acoustic neuroma (malignant tumour of the VIIIth cranial nerve) from which he died.

Matter for the court to decide

The plaintiff's case was based on the general practitioner's apparent forgetfulness in failing to write a referral letter at any of the three visits at which it was alleged that the symptoms were mentioned. It was common ground that it would have been negligent to advise referral, secure the patient's agreement and then do nothing. The defendant's case was that Mr Richardson had been offered a referral but had refused it because he was too busy. Great emphasis was laid on the first of the three entries which described the deceased's employment schedule in terms of working from 6.00 am to 1.00 am and driving 50,000 miles a year. This, it was argued by counsel for the defendant, provided a ready explanation of why the deceased was unable to find the time to attend the hospital. Counsel was able to add that the deceased might also have feared that the specialist advice for the giddiness and deafness might have resulted in suspension of his driving licence, and consequent deprivation of his livelihood.

Held

Just as this book was going to press, it was learned that the plaintiff lost her case on both negligence and causation. The judgment was also available but there was insufficient time left for a proper study of it.

☆ ☆ ☆

SA'D v ROBINSON [1990] 1 Med LR 41

The medical facts

An 18 month old girl sucked hot tea from the spout of a teapot at about 5.45 pm one evening in 1980. Her mother immediately took her to see the local general practitioner and told him the circumstances of the accident. He examined the inside of the mouth and prescribed some medication to soothe the child. The mother and child then went home, collecting the medicine on the way, but during the next few hours the child continued to be in great distress and was salivating copiously. The mother therefore telephoned again, about 8.00 pm, and was answered by another doctor who had come on duty. She reiterated the story to him, including the details of sucking from the spout of the teapot and expressed her concern that the girl might choke on the mucus in her mouth. The duty doctor advised propping the child up with pillows and if the mother was concerned she should telephone again. By 10.00 pm, the child became even more distressed and the duty doctor was called to the house. He examined her and said that although there was no immediate cause for alarm it would be wise for her to be admitted to hospital for observation. He then telephoned the casualty department to warn them of the child's impending arrival. By this stage the child was developing serious difficulty in breathing and was seen on the paediatric ward rather than in the casualty department. There was considerable difficulty in carrying out the necessary endotracheal intubation and inserting an intravenous line. Unfortunately the child had an anoxic fit and suffered irreversible brain damage.

Matter for the court to decide

The court had to decide whether the general practitioner had been negligent when he saw the child on the initial visit to the surgery at 5.45 pm. It also had to decide whether the duty doctor had been negligent, either at the time of the telephone call at 8.00 pm or at the time of the later visit, at which hospital admission was arranged.

Held

(a) In respect of the general practitioner

The trial judge held that the general practitioner was negligent in failing to refer the child to hospital. Evidence showed that he had been told that the child had sucked hot tea from the spout of a teapot, but he seemed not to have recognised the important difference between this and drinking from a cup. The difference was crucial because sucking from a spout might involve the inhalation of steam which could reach the throat directly without burning the mouth. Doubtless this went some way to explaining why the doctor saw little that was abnormal when he examined the mouth at the time of the surgery visit.

(b) In respect of the duty doctor

The duty doctor had been negligent in failing to visit the child when he received the telephone call of 8.00 pm. Like the general practitioner, he should have appreciated the importance of sucking from the spout of a teapot and the dangers that could arise from this.

He was also negligent as regards the admission arrangements at 10.00 pm. He should have ensured that the child was seen at the casualty department rather than on the paediatric ward. Additionally, his telephone call to the hospital should have emphasised the seriousness of the child's condition in view of the history he was given, but he did not appear to realise the significance.

☆ ☆ ☆

SPILLANE v WASSERMAN (1992) 13 CCLT 267

The medical facts

A cyclist was passing through a green set of traffic lights at a crossroads in the city centre in Ontario. A lorry drove straight through the red light and killed the cyclist. In the course of the accident the lorry driver suffered serious head injuries which caused amnesia and he was unable to remember the details of the accident.

The widow and the children of the cyclist sued the lorry driver, his employer and his insurer. However, they also sued the doctors who had previously been treating the lorry driver for epilepsy.

The family and the doctors argued their cases on the basis that the accident had been caused by the driver's failure to drive with proper care, and that his loss of memory after the accident had been caused by the head injuries. Conversely, the insurer's case was that the driver had probably had an epileptic fit and that it was this that had caused the accident.

Matter for the court to decide

The defendants in this action were the driver and the doctors. The court had to decide whether the plaintiff should be awarded damages against either or both of them.

Held

The family succeeded in its action. After hearing expert evidence from both sides, it was held that the accident had probably been caused by the driver suffering an epileptic fit just previously. However, this did not make the accident 'unavoidable', thereby exonerating either the driver or the doctors. The driver had been negligent in being lax with his medication and in not keeping his doctors informed about his condition. Additionally, the doctors had been negligent in not monitoring the condition more closely or reporting his condition to the relevant authorities.

The doctors, one of them a neurologist and the other a general practitioner, were held to be 40% responsible for the accident and the driver was held to be responsible for the other 60%.

☆ ☆ ☆

STACEY v CHIDDY (1993) [1993] 4 Med LR 216

The medical facts

A woman in New South Wales, Australia, consulted her general practitioner in March 1989 with two abnormal lumps in the left breast. An examination was carried out and this confirmed the presence of the lumps. A mammogram and an ultrasound scan were then arranged and these gave normal results, indicating that there was no danger of malignancy. However, it was later pointed out that the tests were not conclusive in that the ultrasound did not confirm that the lumps were cystic, as had been supposed at the time of the clinical examination by the general practitioner. The patient then returned to the doctor in April, was not examined and was merely told that as a result of the tests there was no need for her to worry. She was advised to return at intervals of three months and six months.

In June 1989 the patient re-attended and the breasts were examined with no abnormality being found. In December 1989 she attended again and examination at this stage again showed no abnormality.

Between April and June 1990 the patient became more concerned that the lumps were increasing in size and attended her general practitioner again. At this last attendance, in June 1990, referral was made to a specialist for a biopsy and this demonstrated that the lumps were malignant. Unfortunately, a bone scan showed that the cancer had spread to the spine and a

331

course of chemotherapy was needed. It was established that the damage had resulted in a reduced life expectancy.

Matter for the court to decide

The patient sued the general practitioner on the basis that she was given unjustified reassurance by the negative results. She also believed that she should have been examined at the visit in April 1989 when the results were available and she was told there was no need for alarm. Additionally, she asserted that earlier referral and diagnosis would have resulted in a more favourable prognosis.

Held

(a) At first instance

The court held that the general practitioner was in breach of his duty of care in placing undue reliance on the negative investigations. He was also negligent in failing to examine the patient in April 1989, when he gave the unjustified reassurance.

However, the patient was unsuccessful with the case as a whole, because causation was not established. The judge found, on the balance of probabilities, that the breast lesions in March and April 1989 were not malignant, and this meant that the patient's condition, as regards reduced life expectancy, was unconnected with the negligence at that early stage.

(b) On appeal

The patient, Mrs Stacey, appealed and in view of her reduced life expectancy the hearing was expedited. The appeal was based on two points:

- causation: that is, whether the trial judge was wrong in finding that there was no causal connection between the initial diagnosis of the cysts and the later development of the cancer; and

- loss of chance of cure: in other words, whether the trial judge was wrong to find that any negligence by the doctor made no contribution to the patient's failure to be cured.

The Court of Appeal of New South Wales held that the trial judge had been right in his finding on causation. Among other points it held that:

> ... it was clear that the trial judge found that if the lumps were not palpable and detectable in June 1989 and December 1989, then the malignant tumour detected in June 1990 was not, on the probabilities, relevantly related to the lumps detected in March 1990.

As regards the loss of a chance of cure, it was held that this point could not be raised on appeal because it had not been explored at the trial. Presumably, there cannot ever have been any chance, because it was held that the original lumps were probably benign and so it follows that, even if Mrs Stacey had been referred to a specialist at that stage, no cancer would have been detected and no treatment appropriate to that disease would have been instituted.

Accordingly, the plaintiff's appeal was dismissed.

Clinical note

It is clear that in this case the general practitioner relied upon the negative mammogram and ultrasound findings when he reassured Mrs Stacey that the lumps were benign. The doctor was found to have been negligent in his failure to re-examine the breasts at the follow-up visit of April 1989. On this point, it is worth quoting the commentary by Margaret Puxon QC MD FRCOG on this case (see *Medical Law Reports* [1993] 4 Med LR, p 353):

> *Stacey v Chiddy* underlines the danger that doctors run in relying on technology rather than clinical investigations. Dr Chiddy was confident in his benign cysts because his provisional diagnosis was confirmed by a mammogram and ultrasound which he had ordered and which proved negative. The expert evidence, called on Mrs Stacey's behalf, was to the effect that every such case should be referred to a surgeon, for a clinical opinion, no doubt confirmed by a biopsy.

☆   ☆   ☆

STOCKDALE v NICHOLLS (1992) [1993] 4 Med LR 190

The medical facts

Baby Caroline Stockdale was born six weeks prematurely. She suffered feeding problems and had to stay in hospital for two weeks longer than her mother. The symptoms persisted after the baby went home and she was seen by one of the general practitioners at the surgery premises while her mother was being attended. A week later the symptoms had still not improved and the mother telephoned the general practitioner who arranged for the practice nurse to visit. She duly visited, fed the baby herself and gave the mother some general advice.

That evening the baby vomited and at midnight the parents asked the doctor to visit the house. He did so and gave further advice with regard to feeding. At 4.15 am the baby failed to settle down and looked more unwell. The parents again asked the doctor to visit, as a result of which he examined the child, decided that hospital admission was indicated and provided a letter for this purpose. He also ensured that the parents had access to a car to take them to hospital.

Despite the doctor's visit at 4.15 am, and the giving of the letter, the baby was not taken to the hospital until 7.20 am and she was then seen in the accident and emergency department. She was subsequently admitted to the children's ward but at 10.00 am she had a fit and collapsed. She was diagnosed as suffering from septicaemia and this led to permanent brain damage with severe mental and physical incapacity.

The parents sued the general practitioner for sending the practice nurse in the first place. They also sued him for not arranging hospital admission on his first visit when he had no definite diagnosis. Additionally, they asserted that he should have treated the admission arrangements with greater urgency.

Matter for the court to decide

It fell to the court to decide whether the procedures adopted by the general practitioner fell short of proper standards in respect of these allegations.

Held

Otton J held that:

> ... there is no substance in the criticism that Dr Nicholls failed
> in his duty of care by sending his nurse after the first
> telephone call or that he was negligent in failing to attend
> himself.

Furthermore, there was no indication that any of the physical
signs at the midnight visit warranted admission. Of the last
criticism, the lack of urgency in connection with the admission
arrangements, it was held that there was nothing at that point to
put the general practitioner on notice about urgency. Thus, the
giving of the letter and ensuring that the parents had access to a
car were sufficient steps.

Otton J also observed that this case must fail on causation. By
this he meant that even if the baby had been admitted to hospital
at about 5.00 am she probably would have been admitted to the
ward and the action taken would have been no different.

WHITEHOUSE v JORDAN AND ANOTHER (1981) House of Lords [1981] 1 All ER 267, [1981] 1 WLR 246

The medical facts

A woman was admitted to an obstetric unit for delivery of her
child. The senior registrar decided it was in her best interest to
undertake trial of delivery by forceps. He applied traction on
what he judged to be the right number of occasions and for the
right length of time. Delivery by this method proved impossible
and he therefore undertook a Caesarian section. Unfortunately,
respiration was not properly established after the child's delivery
and this was followed by brain damage to the child.

Matter for the court to decide

It was accepted that the traction that had been applied at the trial of
labour had been the cause of the respiratory difficulties and the

subsequent brain damage. The question therefore arose of whether the obstetrician had been negligent in his use of the forceps.

Held

(a) At first instance

Evidence of fact showed that the obstetrician had made an error of judgment in his use of the forceps. It was therefore held that he had been negligent.

(b) On appeal

The obstetrician appealed against the trial judge's finding of negligence. In the Court of Appeal Lord Denning was extremely sympathetic. He considered the expression an 'error of judgment' and observed that:

> We must say, and say firmly, that, in a professional man, an error of judgment is not negligent.

Lord Denning supported this remark by voicing the fear that:

> ... there would be a danger, in all cases of professional men, of their being made liable whenever something happens to go wrong. Whenever I give a judgment, and it is afterwards reversed by the House of Lords, is it to be said that I was negligent? That I did not pay enough attention to a previously binding authority or the like?

Accordingly, the obstetrician's appeal was allowed and the trial judge's finding of negligence was reversed.

(c) House of Lords

The House of Lords observed that the expression 'an error of judgment' was ambiguous and that it was not possible to infer negligence on that basis alone. Whether or not that error was negligent depended on whether it was of the type that would have been made by a practitioner in that field exercising reasonable care.

All doctors make errors of judgment at times, but they have only been negligent if, in the process, they have failed to exercise a proper standard of care. The point was made thus:

XXVI Table of Cases

To say that a surgeon has committed an error of clinical judgment is wholly ambiguous and does not indicate whether he has been negligent, for while some errors of clinical judgment may be completely consistent with the due exercise of professional skill other acts or omissions in the course of exercising clinical judgment may be so glaringly below proper standards as to make a finding of negligence inevitable.

The House of Lords reviewed the evidence of opinion to which reference had been made at the court of first instance. It found that the error of judgment the obstetrician had made was of the type which could have been made by any practitioner in this field, even when he was operating with a reasonable level of care. This particular error of judgment had not been negligent.

WIPFLI v BRITTEN (1984) 13 DLR (4th) 169

The medical facts

A general practitioner in British Columbia was supervising a woman's pregnancy. He failed to diagnose the fact that she was carrying twins, one of whom was the plaintiff. The first twin, a boy, was delivered by Caesarean section and this was accompanied by considerable difficulty. It was only when the resident obstetrician was trying to remove the placenta that he discovered the existence of the second twin, a girl. Unfortunately, she was born with brain damage. It was alleged that the brain damage had been caused at the time that the placenta was removed.

Matter for the court to decide

It was clearly most unlikely that the damage to the second twin would have occurred if the resident obstetrician, who had not been involved in the antenatal care, had been informed that the mother was carrying twins. The question therefore arose of whether the general practitioner had fallen short of proper standards by not so informing him.

Held

The general practitioner had been negligent in his management of the pregnancy. If he had diagnosed twins earlier, the labour would have been managed differently and the second twin would have been much less likely to have developed brain damage.

(iii)   Causation

(For a discussion of this subject see Chapters IV to VII)

Barnett v Chelsea and Kensington Hospital Management
    Committee, 1968
Bonnington Castings v Wardlaw, 1956
Fanguy v United States of America, 1984*
Hotson v East Berkshire Health Authority, 1987
Lawson v Laferriere, 1991*
Loveday v Renton and Another, 1988
McGhee v National Coal Board, 1973
Marsden v Bateman, 1991
Norberg v Wynrib, 1988*
Robson v Ashworth, 1987*
Rothwell v Raes 1988*
Sigouin v Wong, 1988*
Wilsher v Essex AHA, 1988
Wilson v Vancouver Hockey Club, 1985*

* Denotes Commonwealth or American case

BARNETT v CHELSEA AND KENSINGTON HOSPITAL MANAGEMENT COMMITTEE (1968) [1968] 1 All ER 1068

The medical facts

A man who had been subjected to arsenic poisoning was seen at the accident and emergency department of his local hospital with vomiting. The person in charge of the department contacted the doctor and asked him to see the patient for assessment. He refused and the patient was sent home, but later died.

The widow sued the accident and emergency doctor, on the basis that he was negligent in failing to attend a patient who had been admitted with a history of vomiting.

Matter for the court to decide

The widow was successful in showing that the doctor had been negligent. She had no difficulty in showing that no responsible body of medical opinion would have approved the failure to attend a patient in this condition. However, the court then had to decide whether that negligence affected the outcome.

Held

The court held that the case must fail on causation. It was established that even if the patient had been attended promptly by the accident and emergency doctor he would still have died because too long a period of time had elapsed between the ingestion of the arsenic and any treatment the doctor might have been able to give.

BONNINGTON CASTINGS v WARDLAW [1956] 1 All ER 615

The facts

A firm's employee was engaged in silicone dressing and after a period of some years he developed pneumoconosis which was caused by long-term exposure to dust in the working atmosphere. He was able to show that his employers had been in breach of their statutory duty to maintain the level of dust at, or below, a certain figure so as to ensure a safe working environment. He sued his employer on the basis of this breach combined with his development of the disease which had clearly followed the dust inhalation.

Matter for the court to decide

The court was faced with reaching a decision on causation in this case. The defendants showed successfully that the employee had spent part of his working time in other parts of the premises where the dust was present in the atmosphere but was at a level that was well within the figures prescribed by the regulations. There could be no doubt that the pneumoconiosis had been caused by the sum of all the dust the employee had inhaled during the course of the time he spent on the defendant's premises. Part of that dust was labelled as 'guilty dust', because it was inhaled in an area where the level was unacceptably high, and the other part of it was labelled 'innocent dust', because it was derived from an area where the level was perfectly safe.

Held

The court held that the plaintiff should succeed on causation. Although it was accepted that part of the inhaled dust was unrelated to the negligence it was considered that he should succeed because the dust which was associated with the negligence had made a material contribution to the damage.

FANGUY v UNITED STATES OF AMERICA (1984) 595 F Supp 486

The medical facts

This case concerned a man who attended a hospital in Louisiana with symptoms in his legs and who was sent home with sleeping pills and an arrangement to return four days later. Both legs later had to be amputated because of peripheral vascular disease. The patient claimed that the hospital had been negligent in not arranging admission at his first attendance and that, if he had been so admitted, the amputations would probably have been avoided.

Matter for the court to decide

The court held that the hospital had been negligent in not arranging admission on the first attendance. However, it also had to decide whether the loss of the legs was caused by that negligence.

Held

The court held that:

> ... negligence was not, however, shown to have been a proximate cause of the patient's injuries which resulted in amputation but, rather, evidence was to effect that progression of the patient's peripheral vascular disease had already passed stage where his leg could be salvaged by bypass surgery.

HOTSON v EAST BERKSHIRE HEALTH AUTHORITY (1987)
[1987] AC 750, [1987] 2 All ER 90A, [1987] 3 WLR 232

The medical facts

A 13 year old boy fell from a tree while playing with his friends, and hurt his leg. He was seen at the accident and emergency department at the local hospital but no serious injury was thought to have occurred and he was sent home without an X-ray. He continued to have pain in the hip for the next five days and at the end of this time his general practitioner sent him back to the hospital for review. On this occasion he was X-rayed and this demonstrated a fracture of the neck of the femur. Despite treatment for the condition being commenced at this stage the complication of avascular necrosis of the head of the femur developed and this caused a fair degree of disability in the long term.

The boy sued the hospital on the basis that an X-ray should have been taken on the initial visit and that, if it had been taken, the fracture would have been diagnosed promptly and treatment would have been given which would have avoided the risk of the avascular necrosis.

Matter for the court to decide

The boy succeeded on negligence because he was able to produce expert evidence that the failure to take the X-ray in those circumstances was negligent. However, the court then had to assess the strength of his case on causation.

Held

(a) At first instance

The trial judge accepted expert evidence for the defendants that even with good treatment there was a 75% chance that the avascular necrosis would have occurred. From this standpoint it was argued that the negligence only deprived the boy of a 25% chance of cure. In view of this, the trial judge awarded him 25% of full damages. He was allowed £11,500, compared to the figure of £46,000 that had been the assessment for full damages.

(b) On appeal

The defendants appealed on the basis that they should not even have to pay the one-quarter figure because the plaintiff had failed to show that it was more than 50% likely that with good treatment he would have been cured. The Court of Appeal rejected this argument and allowed the boy to retain his one-quarter figure.

(c) House of Lords

This case gave their Lordships the opportunity of defining the present state of the law on causation in 'lost opportunity' cases. Lord Ackner took the line that to allow a proportionate approach to these cases, rather than an 'all or none' approach, would 'give rise to many complications in the search for mathematical and statistical exactitude'. Following this reasoning, their Lordships allowed the defendant's appeal and the boy lost even his one-quarter share as he had failed to prove his case on causation 'on the balance of probabilities'.

☆ ☆ ☆

LAWSON v LAFERRIERE (1991) 6 CCLT 119

The medical facts

In 1971 a woman saw her doctor about a lump in the breast and a biopsy confirmed that it was cancerous. Unfortunately, the defendant doctor failed to inform the patient of the result and it was not until 1975 that she found her health to be deteriorating from widespread disease. She died in 1978. She sued the doctor on the basis that there had been negligence in failing to inform her of her biopsy results and that, if she had been so informed, she would have had treatment which would have saved her life.

Matter for the court to decide

The court held that the doctor had been negligent in failing to advise his patient of the biopsy result. The question then arose of whether any treatment following this would have resulted in her life being saved.

Held

(a) At first instance

The trial judge held that the negligence did not cause the death because all that had happened was that she was deprived of the chance of being cured. In other words, there was no certainty that she would have been cured even if she had been treated promptly.

(b) On appeal

The Court of Appeal of Quebec took a different view and found the doctor liable in damages for the lost opportunity. It was

> ... of the opinion that the Civil Law recognised that any harm resulting from the loss of a chance be compensable.

This woman was

> ... deprived of the chance of obtaining the treatment necessitated by her state of health.

The damages figure was fixed such that it reflected the degree of lost opportunity.

However, one judge, dissenting, remarked that:

> ... it was not certain, nor indeed probable that a cure or remission would have been obtained. Consequently, no cause or relationship between the fault of the defendant and the harm suffered had been established.

International note

The report in this case observed that:

> In France and Belgium there is a tendency on the part of the courts to focus on the chance itself and to compensate in accordance with the degree of probability of it occurring. In Quebec, depending on the degree of probability, the trend is to concentrate on the actual result of the lost chance. If it were probable that a particular result would eventuate, then total

indemnification would be awarded. Thus it is not necessary to rely on the artificial notion of an intermediate damage called the lost chance.

The English approach to the lost opportunity cases has been discussed in some detail in Chapter V of this book, with particular reference to *Hotson v East Berks HA* (1987). The argument in favour of the proportionate approach to the award of damages is considered by Walter Scott in *Modern Law Review*, July 1992 pp 521-25.

☆ ☆ ☆

LOVEDAY v RENTON AND ANOTHER (1988) [1990] 1 Med LR 117

The medical facts

A large number of claims were made by children who had suffered brain damage following DTP vaccination. It was the pertussis (whooping cough) element of the vaccine that was alleged to have been responsible for the damage. The children wished to sue both the person who administered the vaccine (often the general practitioner) and the manufacturer.

The manufacturer of the vaccine could not be identified in this particular case, but the Wellcome Foundation had a legitimate interest in the case because, at the time of the trial, they were the only manufacturers of the vaccine in the UK. They were therefore joined as defendants.

As is usual in group actions of this kind, one particular plaintiff, Susan Loveday, was chosen as the lead case.

Matter for the court to decide

Clearly, for Susan Loveday to succeed in this case she had to establish both negligence and causation.

(a) Negligence

This point never came to trial because causation was tried as a preliminary issue.

345

However, in passing it was observed that the plaintiff would have had great difficulties in this area. It was accepted that the existence of a manufacturer's leaflet which specifies certain contraindications tends to mean that they represent a reason for not administering the drug, but it does not necessarily mean that it amounts to negligence to give it. By this is meant that a responsible body of medical opinion might well believe that the advantages to be gained from having the vaccine outweigh the very slight chance of an adverse reaction occurring in the face of that contraindication.

(b) Causation

The plaintiff suggested various biological mechanisms to explain the damage, such as febrile convulsions, anaphylactic shock and neurotoxic effect. The suggestion was that the vaccine could cause a febrile convulsion, which in turn could cause brain damage.

Held

The trial was on the issue of causation only, and it was held that:

(a) pertussis vaccine could occasionally cause a febrile convulsion but there was no evidence that this could cause brain damage; and

(b) both anaphylactic shock and neurotoxic effect were extremely unlikely explanations for brain damage.

Thus the plaintiff had failed to show, on the balance of probabilities, that the vaccine could be responsible for the brain damage.

☆ ☆ ☆

McGHEE v NATIONAL COAL BOARD [1973] 1 WLR 1

The facts

An employee of the Coal Board was engaged in bricklaying below ground. This involved exposure to a considerable amount of brick dust and coal dust during the course of the shift. The Coal Board were under a statutory duty to provide pit-head showers so that employees did not have to leave the premises with their skin in contact with clothes that were contaminated with abrasive dirt.

The plaintiff in this case developed dermatitis over his back and shoulders and sued the Coal Board on the basis that its failure to provide the showers was responsible for the development of the dermatitis.

Matter for the court to decide

It was accepted by the plaintiff that there was no certainty that the dermatitis was caused by his having to wear dirty clothes as he cycled home from work. It was conceded that many people develop dermatitis without any such provocation.

The court therefore had to decide whether the likelihood of the dermatitis being caused by the wearing of the dirty clothes was sufficient to justify compensation.

Held

Expert evidence for the plaintiff showed that the wearing of the dust-contaminated clothes materially increased the risk of the development of dermatitis. The court therefore found for the plaintiff even though it was perfectly possible that the dermatitis would have developed in any event.

MARSDEN v BATEMAN (1991) [1993] 4 Med LR 181

The medical facts

A woman gave birth to a baby at home and was attended by her general practitioner. Following the birth, the baby was very pale, was gasping for air and had a low Apgar score. The next day the general practitioner was called to visit again because the baby was breathing noisily. On his arrival, the doctor looked at the baby but did not examine her. He told the parents that he thought the noise was caused by some inflammation in the throat which had followed the removal of debris at the time of the birth. After the doctor left, the midwife was called twice and was told that the baby was very slow to feed. There was no improvement that night and she continued with noisy and rapid breathing. It was established that neither the general practitioner nor the midwife had taken the baby's temperature or checked her blood sugar level.

Two days later a different midwife called. She contacted a consultant paediatrician, who arranged immediate hospital admission.

The parents sued the general practitioner on the basis that he had been negligent in not arranging for admission during the three days which followed the birth. Additionally, they asserted that the mental incapacity that the baby was later found to have was caused by hypoglycaemia and that this should have been detected during that early period.

Matter for the court to decide

The defending general practitioner admitted negligence in that he should have arranged earlier hospital admission. However, he denied causation, on the basis that the baby's disabilities had been caused by an abnormality in the brain which had arisen *in utero*. The court therefore had to decide whether it was the hypoglycaemia or the congenital abnormality which was more likely to have been the cause of the disabilities.

Held

After hearing expert evidence, the court held that hypoglycaemia was unlikely to be the cause of the brain damage and that it was much more likely to have been caused by the congenital abnormalities in the brain. The judge observed that:

> There is nothing in the experience of any of the five experts or in the literature which enables me to take the view that, in the absence of coma, convulsions or apnoea, significant brain damage is capable of resulting from hypoglycaemia.

Furthermore, the allegations that hypoglycaemia ever did exist were poorly founded. Readings by Dextrostix in hospital were not hypoglycaemic, and it was therefore thought that hypoglycaemia was unlikely to have occurred during the 24 hours that followed the birth.

☆ ☆ ☆

NORBERG v WYNRIB (1988) 50 DLR(4th) 167

The medical facts

A general practitioner in British Columbia prescribed a drug to an addicted patient in exchange for sexual favours. The patient was later convicted of an offence of obtaining duplicate prescriptions from several doctors, and sued the doctor for battery and for negligence.

Matter for the court to decide

In this case, the court had to decide whether the girl had a case against the doctor in battery or in negligence.

Held

The court found that there was no case in battery because she had consented to the sexual acts; and there was no evidence that her addiction had deprived her of the ability to reason.

Her action in negligence also failed because there was no evidence that she had suffered physical injury as a result of the prescriptions. This was despite the fact that the doctor's conduct had been disgraceful and unprofessional.

☆ ☆ ☆

ROBSON v ASHWORTH (1987) 40 CCLT 164

The medical facts

A man from Ontario was under the care of his general practitioner in 1982 for depression. He also suffered from alcohol abuse and from stress, caused by a combination of financial and marital difficulties. One of his symptoms was insomnia. The general practitioner treated this with Seconal (a barbiturate sleeping tablet), and the court held that the last prescription the general practitioner supplied was negligent when considered against the other circumstances of the case. Soon after the final prescription was supplied the patient took his own life, and the widow later sued the general practitioner on the basis that his negligent prescription had caused the death.

As a matter of public policy, the trial judge dismissed the action in view of the concept of an individual's responsibility for his own actions. He added that, even if the action had succeeded, the deceased's share of responsibility for his own death would have been set at 90%.

The widow appealed, on the basis that the doctor has failed to diagnose and treat her husband's alcoholism. She asserted that alcohol abuse had contributed materially to his nervous breakdown and subsequent suicide.

Matter for the court to decide

The Court of Appeal in Ontario had to decide what had caused the death by suicide. It was accepted that the insomnia had led to a nervous breakdown, and that this in turn had precipitated the suicide. However, the question arose of whether the alcohol abuse was primarily responsible for the insomnia, as alleged by the plaintiff, or whether it was the stress itself which had caused the insomnia.

Held

The Court of Appeal held that the alcohol had only been a minor contributor to the insomnia. The judge held that the insomnia had been primarily caused by stress which was attributable to the financial and marital difficulties of the deceased. The plaintiff's appeal was therefore dismissed, as the case clearly failed on causation.

☆　☆　☆

ROTHWELL v RAES (1988) 54 DLR (4th) 193, (1989) 59 DLR (4th) 319

The medical facts

A baby in Ontario was subjected to a routine immunisation procedure. This involved injections at the age of 3, 4 and 5 months. One of the components of the vaccine was pertussis (whooping cough). Soon after the third injection the baby was suspected of suffering from a developmental abnormality. He was assessed by a paediatric neurologist, who remarked in the discharge summary that:

> ... it was felt that on the basis of the results of the investigations and the history of the parents, the possible diagnosis was post-pertussis encephalitis.

The neurologist subsequently said he was of the opinion that the neurological condition had two possible explanations. One was that it had existed since birth and the other was that it was a reaction to the immunisation. He added that:

> ... this is a well recognised entity likely due to the pertussis component and can produce severe brain damage.

Unfortunately, the baby was later found to be blind, almost deaf and severely retarded, both physically and mentally. There was no prospect of improvement and he was likely to need long-term nursing care.

Matter for the court to decide

The first issue was whether the general practitioner responsible for the course, or his locum who gave two of the injections, or the manufacturer who had issued the data sheets with warnings, had been negligent in any way. However, for the purposes of the trial, the main issue was that of causation. Causation concerned the likelihood that it was the pertussis immunisation, rather than some other cause, that had been responsible for the neurological handicap.

Held

The action was dismissed. It was held that the burden of proof was on the plaintiffs to establish, on a balance of probabilities, that the brain damage had been caused by the vaccine. They failed to discharge the burden. It had clearly been tempting for the plaintiff to adopt the proposition *post hoc ergo propter hoc* ('after this, therefore on account of this').

A large amount of literature was presented to the court. One case study involved 134,000 children vaccinated for pertussis, and who had been compared with 133,000 who had not been so vaccinated. This was regarded as the most complete and careful study and yet it had not managed to eliminate the possibility of bias and chance. The general consensus in this study was that it had failed to show any causal link between pertussis and neurological illness. Most of the cases of brain damage in the study had been attributable to causes other than immunisation.

An additional point was added that, if brain damage ever was caused by pertussis vaccination, it was much rarer than damage caused by whooping cough itself.

☆ ☆ ☆

SIGOUIN v WONG (1988) 46 CCLT 159

The medical facts

A doctor prescribed Cafergot to a woman for the relief of migraine. He knew she was pregnant and should have realised that this drug, which contains ergotamine, is contra-indicated in pregnancy, as it constricts the blood vessels and may harm the foetus. When the child was born he was diagnosed as suffering from pachygiria. This is a congenital abnormality of the brain that causes mental retardation and physical disability. The patient, together with her husband and the child, sued the doctor on the basis that his negligent prescription had caused the damage to the child.

Matter for the court to decide

There was no doubt that the doctor had been negligent in prescribing this particular drug to a woman in pregnancy. However, the court had to decide whether this particular drug had caused the damage.

Held

The court held, after hearing expert evidence on the matter, that the brain damage was more likely to have had a genetic origin than to have been caused by the Cafergot. The family bore the burden of proof, had failed to show that the negligence had been causative of the damage, and their claim was therefore dismissed.

☆ ☆ ☆

WILSHER v ESSEX AHA (1988) House of Lords [1988] 1 All ER 871, [1988] 2 WLR 557

The medical facts

This was a case of a child who had been born prematurely. He was treated in an incubator and was given supplementary oxygen. The oxygen concentration in the blood was monitored by means of a catheter, which should have been placed in the umbilical artery. Unfortunately, the catheter was inserted negligently and it lay in the umbilical vein. This meant that the oxygen readings derived from it were unduly low and, in response to those erroneous readings, the child was given an excess of the gas. He was later found to have developed some degree of blindness and it was well recognised that the delivery of excessive oxygen to a premature baby was harmful to the retina and could damage the sight.

Matter for the court to decide

There was no difficulty in this case with liability in terms of the negligent misplacement of the catheter, but there was plenty of room for argument on causation. The plaintiff's case was that excessive oxygen administration had long been recognised as a cause of retinal damage giving rise to blindness, and this very side effect had materialised.

Held

At first instance and in the Court of Appeal, the plaintiff succeeded on both negligence and causation. However, the defendants appealed to the House of Lords.

The defendants were able to show that there were five other possible causes for the blindness that were all related to the prematurity and none of which were related to the negligence. The House of Lords held that the plaintiff had therefore failed to prove his case on causation because he had not succeeded in showing that the negligent cause was the one which was more than 50% likely to have been responsible for the damage.

WILSON v VANCOUVER HOCKEY CLUB (1985) 22 DLR (4th) 516

The medical facts

A professional hockey player found he had a mole on his arm. He thought this was changing colour part of the way through the season in February 1979. He was seen by the team doctor who said it should be investigated at the end of the season. In view of this, he referred the plaintiff to a specialist in May of that year. The mole was found to be cancerous and necessitated the excision of an area of skin 10 cms in diameter. The plaintiff's experts argued that, if he had been referred promptly in February, the area of excision would only have been 5 cms in diameter, thereby taking a shorter time to heal. The healing time required for the larger excision had the effect that the patient was unable to play hockey for the whole of the following season and by this stage his career was over.

Matter for the court to decide

The court had to decide whether the three-month delay incurred in referral caused the patient to need a 10 cm excision rather than a 5 cm one.

Held

The court held that the three-month delay made no difference to the size of the excision. The lesion had been reported by the pathologist as being a level III lesion but there was some argument that it was perhaps borderline level II/III. However, the important point was that a 10 cm excision would have been necessary regardless of whether it had been level II or level III and it would at the very least have been level II when the patient was first seen by the club doctor.

(iv)   Consent

(For a discussion of this subject see Chapter X)

* Denotes Commonwealth or American case

CANTERBURY v SPENCE (1972) 244 F 2d 772

The medical facts

A young man had a history of backache and was seen by a neurosurgeon. There was little to find on examination and a myelogram was ordered. This showed a 'filling defect' in the region of the fourth thoracic vertebra, and the surgeon recommended a laminectomy. The patient agreed to go ahead with the procedure but made little inquiry into its exact nature. Unfortunately, there were a number of post-operative complications and the end result was that years after the operation the patient found himself hobbling about on crutches, a victim of paralysis of the bowels and urinary incontinence.

The patient sued the neurosurgeon for failing to obtain his informed consent to the laminectomy.

Matter for the court to decide

In this case, the court had to decide:

> ... whether a 1% possibility of paralysis resulting from laminectomy was peril of sufficient magnitude to bring a disclosure duty into play.

Held

(a) At first instance

The trial judge held that, at least according to the 'doctor-orientated' approach, it was common practice not to disclose a risk of this small magnitude, especially as the patient had not made any particular inquiry.

(b) On appeal

The patient appealed against this decision and it was held that the 'patient-orientated' rule should apply, whereby a patient should be told of all risks a reasonable patient in that situation would want to know. It was irrelevant that most doctors in this situation would not have made the disclosure.

With regard to the court's preference for a 'doctor-orientated' or 'patient-orientated' approach, judgment was given to the effect that:

> 8. It is prerogative of patient, not physician, to determine for himself the direction in which his interests seem to lie.

As regards the significance of whether or not the patient made any direct inquiry, the judgment was:

> 12. Physician's duty to inform patient is not dependent upon patient's request for disclosure.

Nevertheless, the court did recognise that there could be situations in which a patient might be harmed by disclosure:

> 27. Where patient would become so ill or emotionally distraught on disclosure as to foreclose rational decision, or complicate or hinder treatment, or perhaps even pose psychological damage to patient, portents of such type may justify physician in action he deems medically warranted; critical inquiry is whether physician responded to sound medical judgment that communication of risk information would present threat to patient's well-being.

Note on comparative cases

This case should be contrasted with the English case *Sidaway v Board of Governors of Bethlem Royal Hospital and the Maudsley Hospital* (1985), in which a 'doctor-orientated' approach was used. The recent case of *Rogers v Whitaker* (1992) may also be considered.

☆ ☆ ☆

MITCHELL v McDONALD (1987) 40 CCLT 266

The medical facts

A woman in Alberta consulted her doctor complaining of back pain which had not responded to conservative treatment. The plan was to give two cortisone injections into the posterior aspect of the chest in an attempt to alleviate the pain. While one of these injections was being given the needle unfortunately punctured a lung and she suffered a pneumothorax. She sued the doctor for negligence in giving the injection and for failing to obtain her informed consent. Evidence was disclosed that when she found the injection painful she cried out 'for God's sake, stop' but that the doctor continued with the procedure. She then left the doctor's office and became breathless but when she returned he merely gave her a Valium injection. Later that day she was admitted to hospital for treatment of the pneumothorax and subsequently underwent a restorative operation by another specialist.

Matter for the court to decide

The court held that there had been no negligence in puncturing the lung during the procedure because the pneumothorax was 'an unfortunate mishap of rare incidence'. It happened because, by chance, the needle hit a blister within the lung which in turn had been caused by the patient's smoking-induced emphysema.

However, the question arose of whether the patient had given her informed consent and whether, when she later cried out 'for God's sake, stop' she had withdrawn the consent.

Held

The court held that she had given her implied consent to the procedure before it was started. She was familiar with cortisone injections and had on this occasion expected one to be given. Furthermore, when she cried out, the damage had already been done and so it was too late for the consent to be withdrawn. Additionally, the court added that such a cry was nothing more than a plea to stop hurting her rather than an express withdrawal of consent to the treatment.

☆　☆　☆

PRECOURT v FREDERICK (1985) 481 NE 2d 1144

Medical facts

A patient in Massachusetts was on treatment with steroids from the doctor and suffered damage to both hips from aseptic necrosis. He sued the doctor on the basis that the risk of this side effect should have been disclosed by the doctor so as to have given him the opportunity of refusing the treatment.

Matter for the court to decide

The court had to decide whether the doctor fell short in not informing the patient of the risk of aseptic necrosis as a side effect of steroid treatment.

Held

(a) At first instance

The trial judge held that the doctor offered an unacceptable standard of care by not warning the patient about the possibility of the side effect.

(b) On appeal

The doctor appealed and the court then held that the patient presented no evidence of likelihood that he would develop aseptic necrosis after taking steroids, or that the doctor should have known that the risk was anything other than negligible. The decision was therefore reversed.

Two parts of the judgment are worth quoting:

1 Physician has duty to inform patient regarding possible risk of treatment only if physician has, or reasonably should have, information about risk that he reasonably should have recognised that patient would consider important in deciding to undergo proposed treatment.

2 Materiality of information about a potential injury resulting from treatment, for purposes of determining whether physician has duty to inform patient about potential injury, is function not only of severity of injury, but also of likelihood that injury will occur; regardless of severity of potential injury, if probability that injury will occur is so small as to be practically nonexistent, then possibility of that injury occurring cannot be considered a material factor of a rational assessment of whether to engage in activity that exposes one to potential injury.

☆ ☆ ☆

RANDOLPH v CITY OF NEW YORK (1987) 507 NE 2d 1144

The medical facts

A woman, who was a Jehovah's Witness, was admitted to hospital for the birth of her child and needed a Caesarian section. She had given express directions that she did not want to be treated with a blood transfusion. During the operation it became apparent that a transfusion was clinically indicated, but the doctors, in view of the patient's expressed wishes, refrained from giving such transfusion and the patient died. The widower brought an action against the hospital and the doctor for his wife's death.

Matter for the court to decide

At first instance, the Supreme Court, New York County, found the hospital and the doctor each 50% liable. They both appealed, on the basis that they had co-operated with their patient's request.

359

The Appeal Court therefore had to decide whether the patient's previously expressed wish was a justification for withholding life-saving treatment.

Held

The Court of Appeal of New York held that the doctor's failure to administer the blood transfusion, in view of the patient's religious beliefs, could not form the basis of a medical malpractice action.

☆ ☆ ☆

ROGERS v WHITAKER (1992) 67 ALJR 47

The medical facts

A woman lost the sight of her right eye as a result of an injury in childhood. Despite this handicap she had little difficulty in living a normal life, and she happened, when in her forties, to attend a specialist for an eye examination. That specialist offered her an operation which would both improve the appearance of the injured eye and stood a good chance of regaining the sight in it. It so happened that this particular patient was not someone who approached major decisions affecting her health lightly. She was also reluctant to take professional advice on trust. Evidence at trial showed that she subjected the surgeon to unusually extensive questioning about any possible disadvantages or complications of the proposed operation. Expert evidence at trial also showed that there was a recognised 1 in 14,000 chance of the other eye being affected by the condition of sympathetic ophthalmia. In that condition it becomes infected through transfer from the eye that is the subject of the treatment and which is itself at risk. The important point was that if this extremely remote risk materialised it would convert the patient from a one-eyed person to a blind person. For some reason that never became apparent, the surgeon did not bother to mention this risk, and the patient agreed to go ahead with the operation.

Unfortunately, the risk materialised and the patient was rendered blind.

Matter for the court to decide

Expert evidence for the defence showed that there was a significant proportion of eye surgeons who would not have mentioned a risk as rare as this one when discussing an operation with a patient. If this line of thinking had been followed, the plaintiff would have lost her case on the basis of the rule laid down in the earlier English case of *Sidaway v Board of Governors of the Bethlem Royal and Maudsley Hospital* (1985).

However, the plaintiff argued that this was the wrong test. She asserted that the proper test to apply was whether a reasonable patient, in this particular situation, would have wanted to know of such a risk. She would then have to show that, if she had been so warned, she would have declined the operation.

Held

The court reviewed the British rule in *Sidaway* and held that this was not applicable to Australian law. It thus distinguished between the 'doctor-orientated' rule in *Sidaway* and the 'patient-orientated' rule that was under discussion in this case. It held that the 'patient-orientated' rule should apply and found for the plaintiff. The plaintiff had little difficulty in showing that, if she had been warned about this serious side-effect, she would have declined the operation. In this respect, her case was made stronger by the fact that the loss of her remaining eye would render her blind and by the fact that she had successfully shown how her personality dictated a very cautious approach to such matters.

Note The patient-orientated rule had been used two decades earlier in the American case *Canterbury v Spence* (1972).

SIDAWAY v BOARD OF GOVERNORS OF BETHLEM ROYAL HOSPITAL AND THE MAUDSLEY HOSPITAL (1985) [1985] AC 871

The medical facts

A woman developed symptoms caused by pressure on one of the nerve roots in the cervical part of the spinal cord. She was much troubled by pain in the arm and shoulder. She was seen by a neurosurgeon, who offered her an operation on the relevant part of the spine with the object of relieving the pain. Unfortunately, there was a technical difficulty with freeing one of the nerve roots and the spinal cord itself was damaged. This subjected her to a disability which had much more impact on her than the original pain of which she complained.

There was no evidence of negligence with regard to the operative technique but the patient sued the neurosurgeon on the basis that he had not warned her about the side effect which, in the event, materialised.

Matter for the court to decide

The court had to decide whether the neurosurgeon fell short of proper standards by failing to warn his patient of this particular side effect. Expert evidence for the defence showed that the risk of its occurrence was less than 1%.

Held

The defence showed successfully that there was a responsible body of medical opinion which would not have disclosed this risk. It argued that many neurosurgeons considered it wrong to frighten the patient unduly by giving warnings about serious side effects that were very unlikely to happen. Against this background, the plaintiff's claim was dismissed as she had failed to show negligence in relation to the information she was given when her consent was obtained.

Note This case demonstrates the British 'doctor-orientated' approach to consent and should be contrasted with the American 'patient-orientated' rule that was applied in *Canterbury v Spence*

(1972) and which was also applied in the recent Australian case *Rogers v Whitaker* (1992).

☆ ☆ ☆

THAKE v MAURICE (1986) [1986] QB 644, [1986] 1 All ER 479, [1986] 2 WLR 337

The medical facts

A couple had completed their family and the husband asked a surgeon to carry out a vasectomy. The operation was duly performed, but the couple were not warned about the possibility of later recanalisation by which fertility could be restored without any question of negligence at the time of the original operation. Some time after the operation, the wife developed symptoms of early pregnancy but dismissed the possibility, relying on the reassurance she had earlier received that her husband was sterile. When the symptoms persisted she consulted her general practitioner who confirmed the pregnancy, but it was too late for her to have a termination.

The couple sued the surgeon, not for a negligent technique at the time of the operation, but rather for his failure to inform the husband that recanalisation was a possibility. The couple argued that, if they had been so warned, the wife would have sought advice at an earlier stage in the pregnancy when it would have been possible to have had a termination.

Matter for the court to decide

The court first had to decide whether or not the surgeon fell short in failing to inform the couple about the possibility of recanalisation. Secondly it had to decide whether the wife, if she had been so informed, would have sought advice sufficiently early to have had a termination and whether she would have requested one.

Held

The court held that the surgeon was negligent in failing to disclose the possible risk of recanalisation and it found for the plaintiff on the basis that, as her family was complete, she would have requested a termination if she had been offered one in good time.

(v)   *Res ipsa loquitur*

(For a discussion of this subject see Chapter XI)

Cassidy v Ministry of Health, **1951**

CASSIDY v MINISTRY OF HEALTH **(1951) [1951] 2 KB 343, [1951] 1 All ER 574**

The medical facts

A patient was having difficulty in using his hand properly. His general practitioner diagnosed Dupuytren's contracture. This affected two fingers of his hand such that the flexor tendons were tight and prevented proper extension of the fingers. The doctor referred him to a hospital specialist, who arranged admission and a subsequent operation. After the procedure had been completed the whole hand was bound up, but when the dressings were later taken off the patient found that all four fingers were stiff. He had considerable difficulty recovering proper use of the hand and he sued the surgeon.

Matter for the court to decide

At first instance, the trial judge found for the defendants. The plaintiff had been unable to sustain the burden of proof of showing that a negligent technique had been used in the operation.

However, he appealed, on the basis that it was impossible for him to acquire all the relevant facts of the operative technique. He asserted that *res ipsa loquitur* should apply, on the basis that his entry into hospital with two stiff fingers, and his departure with four stiff fingers, was of itself highly suggestive of negligence.

Held

Lord Denning, in the Court of Appeal, approved the application of *res ipsa loquitur* and allowed the plaintiff's appeal.

(vi) *Novus actus interveniens*

(For a discussion of this subject see Chapter XIII)

Prendergast v Sam & Dee, 1989

PRENDERGAST v SAM & DEE [1989] 1 Med LR 36

The medical facts

Mr Prendergast was an asthmatic man who visited his general practitioner fearing he was developing a chest infection. The doctor decided to prescribe a Ventolin inhaler and Phyllocontin tablets for the bronchospasm, and to add a seven-day course of Amoxil capsules in a strength of 250mg one to be taken three times a day.

The patient took the prescription to the pharmacy (Sam & Dee Ltd) for it to be dispensed. Unfortunately, the pharmacist misinterpreted the handwriting for the drug Amoxil and thought that the doctor had intended Daonil. The patient took the drugs as directed by the label on the bottle.[45]

Daonil is an oral hypoglycaemic agent for reducing the blood sugar level in diabetic patients. When the patient took this drug, in place of the intended Amoxil, it had the effect of lowering his blood sugar to the extent that he suffered permanent brain damage.

Matter for the court to decide

The medical difficulty in this case was quite straightforward. The doctor had intended the patient to have an antibiotic but he was accidently given an hypoglycaemic agent. The plaintiff therefore considered that there were two possible defendants:

(i) the doctor who was allegedly negligent in not writing the word 'Amoxil' clearly; and

---

45 A copy of the handwritten prescription for Amoxil, and the label that appeared on the container of the drug which the pharmacist dispensed, can be seen on p 367.

A reproduction of the photocopied prescription form and medicine label which was before the court.

Reproduced by kind permission of Oxford University Press

(ii) the pharmacist who was allegedly negligent in either mis-reading the drug name or, alternatively, in not contacting the doctor to clarify the uncertainty.

The court therefore had to decide whether either, or both, defendants were to blame for the damage that the wrong drug had caused. Additionally, if both were to blame, the question would arise of apportioning the blame.

Held

(a) At first instance

The trial judge held that the general practitioner had been negligent by failing to write the word 'Amoxil' sufficiently clearly. He also held that the pharmacist had been negligent in failing to refer to the prescribing doctor in case of uncertainty.

The question of apportionment then arose, and the judge held that the doctor bore 25% of the responsibility. The pharmacist's difficulty in defending the case was aggravated by the fact that there were a number of features on the written prescription to have put him on notice that the intended drug was very unlikely to be Daonil. One of them was the fact that a strength of 250mg was specified whereas Daonil is usually supplied in a 5mg strength. A further point was that 21 tablets were prescribed whereas Daonil is normally given in much larger numbers (say 100) for long-term treatment in diabetics.

(b) On appeal

The case was held at first instance in March 1988 but in February 1989 the doctor appealed. He argued that 'the chain of causation' had been broken. By this he meant that however bad his handwriting, it was not foreseeable that his patient would suffer brain damage as a consequence. The Court of Appeal considered this but dismissed his appeal on the basis that writing a word which could be construed as Daonil did make the ultimate damage foreseeable.

(vii) Contributory negligence

(For a discussion on this subject see page 207)

Fredette v Wiebe, 1986*

* Denotes Commonwealth or American case

FREDETTE v WIEBE (1986) 29 DLR (4th) 534

The medical facts

The plaintiff was a 17 year old high school student in British Columbia who was single and about one month pregnant. She went to her general practitioner to have an abortion. The procedure was carried out properly and was known to have a failure rate of less than 1%. After the operation she was told to return in two weeks for a post-operative examination. This was one of two safeguards intended to ensure that the procedure had been successful, the other safeguard being that the doctor would shortly thereafter see a report of tissue removed at operation.

Unfortunately, the girl failed to return for her two-week check-up and the doctor also failed to see the report on the tissue until it was too late for her to have a vaginal termination. The girl contended that if the general practitioner had been sufficiently careful to check the laboratory report he would have recalled her when she was still only nine weeks pregnant and she could then have had the original operation repeated.

Matter for the court to decide

The court decided that the doctor had been negligent in not examining the laboratory report in good time, but it also had to decide whether the girl had been contributorily negligent in failing to attend a fortnight after the procedure, as she had been instructed. It was acknowledged that, if she had so attended, she would have learnt that she was still pregnant, and that this would have provided the opportunity for doing the operation again.

Held

The court held that the girl was contributorily negligent in failing to return after the allotted interval.

369

Conversely, the court held that she was not at fault for failing to mitigate her damage by either having a second abortion after she discovered she was still pregnant, or by offering her twins for adoption at a much later date after their births. The court went on to point out that even though a woman may want a termination when she is in the early stages of pregnancy, it is unreasonable to expect her to continue with the same state of mind. It pointed out that a change of mind 'is likely to a large extent to be caused by a process linked to the physical advance in her pregnancy'.

(viii) Criminal negligence

(For a discussion of this subject see Chapter XIV)

R v Prentice and Sullman, 1993

R v PRENTICE AND SULLMAN (1993) [1993] 4 Med 2R 304

The medical facts

This case concerned a 16 year old boy who was suffering from leukemia. He was under the care of a hospital specialist and was part of the way through a course of cytotoxic drugs. He received an intravenous injection of Vincristine each month and an intrathecal injection of Methotrexate on alternate months. On the occasion with which the case is concerned the boy was duly admitted to the ward for his routine procedure to be carried out. The task was delegated to two junior doctors. They were both inexperienced and there was a misunderstanding about the route of administration of the two drugs. They carried out the procedure together, that is with one supposedly supervising the other. The misunderstanding caused the injection of both drugs into the spine and the patient died.

At first instance, both young doctors were convicted of manslaughter.

Matter for the court to decide

Both junior doctors appealed and the Court of Appeal was faced with analysing the case to decide whether the degree of negligence involved fell within the ambit of the civil concept of negligence, or whether it was sufficiently severe to justify the sanction of the criminal law.

Held

The case law on criminal negligence since the end of the 19th century was examined in detail and a decision was made to adopt the test in *Andrews v DPP* (1937). In that case, the judge explained to the jury the degree of negligence they must find to justify bringing it within the category of a criminal act. He explained this to the jury in terms that:

371

... simple lack of care such as will constitute civil liability is not enough: for the purposes of the criminal law there are degrees of negligence; and a very high degree of negligence is required to be proved before the felony is established.

Lord Taylor of Gosforth, in an attempt to identify the various categories of mental attitude that would make a case qualify as criminal negligence, specified the following states of mind:

(a) indifference to an obvious risk of injury to health;

(b) actual foresight of the risk coupled with the determination nevertheless to run it;

(c) an appreciation of the risk coupled with an intention to avoid it, but also coupled with such a high degree of negligence in the attempted avoidance as the jury considers justifies conviction;

(d) inattention or failure to advert to a serious risk that goes beyond 'mere inadvertence' in respect of an obvious and important matter which the defendant's duty demanded he should address.

The Court of Appeal held that the negligence of the two junior doctors did not fall within any of these four categories. Accordingly, their convictions for manslaughter were quashed.

INDEX OF CASES

Page numbers in ordinary type indicate the points at which a case is mentioned in the text.
*Page numbers in **bold type** refer to the entry of the case in part C, the case law section, where a fuller description is given.*

SUBJECT INDEX

SUBJECT INDEX